Praise for DOCTOR WHO PSYCHOLOGY, FIRST EDITION

"A cracking read. They know their Who inside an
cable. Much of it concerns subjects close to my h
every time…. This is an exceptional example of w
legitimate genre." —*The Psychologist* (British Psy

T0043992

"This book is a must-read for every Whovian!" —*Night Owl Reviews*

"Collection of essays by psychologists and mental health professionals of varying degrees and angles, all of whom are huge fans of the Doctor…. These hyperintelligent superfans deliver intriguing insights on a variety of topics." —*Midlife Crisis Crossover*

"This is a must-read for Who fans. The diverse range of topics and in-depth analysis will have you wanting to watch all the Doctors over again." —*The Beguiled Child*

ABOUT THE POPULAR CULTURE PSYCHOLOGY BOOK SERIES

"The Popular Culture Psychology series . . . aims to make 'boring' science fun by showing how real-life science might explain some of the things we see in films and television." —*Kirkus Reviews*

"Absolutely fantastic!" —*Retroist*

"Super interesting and inspired me." —PBS *Braincraft*

"What's great about the books . . . is that they are amenable for both casual reading and deeper study alike." —*Pop Mythology*

"They are fascinating." —*Literary Hype Woman*

"The perfect blend of insightful scholarship, pop-culture savvy, and bloody good fun. Highly recommended!" —**Jonathan Maberry,** *The New York Times* **best-selling author**

FURTHER PRAISE FOR TRAVIS LANGLEY'S WORKS

"Popular culture's greatest mind." **—Joe Wos, Emmy-winning PBS host**

"This man is a genius!" **—Stan Lee**

ABOUT *Spider-Man Psychology: Untangling Webs*

"Friendly neighborhood psychologist Travis Langley and his fantastic team explore the amazing minds of Peter Parker, Miles Morales, and many more in this spectacular edition of all things Spider-Man!" **—E. Paul Zehr, PhD, author of *Becoming Batman, Chasing Captain America,* and more**

"If you're a fan of Spider-Man, this book will fascinate you, as the essays illuminate our understanding of exactly what makes Peter Parker and the people around him tick. Highly recommended." **—Michael A. Burstein, "The Friendly Neighborhood of Peter Parker" *Webslinger* writer, Hugo and Nebula finalist, Astounding Award winner**

ABOUT *Stranger Things Psychology: Life Upside Down*

"Stellar anthology . . . eye-opening . . . The entries mix genuine appreciation with measured critique, taking seriously the complex issues powering the show's plot, without undercutting its overall entertainment value. Fans looking to delve deeper into the show will devour this." **—Publishers Weekly**

"Look into the psyche of *Stranger Things* and get ready to see the show in a whole new way, uncovering new insights and perspective into the characters, the '80s, and ourselves. Be ready to have your perception turned . . . Upside Down. I really liked it." **—Gail Z. Martin, author of the Deadly Curiosities series**

"The book has a unique platform of being able to introduce complex psychology ideas such as boundary ambiguity and counterfactual thinking through something easily digestible as *Stranger Things.*" **—Red Carpet Report (RCR News Media)**

ABOUT *Batman and Psychology: A Dark and Stormy Knight*

"It is a terrific book." **—Dennis O'Neil, Batman comic book writer/editor**

"Scholarly and insightful . . . His professional credentials, mixed with his love for comic books and the character of Batman, create a fascinating, entertaining, and educational read." **—Michael Uslan, Batman film series originator and executive producer**

"A modern classic." **—Mark D. White, author of *Batman and Ethics***

"Possibly the most fascinating book I have ever read." **—Chelsea Campbell, author of the RenegadeX series**

"Marvelous!" **—Adam West, actor**

"Definitely a book worth looking for." **—Kevin Smith, filmmaker**

DOCTOR WHO
PSYCHOLOGY

TIMES CHANGE

THE REGENERATED SECOND EDITION
REVISED AND UPDATED

ALSO BY TRAVIS LANGLEY

Batman and Psychology: A Dark and Stormy Knight (1st & 2nd editions)

ANTHOLOGIES

Spider-Man Psychology: Untangling Webs

Stranger Things Psychology: Life Upside Down

The Joker Psychology: Evil Clowns and the Women Who Love Them

Black Panther Psychology: Hidden Kingdoms

Westworld Psychology: Violent Delights

Daredevil Psychology: The Devil You Know

Supernatural Psychology: Roads Less Traveled

Star Trek Psychology: The Mental Frontier

Wonder Woman Psychology: Lassoing the Truth

Doctor Who Psychology: A Madman with a Box (1st edition)

Game of Thrones Psychology: The Mind is Dark and Full of Terrors

Captain America vs. Iron Man: Freedom, Security, Psychology

Star Wars Psychology: Dark Side of the Mind

The Walking Dead Psychology: Psych of the Living Dead

DOCTOR WHO
PSYCHOLOGY

TIMES CHANGE

THE REGENERATED SECOND EDITION
REVISED AND UPDATED

TRAVIS LANGLEY, PhD, EDITOR

FOREWORD BY KATY MANNING
(COMPANION ON *DOCTOR WHO*)

TURNER
PUBLISHING COMPANY

TURNER PUBLISHING COMPANY
Nashville, Tennessee
www.turnerpublishing.com

Cover design by M.S. Corley
Book design by William Ruoto

Library of Congress Control Number: 2023939924

Printed in the United States of America

to Nicholas

He introduced me to comic cons,
I introduced him to *Doctor Who*,
and we've lived in a different
timeline ever since.

Contents

About the TARDIS Crew

Editor

 **Travis Langley, PhD,** series/volume editor, distinguished professor of psychology at Henderson State University, has been a child abuse investigator, courtroom expert, and *Wheel of Fortune* game show champion. A popular keynote speaker for the American Psychological Association, Amazon, and other organizations, he speaks regularly at events throughout the world, discussing heroism and the power of story in people's lives. *Psychology Today* carries his blog, "Beyond Heroes and Villains."

The *New York Times, Wall Street Journal, Saturday Evening Post,* CNN, MTV, and hundreds of other outlets have interviewed him and covered his work. He has appeared as an expert interviewee in documentary programs such as *Necessary Evil, Legends of the Knight, Superheroes Decoded, Pharma Bro, AMC Visionaries: Robert Kirkman's Secret History of Comics,* and Hulu's *Batman & Bill.* Online, he's easy to find. Look for Travis Langley as **@Superherologist** or **@DrTravisLangley**. At conventions, you may find him cosplaying as the War Doctor, the first Doctor known for sporting a beard (and in the morning, Travis's hair sticks up the same way).

Interior Illustrator

Marko Head is an artist living in the Rockies. As illustrator and storyboard artist, he has worked on projects for HBO, Paramount, NBC, BuzzFeed, Warner Bros., Noggin, *Sesame Street*, and more. His artwork has appeared in Rooster Teeth's *Death Battle* playing card game, the graphic novel *Kill the Freshman, The Workday Comic*, and the book *Batman and Psychology: A Dark and Stormy Knight*. Along with many celebrated creators, he scripted and illustrated official *Dig Dug* webcomics for Namco Bandai's ShiftyLook project.

Other contributors' biographies appear at the ends of their respective chapters. Keep up with these books through the Popular Culture Psychology page at **Facebook.com/ThePsychGeeks.**

Acknowledgments

Our Companions

Tim Cogburn and Harlan Ellison introduced me to *Doctor Who*, whether they ever knew it or not. When we were kids, Tim told me about this British television program that author Ellison had praised as "the greatest science fiction series of all time"[1] when relatively few Americans knew it existed. Intrigued, I sought out *Doctor Who* novelizations before I ever saw the show. Who was your first Doctor? For some of this book's writers, it was a classic Doctor such as Tom Baker (Fourth Doctor) or Colin Baker (Sixth), while others discovered it through twenty-first-century Doctors such as Christopher Eccleston (Ninth) or David Tennant (then Tenth). Mine was my mental version based on novels that did not indicate which Doctor they featured.

All of us who wrote this book thank everyone who has let us explore our relative dimensions in mind on page: on the first edition, Connie Santisteban and Kate Zimmermann; on the second, Turner Publishing's Amanda Chiu Krohn, Ryan Smernoff, Claire Ong, Tim Holtz, Kitty Chibnik, and once again Who-lover Connie. My literary agent, Evan Gregory of the Ethan Ellenberg Literary Agency, handles more details than readers probably want to know. We thank Daniel Thompson and others for our author photos. Marko Head, who previously illustrated *Batman and Psychology: A Dark and Stormy Knight*, returns with outstanding illustrations once again. The episode transcripts Christina Luckings posts at chakoteya.net have been a world of help. We always rewatch the scenes ourselves, but the transcripts have helped when we're checking and double-checking source material.

For serving as our muses, mentors, devil's advocates, founts of knowledge, ground support, and most valued companions, we thank Renee Couey; Ron Currie; Vic Frazao; Jeffrey Henderson; Chris Hesselbein; Nadine Kofman and Bill Welch; Nicholas, Alex, and Spencer Langley; Sharon Manning; Dustin McGinnis; Nick Robinson; Bethany, Luca, and Fermina San Juan; Mike Silberback; Nicki Wortman; "more Dax;" and my wife, first reader, and best friend, Rebecca M. Langley. Our faculty writers group provided crucial feedback: Angela Boswell, Andrew Burt, Maryjane Dunn, Martin Halpern, William Henshaw, Megan Hickerson, Michael Taylor, and Shannon Wittig. Madelyn Byrd, Shelly Clevenger, Sara Ebert, Molly Jessup, Adam Korenman, Paul Patacek of the Krewe du Who, Jessica Tseang, Faith Whiteside, and Beth Woodward have joined us or invited us onto convention panels where we shared our thoughts and love for everything Whovian. Grant Imahara brought me to Adam Savage's Comic-Con party where I made many fine friends, including Matt Munson who assembled the "Post-Time War Stress Disorder" chapter's team (and helped me complete my War Doctor cosplay). We miss you, Grant. For reasons diverse and sometimes paradoxical, Eric Bailey, Austin and Hunter Biegert, Jeff Ewing, Neil Gaiman, Katrina Hill, Maurice Lamarche, and Paul McGann deserve mention and appreciation.

More than half a century ago, Sydney Newman and Verity Lambert gave us *Doctor Who*, created with C. E. Webber and Donald Wilson. Showrunners Russell T. Davies and Steven Moffat hurled it into the current millennium for new generations to enjoy. Ron Grainer composed the original *Doctor Who* theme, but it was Delia Derbyshire (assisted by Dick Mills) whose arrangement transformed the music into something eerie, haunting, unforgettable, and fun. We owe a great debt to the thousands of people who have worked on *Doctor Who* over the years—so many actors, writers, directors, producers, designers, crew members, and more. *Doctor Who* audio drama star Chase Masterson is a fine friend. We cannot say enough to thank television stars Peter Capaldi, Peter Davison, Christopher Eccleston, Michelle Gomez, Alex Kingston, Pearl Mackie, Sylvester McCoy, Billie Piper, Matt Smith, David Tennant, and Jodie Whittaker for speaking with

Aaron Sagers and Jenna Busch while we were writing editions of this timey-wimey book.

The world met the Doctor in the form of actor William Hartnell (First Doctor), but it was Patrick Troughton (Second Doctor) who showed us how greatly the character could change and then Jon Pertwee (Third Doctor) who brought the Doctor to our contemporary world. This book's foreword by Pertwee's companion, Katy Manning, who worked with all of the first three and several who came later, is a special treat. Thank you, Katy.

Thank you, all.

Let the madness ensue.

Foreword

The How, Not Why, of *Who*

Katy Manning

(Companion on *Doctor Who*)

I have never been a "why" questioner—there lies a path to unanswerable conjecture—but rather a "how" questioner. "How" takes you down the path of logic, learning, and understanding.

Being involved in television in the late '60s/early '70s as a young actress was a stimulating and exciting path of technological experimentation, especially in a program like *Doctor Who* that I had watched from its conception in front of and from behind the sofa! It required space travel to other planets, aliens, electronic music, and "otherworldly" sound effects. The hero was a nomadic two-thousand-year-old man with two hearts who traveled in time and space via a blue police box! A genius concept, allowing limitless adventures and possibilities into the world of fantasy and imagination. Computers were in their infancy, entire rooms of massive machines looking somewhat like Boss in *The Green Death*.[1] Cameras were big and cumbersome, so to achieve what they did during the '60s in black and white was all due to the remarkable creativity of the enthusiastic, dedicated technical teams with a great deal of trial and error and a very small budget—often with little time and difficult, barren winter locations. Last-minute lines like "freak weather conditions in Dungeness" covered the problem of two days of snow, rain, thick fog, and bright sun! I even had hot water poured around my thin suede boots to unfreeze them from the ground. Once we were in the studio for recording, there was a very strict 10 p.m. curfew, and, with special effects to be done in the studio, it was always a tense time where actors had to be sure of achieving performances in one take. When Barry Letts took over as producer in 1970, he fought relentlessly with the powers that be to obtain a little extra money to experiment with the development of special effects and really take this unique program forward. Alien masks were given from the makeup department over to the special effects department, using anything and everything to achieve this end.

The Earthbound Doctor

When I joined *DW* in 1971,[2] it was the beginning of many new things but very importantly the first year of *Doctor Who* in color. Color separation overlay, too (now green screen), was in its infancy and would add so much possibility. (I was put in front of three different-colored screens while it was being perfected.) Barry also wanted to open up *Doctor Who* to a wider audience and age group, which he did with resounding success, building a cult following and soaring ratings. Barry Letts and his right-hand man, the incorrigible scriptwriter/editor Terrance Dicks, introduced the Doctor's Moriarty in the shape of the Master, played to perfection by Roger Delgado. Real members of the army and navy were used in several episodes. Richard Franklin was introduced as Captain Mike Yates to strengthen the UNIT team led by Nicholas Courtney as the quintessential Brigadier ("chap with wings, five rounds rapid"),[3] and John Levene as Sergeant Benton. It was a risk to banish the Doctor to the planet Earth by the Time Lords. However, it really gave UNIT a solid part to play. After all, in our limitless imaginations, aliens are to be expected on other planets, but it takes a whole new twist when a policeman rips off masks to reveal faceless Autons, troll dolls come to life and kill, or a man is even devoured by a blowup black plastic chair.[4] Completely nonhuman Daleks lurking beneath our cities[5] or the summoning up of the Devil in a picturesque country village church[6] is perhaps more frightening and unexpected on the planet we inhabit. Story lines followed subjects like the slow destruction of the planet Earth through chemicals and financial greed.[7] Interesting to me and indeed perhaps the Doctor was that all the scientific progress we make is useless without moral progress on any planet.

Jo Grant and Her Doctor

The casting of Jon Pertwee as the Third Doctor was inspired—an actor known mostly through radio and light entertainment, a master of character voices, and a real adventurer in his private life. All these talents added to the depths of character Jon brought to "his" Doctor, his first truly dramatic role: a swashbuckling dandy with a wonderful ethereal quality, a dark secret side, and a desire for justice and peace, but always an otherworldly twinkle in his eye. A man we could trust. It was an honor to be cast alongside him, as I had grown up admiring his work. We instantly became fast friends and I learned so much about everything from this wise and wonderful man. This played out onscreen. I was working on a series (my first role out of drama school) for ITV and I was not available during the original auditions, so by the time I appeared, the role of Jo Grant had been shortlisted to three. After a lone improvised scene, I was cast! A nineteen- or twenty-year-old niece of a high-up member of UNIT—who was hired not because of her ability but because of nepotism, she had done a short training course with UNIT, escapology, Sanskrit, and some dubious GCE (HSC)—results! Jo could ask the questions on behalf of the younger viewers and non–sci-fi boffins, and appeal to the teenagers as a trendy miniskirted, platform-booted, beringed girl of the '70s. She was foisted onto the Doctor. She was resourceful, brave, cheeky, disobedient, and a little clumsy; didn't scream much; didn't always agree with the Doctor, but (as in *The Daemons*) was prepared to lay down her life for the man she learned to love and respect. In turn, she brought out the nurturing side of the Doctor's character and she grew up onscreen in our living rooms, ending her tenure by marrying a Nobel Peace Prize–winning eco warrior—a younger version of the Doctor, a professor played excellently by my then-real-life-fiancé Stewart Bevan. In a beautifully crafted script, her meeting with her professor mirrored Jo's first clumsy meeting with her Doctor.[8] There was no other part I could have played where my powers of imagination were so deeply tested, where I could have learned so much from both the technical teams and my fellow actors, or where I could have done stunts in the safe hands of the incredible and patient boys from Havoc, led by Derek Ware. Jon insisted on doing the majority of his own stunts and I was never far behind! He was an absolute joy to spend every day with and was a strong, committed team leader.

The First Three

When *The Three Doctors*[9] came about, a first in bringing their past re-generations together, I felt extremely privileged to be working with the Doctors I had grown up watching. Sadly, William Hartnell, who set the bar high as the First Doctor and who I believe created some of the traits given to the future Doctors, was ill and his filming was done without us. Patrick Troughton as the Second Doctor was a very different actor than Jon. Pat was what we used to call a classical actor, with a huge career in theater behind him and a wonderfully naughty sense of humor. He liked to improvise around the script, whereas Jon liked to know exactly what was going to be said and what he was going to respond to. Their differences were soon overcome with respect for each other's choices in playing the Doctor. Watching these two very contrasting but great actors weave their magic was a master class. Pat's Doctor may have seemed discombobulated, but this cleverly concealed the twinkling genius beneath the surface. The clothes that each actor wears as the Doctor help define his take on the character.

New Doctors

This pioneering show prompted so many to enter the world of act-ing, producing, writing, and directing—way too many to name. For others, *Doctor Who* brought a magical, trustworthy hero into their lives and living rooms. The genius Russell T. Davies, a massively keen boy fan, was the champion who regenerated *Doctor Who* back onto our screens after a well-deserved rest—bringing with him all the modern technology, along with brilliant scripts and casting. Amongst this, he also created marvelous spinoffs, including *The Sarah Jane Adventures* with the unrivaled Lis Sladen. So, after forty years, I had the privilege of working with a young Matt Smith's Eleventh Doctor, yet again putting a totally unique and delightfully physical stamp on the character of the Doctor.[10] Though a younger actor, there was something extremely comforting and familiar about him as my Doctor. He was so warm and generous, and allowed me great freedom in our emotional scenes together. An unforgettable time shared with Lis and a script that encompassed Jo's life forty years on—perfection.

On audio, I have played Jo Grant with Sylvester McCoy's Seventh Doctor, a lighter and enjoyably clownish take on the character. I played Iris Wildthyme with Peter Davison's Fifth Doctor—a younger, gentler Doctor—and Colin Baker's more bombastic Sixth Doctor,[11] and talked with Peter Capaldi, the Twelfth Doctor, about his inspired performance and layering of the Doctor. More recently, I have worked with the incomparable Tom Baker, the Fourth Doctor. I could not ask for more! It seems to me, watching all the actors who have brought their innovative expertise to our screens, that one of the Doctor's two hearts belongs to the character and the other to all the brilliant actors who brought the Doctor so strongly and believably into the hearts of the viewers, now seen and loved in more than a hundred countries around the world.

So the question of why *Doctor Who* is still so popular after all these years is impossible to answer. All *Doctor Who* fans will have their own take on that and indeed who their favorites are. But, for me, "why" or even "who" matters not at all. I shall just continue to watch, enjoy, and marvel at the phenomenon of the *Doctor Who* kiss, the love that everyone who has ever been involved or watched *Doctor Who* has.

Katy Manning's career has spanned over fifty years and three countries. Her extensive television work began with John Braines's groundbreaking series *Man at the Top*. During this time, Katy was given the role of Jo Grant in *Doctor Who* alongside the unforgettable Third Doctor, Jon Pertwee, a role she revisited some forty years later in *The Sarah Jane Adventures,* starring Elisabeth Sladen with Matt Smith as the Eleventh Doctor. Katy's theater credits extend from London's West End to Sydney's Opera House. She returned to the UK with her critically acclaimed one-woman show about Bette Davis, *Me and Jezebel.* Katy has voiced numerous cartoons, including the award-winning *Gloria's House* as the ten-year-old Gloria. She has hosted her own interview show and directed two major musicals and several other plays. For over a decade, she has recorded for Big Finish as Jo Grant in *The Companion Chronicles* and as Iris Wildthyme in her own series, and guested on *The Confessions of Dorian Gray, Doctor Who Short Trips, Dracula,* and *The Lives of Captain Jack Harkness.* Katy wrote and performed *Not a Well Woman* in New York and LA, recorded by Big Finish. More recently, Katy appeared on *Casualty* and for Bafflegab recorded *Baker's End* with Tom Baker.

For the BBC's 100th anniversary, Katy appeared as Jo Grant Jones once more, this time at a gathering of former companions, and got the final word to the group.[12]

Introduction to 1st Edition
Doctor Who Psychology: A Madman with a Box

Madness in Who We Are

Travis Langley

> "I thought—well, I started to think—that maybe you were just, like, a madman with a box."
> —Amy Pond (Karen Gillan), companion to the Eleventh Doctor[1]

> "A possible link between madness and genius is one of the oldest and most persistent of cultural notions; it is also one of the most controversial."
> —psychologist Kay Redfield Jamison[2]

 Think outside the box. No matter how deceptively large your box might be, no matter how many swimming pools and libraries and strikingly similar corridors it might hold, and no matter where it might take you or when, be ready to step outside and look around. This kind of thinking takes the Doctor away from Gallifrey[3] and carries the Time Lord from one adventure to another instead of merely observing history and the universe from a place of greater safety inside. Rather than stick with the tried-and-true, the Doctor tries something new. Copernicus, Galileo, Mozart, and countless others down through the millennia have been called "mad" for making novel claims, challenging established ideas, and trying something new. When the TARDIS (embodied in a woman) calls the Doctor the only Time Lord "mad enough"[4] to run away from Gallifrey with her, is she calling this thief who stole her insane or is she talking about the Doctor's unconventionality?

What is madness? Psychiatrist Thomas Szasz has repeatedly accused the mental health profession of perpetuating myths about mental illness by describing any aberrant, disconcerting, outrageous, or otherwise unconventional behavior as "illness" or "disease."[5] Diagnosticians evaluating whether clients' behavior is bizarre or unhealthy must take into account what is considered normal for each client's environment, social class, or culture.[6] The Doctor's supposed madness does not refer to regeneration-induced chaos in memories and personality because that's normal for Time Lords. The Doctor is even called "mad" by their standards.[7] The qualities deemed inappropriate by their standards, however, may be heroic by ours. Scientific and artistic originality are not the only forms of unconventionality to get someone slapped with a label of madness. Standing up for what's right can, too, and the Doctor's fellow Time Lords with their vaunted—and easily sidestepped—noninterference policy are not well known for doing what's right for others.

By any standards, the Doctor is an unconventional hero whose thinking may be divergent, convergent, deductive, inductive, logical, and illogical—or at least unconstrained by anyone else's rules of how to follow a logical train of thought. The Time Lord engages in a lot of *heuristic thinking*, taking mental shortcuts because of having too little patience for more methodical, meticulous, *algorithmic analysis*.[8] Taking shortcuts in decision-making leads to more mistakes but, to be fair, the Doctor's heuristics are based on foundations more solid than ours tend to be. This hero charges in with little or no plan,[9] tries something, tries something else, and continually adapts to circumstances because of having the sheer ability and experience to make it all work out in the end (most of the time) and a personality that simply lacks patience.

What is the Doctor's personality? Given how many different incarnations have appeared, can we even say the Doctor has "a" personality? And how can an unconventional hero with an unconventional personality (or personalities) help us look at human psychology, and can we really use our own psychology to look at someone so fantastic? The Doctor, of course, is not just any ancient, time-traveling alien. This is an ancient, time-traveling alien who grows fascinated with us. We can use our sense of psychology to look at this character and we can use this character to look at our psychology, because all the Doctors judge themselves by looking at us. If there's a bit of bedlam in us all, then letting it out can sometimes be creative, constructive, and good for us—a kind of madness or passion that is not a mental disease at all.

> "There's something you better understand about me, 'cause it's important and one day your life may depend on it: I am definitely a madman with a box."
>
> —**Eleventh Doctor (Matt Smith)**[10]

> "The madman is a waking dreamer."
>
> —**philosopher Immanuel Kant**[11]

> "Anybody remotely interesting is mad in some way or another."
>
> —**Seventh Doctor (Sylvester McCoy)**[12]

Introduction to 2nd Edition
Doctor Who Psychology: Times Change
Change and Renewal

Travis Langley

Known to us and most characters by no truer name, the Doctor travels through the universe and history, usually accompanied by an attractive Earth woman, although there have been men, some nonhumans, a couple of robots, and one Cyberman head along the way. Three years into the show's early run, producers recast the role. The showrunners introduced *regeneration,* then known as *renewal.* William Hartnell's version would become retroactively known as the First Doctor, and Patrick Troughton (who looked nearly nothing like Hartnell) as the Second Doctor. The character's renewal gave the program itself the potential for endless change and renewal. Without yet realizing the magnitude of this gimmick, they'd imbued the Doctor's story with endless life.[2]

Before we wrote the first edition of *Doctor Who Psychology*, journalist Alan Kistler interviewed me for *Doctor Who: A History*, a book celebrating what was then the show's fifty-year history. He asked me how the Doctor's fantastic regeneration ability related in any way to real human nature. I shared some thoughts:

> We know from *The Three Doctors*[4] that Hartnell's Doctor is the first one; he didn't have previous versions of himself we didn't see. So when the Second Doctor arrives, this is someone who's just experienced regeneration for the first time and wasn't really expecting it that day. It makes sense that, at least at first, he feels disconnected from his old self. People who've had serious facial reconstructive surgery can experience a depersonalization effect. When people change their names, it can take a while to adjust to that concept emotionally. The temporary, partial amnesia that usually happens during regeneration can also enhance this. People who've suffered amnesia or brain damage will sometimes refer to who they were before the change as a different person. As his memories settle back into place, he feels more connected to his past.[5]

Despite a later glimpse of eight unfamiliar faces that may have belonged to other past incarnations in the serial *The Brain of Morbius*,[6] the anniversary special *The Five Doctors* reaffirmed that the First Doctor was still considered *the* first, "the original, you might say,"[7] with no room left for unknown Doctors in the sequence between himself and the Fifth. Even that can change.

Each new Doctor seems to emerge with characteristics formed in reaction to the character's own concerns and uncertainties about the previous incarnation. As the Doctor looks back on the last life just before starting the next, thinking about how things could have been different, the effect might be akin to a person focusing on a topic just before sleep and then having that notion influence their dreams. It also resembles some human expectations about how a cycle of reincarnations might work. The irascible, refined First Doctor grows kinder then changes into a jovial, scruffy replacement. The Fifth Doctor

(Peter Davison) grows unsure of himself and bears the weight of several traveling companions' fates, especially Adric's death, and so he rebounds into the self-assured, perhaps even smug, Sixth (Colin Baker). Haunted by the Time War, the Ninth (Christopher Eccleston) emerges as the most present-focused, the Tenth (David Tennant) becomes "the man who regrets," and the Eleventh (Matt Smith), "the man who forgets."[8] Though relieved a bit of his burden when Doctors unite to rescue Gallifrey from the Time War, allowing himself to think about the War Doctor also makes the Eleventh Doctor realize he has used up all twelve regenerations. Despite his young face, he feels old.

When interviewing people for *Doctor Who: A History* while the program still starred the Eleventh Doctor, Kistler asked if the Doctor should become a woman. I specifically said that, yes, the Thirteenth Doctor should be a woman. Given the Eleventh Doctor's character arc at the time and the fact that twenty-first-century viewers needed to see a Doctor reminiscent of how he began, the character first needed to become an older man again. The Doctor gets a new cycle of regenerations, and the Twelfth Doctor arrives in the form of actor Peter Capaldi, the same age William Hartnell had been when he originated the role (though the original portrayal and Hartnell's health made him seem older). The Twelfth Doctor has unconsciously selected a face that reminds him to save people who seem beyond saving.[9] After suffering more personal losses among his companions than we've witnessed in any previous Doctor, the Twelfth resists regenerating.[10] Once upon a time, he would have been said to suffer *combat fatigue*. These days, we have some other things to say about his complex, repeated grief, as this edition will explain. When he finally welcomes the fresh start, the Doctor's next change is again shaped by concerns on his mind at the time: sexism even among the oh-so-advanced Time Lords.[11]

Between the Master's disgust over learning he will regenerate as a woman and the Doctor's discomfort over reminders of the First Doctor's chauvinism, the Twelfth Doctor is ready to become the Thirteenth. Psychoanalyst Carl Jung said that each man must discover his *Anima*, the archetypal female side of his own personality. Whether we agree with Jung's reasoning regarding the role of the collective unconscious, the Doctor appears to have done so quite literally.

"We can evolve while still staying true to who we are. We can honor who we've been and choose who we want to be next. Now's your chance! How about it?"

—Thirteenth Doctor (Jodie Whittaker)[12]

People can heal many times in body and mind. Recovery, growth, and renewal are not one-time fixes for life's problems because life itself, as mentioned before, must change. New challenges will arise, and that's part of being alive. Each Doctor evolves, then works on other personal issues. Discovering that she has at least one previously unknown incarnation (the more confident and commanding Fugitive Doctor)[13] and that so much more of her own history remains a mystery to her may be why the Thirteenth Doctor regenerates into an aged version of a past self (David Tennant, previously the Tenth Doctor), the one whose time ended most reluctantly, the one who didn't want to go[14] and has a few other areas where the character needs some closure. Finding some solace may help this Doctor reaffirm a sense of identity and finally feel ready to go at last, ready to become an exciting and enthusiastic new self (Ncuti Gatwa, Fifteenth Doctor). The cycle carries on.

We have many new things to say about the Doctor, the companions, and real human nature for this second edition. Obviously the first edition's subtitle, *A Madman with a Box,* no longer will suffice because times change, and so must we. The subtitle, like the Doctor and like us all, gets a makeover. It's time for change and renewal. Now, let's go visit that blue box.

"Let me take it from the top: Hello, I'm the Doctor."

—Fugitive Doctor (Jo Martin)[15]

DOCTOR WHO HISTORY

On the Air: Television

- The classic series debuted November 23, 1963. First serial: *An Unearthly Child* (originally the first episode's title, retroactively assigned as the name of the complete four-part serial).
- Classic series ended December 6, 1989. Final serial: *Survival*.
- Television movie (1996): *Doctor Who*.
- The modern series debuted March 26, 2005. First modern episode: "Rose."

Off the Air: Alternate Timelines

Licensed comic books, comic strips, videos, and novels have adapted television stories and provided original tales not seen on television. Rarely are they canon to the TV show.

Big Finish Productions released audio plays adapted from *Doctor Who* novels in 1998, then started producing original stories the following year. Some feature impersonators who voice different Doctors, but many star the TV actors yet again. Every lead from the Fourth Doctor (played by Tom Baker) through the Tenth (David Tennant) has returned for more adventures, as have other incarnations such as the War Doctor (John Hurt) and Fugitive Doctor (Jo Martin). Continuity within the audio dramas is inconsistent, sometimes contradictory, which the Tenth Doctor attributes to the Time War altering history.[1] Because the television program avoids referring to the audio stories, canonicity is unclear. However, as the Eighth Doctor (Paul McGann) is about to regenerate into the War Doctor in live action, he names audio companions: "Charley, C'rizz, Lucie, Tamsin, Molly: Friends, companions I've known, I salute you."[2]

ROLL CALL: WHO'S WHO

Except where stated otherwise, chronological ages listed here for the Time Lord come from the earliest number mentioned by each Doctor even if they later gave other ages. The actors' ages below refer to how old they were when each performer's first appearance aired.[1]

> *First Doctor*, 236 when he steals the TARDIS according to numbers Romana mentions, therefore Gallifreyan years (played by William Hartnell, 55).
>
> *Second Doctor*, "in Earth terms . . . about 450" (Patrick Troughton, 46).
>
> *Third Doctor*, "several thousand years" (Jon Pertwee, 50).
>
> *Fourth Doctor*, "something like 750 years;" Romana later says he has lost count (Tom Baker, 40).
>
> *Fifth Doctor*, no age given on TV (Peter Davison, 29).
>
> *Sixth Doctor*, 900 (Colin Baker, 40).
>
> *Seventh Doctor*, 953 (Sylvester McCoy, 44).
>
> *Eighth Doctor*, no age given on TV but has spent 700 years traveling in the TARDIS (Paul McGann, 36).[2]

The next few Doctors, introduced since the show's 2005 revival, all state ages younger than the Seventh, with the later-added War Doctor younger than Sixth. How can that be? Perhaps (a) thinking he destroyed Gallifrey prompts the Doctor to switch from Gallifreyan to terrestrial years, (b) they adopt some other dating method, (c) the Time War erases decades from their personal history, or (d) the number resets entirely for reasons unknown.

War Doctor, a.k.a. *Warrior* or *Doctor of War*, 800 (John Hurt, 73).

Ninth Doctor, 900 (Christopher Eccleston, 41).

Tenth Doctor, 903 (David Tennant, 34).

Eleventh Doctor, 907 (Matt Smith, 27).

Twelfth Doctor, 2,000 (Peter Capaldi, 55).

Thirteenth Doctor, "thousands of years, so long I've lost count" (Jodie Whittaker, 36).

Fourteenth Doctor, older (David Tennant, 51).

Fifteenth Doctor, even older (Ncuti Gatwa, 31).[3]

Played by Jo Martin, the Fugitive Doctor turns out to be an earlier regeneration, but her debut reveals neither character age nor sequential order.[4] (While believing she's human Ruth Clayton, she says she's 44.) Whether she precedes the First Doctor or pops up between Second and Third, she is canonically a female Doctor before the Thirteenth and a non-White version earlier than the Fifteenth. Richard Hurndall, 73, and David Bradley, 75, each filled in as the First Doctor while two decades older than William Hartnell had been. Sacha Dhawan, 38, played the Doctor when forced to turn into the Master—an involuntary regeneration not reflective of the true Doctor's preferences or needs.[5] Unconfirmed Doctors include a boy in a barn, the Timeless Child, eight faces projected during a "mind-bending" duel, and Dr. Moon, the 45th Doctor.[6] More certain to be a future Doctor is the Curator, first played by Fourth Doctor actor Tom Baker, 79.[7] If all that doesn't make a fan's head spin, then the Watcher, Valeyard, Dream Lord, and other mysterious manifestations may.[8]

"I think I'm going to need a bigger flowchart."

—**Twelfth Doctor**[9]

I.

THE HEARTS OF WHO WE ARE

We identify ourselves in many ways—among them, how we care for others and whether we'll help them out. When one Time Lord filled with wanderlust chooses the name *The Doctor*, the choice reveals much about who this person is, wants to be, and resolves to become. It is a promise.

"Doctor who? What's he talking about?"
—First Doctor (William Hartnell)[1]

While other areas of psychology might stress how and why we do what we do, personality psychology builds a foundation upon the first question: Who are we?

1

The Who of You:
Interview with Four Doctors and a River on the Core of Personality

Travis Langley & Aaron Sagers

"That's the trouble with regeneration. You never quite know what you're going to get."
—**Fifth Doctor (Peter Davison)**[1]

"To understand what a person is, it is necessary always to refer to what he may be in the future, for every state of the person is pointed in the direction of future possibilities."
—**personality psychologist Gordon Allport**[2]

Stability versus change, one of the classic debates in the psychology of human development, concerns the permanence of "who" we are.[3] Do basic personality traits formed early in life persist through an entire lifetime, or are they all flexible? The person you are at age thirty may be different from who you were at thirteen, and yet you still seem likely to have more in common with who you were back then than with some other individual then or now. The Doctor changes more extremely and more abruptly than most of us might, but as the Eleventh Doctor points out to Clara Oswald right before he becomes the Twelfth, we all change.[4] The Doctor's changes reflect ours. The debate is not over whether change occurs at all. Instead, it is more about whether a person has core traits that will remain deeply ingrained despite all other fluctuations over time.

What Is the Who of You?

Gordon Allport, known as the founder of personality psychology,[5] described individuals in terms of *personality traits*, predispositions to act and react in consistent ways.[6] He observed that some traits tend to go together (*trait clusters*, a.k.a. *personality factors*—covered in chapter 5).[7] He concluded that traits can be what he called cardinal, central, or secondary, depending on how pervasive (infiltrating most aspects of life) and persistent they might be.[8]

Cardinal Traits

A *cardinal trait* is persistent and powerful. Most people do not have this kind of ruling passion that guides everything. Even a particularly friendly person, for whom friendliness is a defining characteristic, probably does not worry daily about finding the friendliest way to brush teeth or eat ice cream. Allport offered sadism as an example of a cardinal trait. Nearly everything the villainous Dominators do seems aimed at hurting others, so in their case, the cruelty seems cardinal. Angel Bob seems no less cruel but possibly only for strategic purposes, trying to unnerve the Eleventh Doctor's group in a specific situation, so we have no basis for judging what that particular Weeping Angel would be like at other times.[9] Fiction often depicts villains as having cardinal traits such as sadism or lust for power, but even they tend to pale in comparison to the single-minded Daleks, driven as they usually are by sheer, murderous hate.[10] When a single trait is all-consuming, the individual with that trait may have a personality disorder because it could interfere with functioning in key areas of life.[11]

Central Traits

Even though most people do not have one trait that affects almost all behavior, each person has a handful of characteristics that each affect a lot of behavior—that person's *central traits*.

In the documentary *The Ultimate Time Lord*, psychologist Mike Aitken told actor Peter Davison (the Fifth Doctor) that even though the Doctor has a dozen "well-established personalities," the character also shows characteristics that carry over from one regeneration to another: steadiness under pressure, risk-taking, extraversion, agreeableness, and possession of an ego that "emerges when a leader is really required" even among the more reserved versions.[12] According to that assessment, these consistent qualities would be the most central traits.

Secondary Traits

Less stable than central traits are the many characteristics that each affect only a little bit of each person's life—the *secondary traits*. Even if someone's love of chocolate is strong and stable, it would be unusual for that preference to affect much of what that person does. The Doctor's love of Jelly Babies candy—first shown by the Second Doctor[13] and most associated with the Fourth[14]—does not show up in every Doctor and does not shape major decisions. It is a quirk, not a characterization. These secondary traits are not at the crux of the stability versus change debate. That has more to do with cardinal and central traits, the ones that answer the first question of who we each truly are.

Who on Who

Journalist Aaron Sagers has interviewed many *Doctor Who* writers and performers.[15] Among his achievements, he broke the news that Tom Baker would appear in the *Doctor Who* 50th anniversary special episode, "The Day of the Doctor," thanks to a revelation from the actor who played the Fourth Doctor, then the Curator, himself.[16] At various fan conventions, Sagers has moderated question-and-answer sessions for *Doctor Who* stars. To help us get to the hearts of "who," he asked five of them about Time Lord identity issues, starting with how they get inside the head of someone so unlike any real humans.

> **David Tennant (Tenth Doctor, Fourteenth Doctor):** I think the process is the same, whatever it is. Every character is a different set of circumstances. Some of them may be based on historical fact or some of them may just come from a script or some might come from your imagination or other people's imagination. With anything, you start with a script and see what else is out there, and

hopefully it coalesces into something that makes a recognizable human being/alien time traveler.

Matt Smith (Eleventh Doctor): Weirdly, with the Doctor, you have got a real person to go on because of years of people doing it and years of stories and years of events. There's a lot of material there.

Sagers: What are the core personality traits of the Doctor? What are the key traits that are shared across regenerations?

Peter Davison (Fifth Doctor): I always thought I wanted to bring a certain naïve recklessness back to the Doctor, a certain vulnerability. I grew up watching *Doctor Who*. My Doctor was Patrick Troughton, and I think he had that. I think it disappeared slightly with Jon Pertwee and Tom Baker. It was something I liked in Patrick Troughton's character, and I wanted to bring that back.

Sylvester McCoy (Seventh Doctor): Funny enough, Patrick Troughton was the first Doctor I saw, but then I lost touch with it because I became an actor. There were no VCRs or ways to record it and keep up with it, and it was never repeated. My distant memory when I arrived in the TARDIS was of Patrick Troughton. Then, I suppose Peter and I are exactly the same!

Smith: I think we're all slightly mental, really. That is what's nice about it when you look across the board. He's always kind of mad.

Alex Kingston (River Song/Melody Pond): I wouldn't call the Doctor a madman.

Smith: That was, I think for me anyway, one of the great virtues of playing him. With most other characters—if you're thinking of him as an alphabet—if you're playing a character and something happens to him, you have to go through A, B, C, D, and then you have to go through F and eventually you get to Z. You go through this whole story. Whereas with the Doctor, you can leap from A without explaining any other letter. The great thing about playing him is he's generally the most intelligent person in the room. He's always the cleverest. He knows the most, which allows him to be the silliest.

Tennant: What I always used to love about the Doctor when I played him were the moments where he'd stop and go, "This is brilliant." There was a sort of joy he felt in facing the little unexplored corners of existence—like the fact that he could stop and celebrate the extraordinariness of a werewolf before it bit his head off. Those moments where he would catch himself and be overcome by the marvelous stuff—there was something in that. I guess what appealed to the Doctor in his companions was a sort of passion similar to that.

Smith: And courage, as well. [The companions] were all quite courageous and defiant. And he needs the antithesis, the balance. He needs someone to tell him, "No, stay away from the werewolf." A central character that is essentially the kind of superhero of the piece, that fixes the world with a toaster and a ball of string. That's how he saves the day: through being mad. That's sort of brilliant.

Kingston: He does it with his smarts, not his guns.

Smith: He is a pacifist, really.

The Doctor Defined?

Who does the better job of pegging a character's essence—actors who played the part or professionals looking on as both psychologists and fans? The more experts that actor Peter Davison spoke with during his attempt to pinpoint who *Who* really is, the more complicated the answer grew.[17] All of these answers are about central personality traits, but they're all complicated by the issue of stability versus change. The Doctor changes more dramatically than we do, but we change too. As several of this book's chapters explain, drastic personality change can occur due to changes in our brains[18] with no regeneration required. Even without traumatic brain injuries, we grow and learn throughout our lives.[19] In this book, we'll explore these issues of who we are from a variety of perspectives, and we'll even contradict each other at times because some of our most human qualities are the most abstract and the most difficult to pin down—yet we should still try. Having the ability to imagine abstraction and complexity, and to ask who we really are, may be the most human qualities of all.

As a couple of our Doctors shared, imagination and sheer humanness lie at the heart of why *Doctor Who* endures.

> **Davison:** It's the endless possibilities, I suppose. I think it appeals to the creative mind, which is why so many people who grew up watching it grew up to work on the show. Showrunners Russell T. Davies, Steven Moffat—huge *Doctor Who* fans. David Tennant—huge *Doctor Who* nerd. It is almost self-perpetuating now. It fires the imagination.

> **McCoy:** They say there are only five stories under the sun, and that mankind's genius is to take these five stories and rewrite them. The story of someone coming from outside Earth, down to Earth, taking on human form, and trying to help in the best way possible, being heroic but at the same time being small and human—that is a very, very attractive story. It has been told over centuries and centuries, going way back.

Aaron Sagers, a National Geographic presenter and former professor at New York State University, hosts *28 Days Haunted* on Netflix and *Paranormal Caught on Camera* on The Travel Channel. He created/co-hosts the *Talking Strange* video/podcast show with Den of Geek. Previous projects include TLC's *Paranormal Lockdown: Evidence Revealed,* Robert Kirkman's *Skybound Happy Hour,* and *Ripley's Road Trip* for *Ripley's Believe It or Not!* In addition to celebrity interviews for the Popular Culture Psychology series, his written works include the book *Rambling and Shambling through the Entertainment of the Unexplained* and articles for *The Chicago Tribune, Miami Herald,* and more.

Travis Langley's bio appears at the beginning of this book.

Left to right: Aaron Sagers, Alex Kingston, Matt Smith, and David Tennant speak to the audience at New York Comic Con. Photo by Charles Cangialos.

A MOMENT WITH JODIE WHITTAKER:

"YOUR ROLE MODELS"

Jenna Busch & Travis Langley

Despite all the Doctor's differences from the rest of us, the character becomes a role model,[20] an example to demonstrate persistence, learning from friends and other companions, inspiring hope that others will do the right thing, and affirming the belief that we might do right too.[21] While we generally think of a role model as someone whose behavior we emulate, one who models the behavior or style we may try to repeat, we also take inspiration from our role models in other ways. We want them to regard us favorably. The Doctor's love and hope for humanity encourages us to show love and hope toward ourselves.

Role models present in observers' own lives are vital, but the influence of positive examples includes role models witnessed indirectly through a variety of media.[22] For example, simply reading about role models' struggles can foster readers' persistence and help them feel more confident about their own chances for success.[23] Stories can help an individual develop a *growth mindset,* a pattern of thinking in which the person understands that, rather than always hindering them, challenges can help them improve their abilities and grow as people.[24]

We asked actor Jodie Whittaker (Thirteenth Doctor) about her Doctor's significance in this regard.[25]

Jenna Busch: How important is this to you?

Jodie Whittaker (Thirteenth Doctor): It's amazing, isn't it? I knew I always wanted to be an actress but never dreamed of becoming the Doctor because it wasn't within the realm of possibility. For little kids, I'm just really excited that, for girls and boys, your role models don't always follow the same gender. We're all pretty similar but come in all shapes and sizes and genders. This is wonderful for fans who have been loyal to the show, to Whovians . . . but for new people who haven't necessarily watched it before, it's an inclusive show.

People feel more inspired by role models with similarities to themselves. Any detectable characteristic can potentially build a sense of similarity. Individuals who grow up without seeing anything distinctive about themselves present in people worthy of admiration may feel less capable of being or becoming admirable themselves. Exposure to *counterstereotypes,* examples of those whose characteristics clearly contradict familiar stereotypes, can improve expectations about others and themselves regarding gender,[26] race,[27] sexual identity,[28] and other role model characteristics. Influential similarities can be more abstract, though, and perceptions of similarities can improve. For example, reading about the struggles of others can help readers empathize with them and feel similar through the shared experience of struggle itself—which, in turn, makes those role models more meaningful and influential to them.[29]

How we love and whom we love can
change throughout the stages of our lives.
Are the Doctors' feelings toward those
closest to them familial, friendly, sexy,
romantic, or something more complex?

2

Love on Board a Big Blue Box

Travis Langley

> "He's the Doctor! He doesn't go around falling in love with people!"
> —River Song (Alex Kingston)[1]

> "Loving someone liberates the lover as well as the beloved. And that kind of love comes with age."
> —memoirist and poet Maya Angelou[2]

"**E**very room you walk into, you laugh at all the men and show off to all the girls," Amy Pond says, asserting that the Eleventh Doctor's alien nature does not make him any less of a "bloke" with a sex drive. When she wonders how many of his companions have been female, young, and "hot," a console screen displays images of previous TARDIS inhabitants. Perhaps in its own bit of mischief, the TARDIS shows only the women, none of the men, and no metal dog.[3]

This Doctor claims not to have noticed how many of the women were "hot." At some points in the Doctor's history, that may be true. The Fourth Doctor tells a countess, "Ah. Well, you're a beautiful woman probably, and Duggan was trying to summon up the courage to ask you out to dinner," so he may not have any personal feelings about her appearance but does observe that someone else finds her attractive.[4] After the Eleventh Doctor (and probably in reaction *to* the Eleventh), the Twelfth shows little ability to recognize age, attractiveness, or many other visual qualities.[5] When he compliments River Song's appearance, she says, "Doctor, you have no idea whether I look amazing or not," but adds that "it's very sweet of you to try."[6] Though she has just met the Twelfth, she knows the Doctor well enough that she considers the Time Lord's obliviousness to beauty to be a deep-rooted trait.

Modern Doctors, those seen since the program returned with the Ninth Doctor in 2005, take more romantic turns than did classic Doctors, but does that make the character genuinely sexual? A person with no sex drive can have romantic interests. An *asexual* individual, one who lacks interest in sexual activity, can want intimate relationships of other kinds. Much as physiological changes due to age, injury, or medication can kill, diminish, or enhance a person's sex drive,[7] so too might regeneration. Classic Doctors often seem asexual and *aromantic* (*a-romantic*, not romantic), and maybe they are. Maybe, though, those versions of the Time Lord simply tend not to have such feelings toward a non-Gallifreyan species.

How much love can two hearts hold? How *does* the Doctor love?

Love over Time

The Doctor's romantic or sexual interests vary with age. This may be circular wherein apparent age can vary at least partly in line with how ready the Doctor is for romance.

"He is the Doctor," Silurian warrior-turned-detective Vastra tells Clara Oswald over tea, admonishing the "impossible girl" for rejecting the Twelfth's new appearance. The mere fact he has changed is not all that makes Clara cross. After all, she has seen a dozen previous Doctors. No, it is because his new face looks old. As far as she knows, previous Doctors all started out young but then some grew older-looking. Vastra chides Clara for this reaction: "He has walked this universe for centuries untold. He has seen stars fall to dust. You might as well flirt with a mountain range."

Clara (Jenna Coleman): I did not flirt with him.

Vastra (Neve McIntosh): He flirted with you.

Clara: How?

Vastra: He looked young. Who do you think that was for?

Clara: Me?

Vastra: Everyone.[8]

By Vastra's reasoning, the Eleventh Doctor's readiness to flirt produced his youngest-looking face when regenerating from the Tenth, but then the Twelfth drops the veil of youth.

The longer the Doctor lives (*chronological age*), the more often this Time Lord regenerates with a younger face (*physical age* or *apparent age*). The age at any point involves two questions: How old is the Doctor, and how old does the Doctor look? Dialogue sometimes answers the first, even if it is not always clear whether the age is in Earth years, Gallifreyan, or some other system—which may explain inconsistencies. The second question may be best addressed by considering the ages at which each actor takes over the role.

Classic Doctors (Pre-Time War)

Early life experiences shape how we relate to others, including how we love. Before the first episode, the Doctor has already lived more than 250 years. Except for possible glimpses of the Doctor as a child, viewers do not see the Doctor before he's an old man stealing a TARDIS.[9] "Such a lonely boy," Reinette (Madame de Pompadour) calls the Doctor's childhood self when the Tenth telepathically links with her. "Lonely then and lonelier now."[10] Not every lonely child grows up to become a lonely adult, but the likelihood for them is higher.[11] Social success, failure, affiliation, affinity, and alienation early in life interact with inborn temperament to mold social actions and needs. The child who connects with family or adults but not peers at least learns social skills. Some will later generalize that to everyone around them, while others may always have trouble opening up to more than a select few people. Once the First Doctor loses all family except for one grand-daughter, he leaves behind everyone else he has ever known.

During early life, the First Doctor has "some experience with the, er, fairer sex."[12] According to Steven Moffat, showrunner for the Eleventh and Twelfth Doctors, the Doctor's "first girlfriend"[13] could be Tasha Lem, a woman who wrestles with the psychopathic side of her nature, or someone like her.[14] Moffat said the great question they never answer is "Who's Mrs. Who?" He said he included the Doctor's Gallifreyan first wife in the count when Clara mentions the Doctor has been "married four times, all deceased."[15] Considering whom that first wife marries, she may be a person of great patience, perhaps as early as their wedding day because the Tenth Doctor calls himself "rubbish at weddings, especially my own."[16]

The Doctor becomes a father and grandfather. Whatever fate has befallen their family, the Doctor will not say.[17] Losing loved ones in traumatizing circumstances (*traumatic loss*)[18] can alter survivors' sense of self and extensive *mindset* (established set of attitudes) or worldview.[19] They may they feel *survivor guilt* for their own continued existence.[20] The Doctor has not *repressed* memories of family, unknowingly locking them away from conscious access, but does *suppress* such thoughts, knowingly pushing them away from conscious awareness.[21] As chapter 6 points out, the Doctor can picture them all when he really wants.

So the First Doctor begins his travels with self-concept fixed on his roles as grandfather and scientist. After years of travels to other worlds, he and Susan reach Earth—where a chameleon circuit makes their TARDIS emulate a police box, then gets it stuck in that form. At this point, the TARDIS is his "ship," and he is years away from growing fond enough for the time machine's intelligence to be adored, much less appreciated as "the Doctor's wife."[22]

The Family Man: The Grandfather in Black and White

When women who traveled with the First and Second Doctors appear among the slideshow on the console screen, the TARDIS does not show Amy that the Doctor looked old back then, and she cannot know that the early Doctors' fondness toward those earliest women was familial. He became a grandfather to them, with nothing sexy about it.

Much as the First Doctor gripes about Ian and Barbara's initial intrusion into the TARDIS or likewise with Polly and Ben later,[23] he quickly grows attached to them. Halfway through the first year, he apologizes to Barbara for acting rudely, and his manner toward them softens.[24] He welcomes each TARDIS passenger's company while they're with him and misses them after they go.[25] When Steven leaves angrily over the Doctor's insistence that they must not change history even to save lives, the Time Lord faces the prospect of traveling alone. Heavy sadness falls over him. The prospect of journeying onward by himself pains him—if only for a moment before Dodo Chaplet blunders in and Steven rushes back to warn the Doctor that police are on the way.[26]

The First and Second Doctors regularly travel with two or three people, including a heroic young man (Ian, Steven, Ben, Jamie) and a granddaughter type who screams well. After granddaughter Susan leaves the show, a succession of surrogates will follow, each an orphan in her mid-teens: Vicki, Katarina, Dodo, Victoria, Zoe. More often than not, the orphan leaves when she finds a new home. Until then, the Doctor serves as foster parent. The two adult women who ride along both join because of the granddaughter figures: Barbara, a teacher trying to inspect student Susan's home life, and Polly, a friend delivering Dodo Chaplet's farewell note.[27] The First Doctor regularly addresses others as "child," certainly because of their age difference but sometimes also because they start to feel like his own children or grandchildren. During the earliest Doctors' time, the companions help meet the Doctor's need for *familial love*.

A grandparent can still have a love life, not that the grandchild necessarily wants to think of them as healthy adults with a romantic or sexual side. Out of all the classic Doctors, surprisingly, it is only the First who clearly opens himself to romance. While visiting Aztecs, he becomes truly smitten with a local sage and philosopher, Cameca, and she falls in love with him.[28] The mere sight of her brightens his day. When Cameca speaks of sharing "a life of bliss with you," full of peace and contentment, the dream pleases him. He cannot stay, though, and she knows. After arguing with Barbara that they must not rewrite history ("Not one line!") by changing fate for any of the Aztec people, the Doctor leaves Cameca behind. He nearly leaves behind a gem she has given him, but reconsiders and takes the souvenir of their romance.

The Mission Man: A Doctor with Assistants and Uninvited Guests

The Third and Fourth Doctors, the earliest to appear in color episodes, have assistants. They embark on missions assigned by organizations in authority—specifically, UNIT (originally the United Nations Intelligence Taskforce) and the Time Lords. These Doctors get assistants. UNIT assigns Liz Shaw and then Jo Grant to work as the Third Doctor's assistants.[29] The Time Lords send Romana to assist the Fourth Doctor on a quest to assemble the Key to Time.[30] The assistants' gender is unlikely to be random. The Doctor does not choose those assistants, though, so the selection reflects sexism either on the part of those who assigned them (like hiring women as secretaries or other positions stereotypical at that time) or in their perceptions of the Doctor himself (thinking he would accept a female assistant more readily than a male). Even the oh-so-advanced Time Lords dispatch Time Lady Romana as the Doctor's subordinate, not partner.

After Jo but well before Romana, though, comes journalist Sarah Jane Smith. She technically becomes the Third Doctor's assistant to get UNIT security clearance, but only *after* the Doctor convinces her to stay. Because previous Doctors never could control the TARDIS, this makes Sarah Jane the first companion whom the Doctor entices by offering to take her anywhere and anywhen she would like to go. Feeling melancholy over Jo's exit,[31] he seeks a friend. The Fourth Doctor will introduce her as his best friend.[32] Sarah may start to romanticize her perceptions of their relationship in hindsight by the time she meets the Tenth, but any love the most alien-seeming Fourth Doctor feels appears *platonic* (caring friendship, no sexual or romantic interest), not even *companionate* as psychologists use the term.[33] Companionate love involves a deeper and more personal use of the word *companion* akin to that of significant other or life partner, not a relationship the Doctor is clearly shown to have.

After Sarah, the Fourth Doctor might prefer to travel alone. He rejects Leela's request to accompany him, then shouts for her to get out as she barges into the TARDIS and hits a switch that makes it take off.[34] Later, Leela talks him into accepting K9 Mark I, Adric stows away in the TARDIS, the Master brings Nyssa to the Doctor when her homeworld gets destroyed, and Tegan, like Dodo before her, rushes into the police box in need of help.[35] Adric and Tegan travel with the

Doctor before he even knows they're in the TARDIS. No, Amy's later insinuation that the Doctor chooses to travel with "hot," young women fares poorly with the Fourth Doctor. In point of fact, the only companions he actively selects are UNIT physician Harry Sullivan (whom the Doctor and Sarah coax into the TARDIS as a bit of a prank) and K9 Mark II—a man and a robot dog that goes by *he* and *it* pronouns.[36]

In support of Amy's insinuation, though, some fans perceived signs of romance between the second Romana and the Fourth Doctor.[37] She takes a turn becoming his best friend, too, but this time with a level of playful banter between equals never repeated in the classic series and little seen in the modern. Romana is a member of the Doctor's own species, after all, a fellow immortal. Her intellect can challenge him, and she shares his culture, moral values, and adventurous spirit. They complete their assigned mission, and yet she stays with him. For how long? Who knows? Their seasons together on the show could span decades of their lives. The Doctor's affection shows in his smile and tone when he whispers, "Psst. You are wonderful." Romana beams.[38] Could such glimpses hint at true companionate love developing between them?

The progression of the Doctor/Romana relationship reflects the actors' relationship behind the scenes. Actors Tom Baker and Lalla Ward played up the romantic side when they appeared as the Doctor and Romana in computer commercials (not canon to the TV show) that suggested hanky-panky in the big blue box. In one ad, the Doctor proposes marriage and Romana accepts.[39] The television episode in which the Doctor calls Romana wonderful aired seven days before actors Baker and Ward married in real life. Alas, the marriage lasted a mere sixteen months, and some of Romana's later frustration may foretell other things that would happen in real life as well. After Romana departs, the Doctor gazes sadly into her vacant TARDIS room.[40]

Wanderer with One Companion

The Doctor's long-running habit of voluntarily traveling with one specific woman at a time begins late in the tenure of the Fifth Doctor, who happened to be played by the youngest actor to fill the role until flirty number Eleven. Initially, the Fifth inherits the Fourth's entourage, then accepts Turlough's request to travel with them only so he can keep an eye on the untrustworthy young man.[41] This Doctor's friendship with one carryover from the Fourth, Tegan Jovanka, evolves. At one point, he abandons her at an airport while he and Nyssa rush off to avoid the airport controller. (Having finally returned Tegan to Earth after months trying to help her get home, they don't know she has reconsidered staying behind.) When Tegan later returns, Nyssa is overjoyed but the Doctor looks annoyed.[42] Nevertheless, the fact that he lets her rejoin prepares him to regard her more favorably. Feeling that we have choice (*perceived volition*) and control over a situation (*perceived control*, even when it's *illusory control*) fortifies our commitment to choices we've already made.[43] When Tegan later rants in frustration that she wants to go home, he calls her bluff, saying, "It's a shame, of course. There were many wonders I wanted to show you."[44] The Fifth Doctor tempts Tegan with what the Third Doctor has pitched to Sarah Jane and most modern Doctors will offer their own companions. So Tegan stays with him and Turlough . . . until eventually she doesn't.

The aforementioned habit of choosing to travel with one person, one woman, at a time begins with the Fifth's final companion, an American, Peri Brown.[45] Nothing romantic manifests through the remainder of the show's original run, though. The arrogant Sixth Doctor looks down on everyone, even those he likes. The Seventh Doctor's relationship with Melanie Bush, then with Ace, is mentor-to-apprentice. His manner seems so professorial that Ace calls him "Professor" from the moment after they meet.[46] Though his lessons can be harsh, their bond grows. His connection with Ace turns paternal, maybe grandfatherly once more. His words to her years later, via A.I. interface, cover both parts of how he sees her: as a student he hopes to teach and as a child he hopes will fly high after she leaves home.[47]

Transitioning Through the Time War

The Eighth Doctor starts all the kissing.

After the original program ended, a TV movie attempted to revive *Doctor Who* with a more amorous, more human Doctor. The Eighth thinks of himself as "half human, on my mother's side,"[48] despite sources that contradict this as his literal heritage.[49] (In fact, the Doctor's Gallifreyan mother possibly shows up later to help Donna's grandfather look out for the Tenth.)[50] Regardless of why the Eighth Doctor views himself as equally Gallifreyan and human, that is in the self-concept of the Doctor who kisses Dr. Grace Holloway several times.

This incarnation suffers post-regeneration amnesia more severely than other Doctors do. As far as this "John Doe" knows at first, he is the same species as anyone around him. Excitement over remembering his identity inspires him to kiss Grace. *Disinhibition*, loss of inhibitions, starts occurring more often during amnesia recovery as loosening restraints on memory accompanies the loosening of other *cognitive* (mental) or emotional restrictions.[51] Amnesia itself can potentially be liberating when the individual forgets reasons for not doing certain things.[52] When Doctors forget who they are, they fall in love. As tour guide Ruth Clayton, the Fugitive Doctor has a husband. As schoolteacher John Smith, the Tenth Doctor wishes to live a long and human life wed to nurse Joan Redfern.[53]

The Eighth Doctor generally keeps out of the Time War until tragic experiences leave him disheartened. "I don't suppose there's a need for a doctor anymore. Make me a warrior."[54] So this "half-human" romantic regenerates into a Gallifreyan warrior whom others call the War Doctor or Doctor of War even though he feels he no longer deserves to be called Doctor at all.

Stories on screen reveal little more about how the Eighth and War Doctors relate to other people. When the War Doctor encounters two of his future selves, he is surprised to witness the Tenth Doctor's private wedding with Queen Elizabeth I.

War Doctor (John Hurt) *(as bride kisses groom)*: Is there a lot of this in the future?

Eleventh Doctor (Matt Smith): It does start to happen, yeah.[55]

Modern Doctors (Post-Time War)

Horrified by the Time War and his part in it, the Doctor grows progressively younger-looking through what should be his last regenerations. In this way, he (still consistently male for a while) runs away from his oldest-looking self to escape into youth, and into a more human nature. Home is where the TARDIS is, and yet, despite returning to Gallifrey so rarely, the Doctor has always called that world home. With Gallifreyans and their planet gone, needs for *affiliation* and *rootedness* (respectively, to unite with others and to have a sense of coming from somewhere to which you can return) ache.[56] Though not from Earth, he declares himself its protector.[57]

End of the Cycle

The Ninth Doctor appears, takes Rose Tyler by the hand, and says to run.[58] He often holds her hand, whether leading her from danger, offering reassurance, or simply walking along—something past Doctors would not do.[59] His time as the Doctor ends with a kiss. Okay, he kisses her as part of the process to transfer energy back into the TARDIS, but he could do that another way. A classic Doctor would have. The Ninth Doctor chooses to kiss her.[60]

The turning point for the Doctor may take place in "The Doctor Dances"[61] (an episode that actor Eccleston discussed with us when interviewed for chapter 20). Rose's comparison between the Doctor and Jack Harkness reveals something of how she sees the Doctor: "I trust him because he's like you, except with dating and dancing." The Doctor objects to her assumption: "Nine hundred years old, me. I've been around a bit. I think you can assume at some point I've danced." He seems unable to dance, though, until glee over successfully saving everyone that night brings it back to him.

Ninth Doctor (Christopher Eccleston): Rose! I've just remembered.

Rose (Billie Piper): What?

Doctor: *(dancing)* I can dance! I can dance!

Rose: Actually, Doctor, I thought Jack might like this dance.

Doctor: I'm sure he would, Rose. I'm absolutely certain. But who with?

At one point in the story, dancing also serves as his euphemism for the human race's procreation and propagation. So when he remembers how to dance, what else awakens in him?

After energy flowing from Rose to Doctor to TARDIS makes him regenerate, no Doctor falls in love more readily than the Tenth, the Doctor forged from that kiss. He loves Rose, falls for Joan while amnesiac, starts falling for Reinette, says Astrid can join his travels *after* she has already expressed interest in waking up with him in the morning, and marries a queen of England.[62] This regeneration is ready to hook up. Although, to the chagrin of Martha Jones, despite her observation that he behaves like a man on a date during their first trip through time, he's not ready for rebound romance right after losing Rose.[63] People who experience divorce, death, and other loss may feel reluctant to "love again."[64] Reasons vary. Many fear risking further loss, others mourn those they've lost so strongly that they cannot yet imagine loving someone else, some feel unworthy, and more than a few worry they've forgotten how. Even the Tenth Doctor, during one early adventure, expresses one such fear to Rose: "Humans decay. You wither and you die. Imagine watching that happen to someone that you . . . "[65] A majority of people reach the point when they do feel ready again.[66] This Doctor does. Probably the most hetero of the modern Doctors, he keeps finding women he can love.

Steven Moffat argues that Rose pulls the Doctor out of depression "and resurrects him as an engaged, heroic figure."[67] She brings him to life. It is not simply the fact that she's there first. And, though universes may keep them apart, his passion for Rose endures. He will not say it. Although, as he burns up a sun just to power up their interdimensional farewell at Bad Wolf Bay, he apparently starts to say it before their call gets cut off.[68] Later, though, Rose gets a Doctor she can keep. The Metacrisis that allows the Tenth Doctor to regenerate without changing faces also creates the so-called Metacrisis Doctor, essentially a full-grown clone except that he is mortal with one heart. Faced with two nearly identical men, Rose asks what the Doctor meant to say that day on the beach. He does not tell her, but his duplicate whispers the answer in her ear. That quiet profession of love cues Rose to embrace the duplicate and welcome this loving part of the Doctor into the rest of her life.[69]

Other kinds of love also matter to this Doctor. He thanks Donna Noble for saving his life many times over simply by being his friend, and though their mutual bond remains platonic, Donna hopes to travel with him for the rest of her life.[70] Family needs linger, too, try as he might to deny them. When he sees Jenny, a full-grown daughter artificially created from his involuntary skin sample, he sees his late family. Caught up in *denial,* the defense mechanism of denying a truth that feels painful,[71] the Doctor at first rejects Jenny. In a rare mention of his lost kin, "the hole they left, all the pain that filled it," he tells Donna that "when they died, that part of me died with them. It'll never come back."[72] Donna tells him he's wrong. His hearts house plenty of room for family again, and he does come to accept Jenny as a daughter.

The Eleventh Doctor builds extended family—after moving past a sort of romantic triangle once Amy understands the depths of her love for Rory and Rory's for her. In addition to his companion—and eventual mother-in-law—Amy Pond, her husband Rory Williams, and their daughter Melody who becomes River Song, the Eleventh assembles a full adventuring party of friends for a few excursions and as allies in time of need.[73] Vastra leads some of those friends in providing him respite and solace while mourning losses, until he's ready to travel again.[74]

The Eleventh Doctor happens to be the Time Lord's flirtiest, kissingest manifestation. He smooches anyone. He dances with anyone, too, including all women and men at Amy's wedding, and has weddings of his own.[75] And yet this version's creator, showrunner Steven Moffat, considered him "more sexless and less of a lad"[76] than other modern depictions. Despite feeling the weight of his centuries, this youngest-looking Doctor can act the most childlike and immature. His flirtatiousness is superficial. He has no follow-through. The mere mention of something as intimate as human conception makes him gulp in discomfort.[77] Though the Eleventh Doctor readily plays the role of

Clara's boyfriend when she "accidentally invented a boyfriend" to keep relatives from pestering her, the next Doctor after him will apologize for the mistake of having ever treated her like he really was one.[78]

The New Cycle

When the Doctor gains a new lease on life, a fresh cycle of regenerations he never expected to have, he trusts Clara enough to show her a face that looks more like he feels: older. Along with turning less flirty, less superficially amiable, the Twelfth Doctor can be the *un*friendliest Doctor since the Time War through a sort of *reaction formation* (displaying the opposite of an unconscious impulse or previous behavior for which one feels guilty).[79] That's not to call him passionless. His temper can be fiery and his loyalty fierce. In terms of more personal treatment, though, he reserves that for those closest to his own kind, one Gallifreyan and one human who also has some Time Lord DNA: Missy and River.[80] The Twelfth Doctor cannot even remember the Tenth's adventure with the fully human Madame de Pompadour.[81]

After regenerating, the question of whether he is a good man haunts the Twelfth Doctor. But when Missy, the Doctor's oldest friend and enemy now regenerated as a woman, offers him an army with the power to determine the outcome of every invasion and war, his ability to reject the temptation gives him the answer: Rather than a good man or a bad man, he is "an idiot! With a box and a screwdriver, just passing through, helping out, learning." He needs no army when he has people to love: "Always them! Because love, it's not an emotion. Love is a promise." The grateful Doctor plants a kiss on Missy, not unlike the first kiss (just the first one) the Eighth Doctor gave Grace when he also gained sudden insight into his own nature.[82] Later, he and Missy put time and work into trying to become friends again.[83]

As for River Song, consider: The Tenth Doctor meets her and the Eleventh marries her, but it is the Twelfth who honeymoons her through a twenty-four-year-long night. Despite calling the Eleventh "my Doctor" and ardently loving him, River believes—and accepts—that he has never loved her back. To criminals who want to use her to bait the Doctor, she shouts that "if I happen to find myself in danger, the Doctor is not stupid enough or sentimental enough, and he is certainly not in love enough to find himself standing in it with me!"—right before she finally realizes the man standing in it with her is the Doctor wearing yet another face. Then comes his turn to deliver her usual greeting, his eyes and tone full of affection: "Hello, sweetie." River has mainly known the boyish Eleventh, but the Twelfth Doctor is a man.

Twelfth's successor, the first female Doctor as far as they can recall, shifts away from romance. Needing friends and missing family, the Thirteenth Doctor becomes the first one since the Fifth Doctor to travel regularly with a group of not one, not two, but three companions. Once she knows them well enough, she calls them her "fam" and, when past companions later join them on an adventure, "extended fam."[84] One of them, Yaz, falls for this Doctor. The Time Lord tries not to notice, in denial once again, but a newer companion calls her on it. Soon, the Doctor discusses this with Yaz.

Thirteenth Doctor (Jodie Whittaker): Dates are not something I really do, you know. I mean, I used to. Have done. And if I was going to, believe me, it'd be with you. I think you're one of the greatest people I've ever known . . . If it was going to be anyone, it'd be you. But I can't.

Yasmin (Mandip Gill): Why not?

Doctor: Because, at some point, time always runs out.[85]

Yaz does not bring it up again. She stays with the Doctor as devoted companion until the time comes for Thirteenth to regenerate into Fourteenth. For Yaz and the Thirteenth, their relationship resembles that of a comfortable couple, and not every couple needs sex and romance to feel fulfilled.[86] This is not simply about the Thirteenth's gender, not within the fiction. The Doctors who start the new cycle of regenerations, those after the Eleventh, aren't wooing mortals. Admittedly, the Thirteenth doesn't show a lot of warmth toward the latest Master, but she's probably disappointed in him for not retaining Missy's personal growth. Whatever feelings this Doctor has for Yaz, do those make her lesbian, bisexual, pansexual, or anything else in sexual or romantic orientation? It's doubtful she feels a need to apply a label. The fact that her earlier, forgotten female self, the Fugitive Doctor, married a man gives the Thirteenth Doctor not one whit of concern.

Among genderbending Time Lords, it is not queer to be queer.

The Doctor's Wife

One psychological model of love, the *triangular theory of love*, holds that love can be understood in terms of three components: *intimacy* (feelings of closeness), *passion* (in this context, drives leading to romance, attraction, or sex), and *commitment*.[87] Though the Doctor gets closer to the companions than to anyone else, the Time Lord's secrecy frustrates them. Ironic as it may seem for the immortal who keeps moving on from companions, rarely looking back, though, commitment is one of the strongest aspects of the Doctor's love.

The commitment component differs in the short or long term, regarding how powerfully one person commits to another for now versus planning to maintain that for the duration. The Doctor is powerfully committed to companions on hand but avoids thinking much about where they're going. When Rose asks if he'll leave her behind one day like Sarah Jane, the Tenth Doctor at first says that will not happen to her and yet, seconds later, admits the problem: "You can spend the rest of your life with me, but I can't spend the rest of mine with you. I have to live on. Alone."[88] In the here and now, the Doctor is committed. In one example, Clara attempts to betray the Twelfth Doctor in order to change time and save her boyfriend, then assumes he is done with her. He scoffs, "Why? Do you think I care for you so little that betraying me would make a difference?"[89] This may play a part in the Doctor's reluctance to give up on the Master.

Of the triangular theory's three components, how many of them does the Doctor feel? Ever? Not everyone feels them all. Not everyone can. A human who has spent a long adulthood without getting close to anyone else, without disclosing much about themselves, does not fully overcome intimacy issues. One who has lived without desiring sex and romance is unlikely to turn into a lascivious lover late in life.[90] And the Doctor has had centuries to establish traits. Even so, surprises happen.

Drives can fluctuate, people can change, and regeneration can rewrite it all. The Doctor comes closest to feeling all three, as much as possible, toward one figure, arguably the nearest thing to a significant other: "the Doctor's wife," the TARDIS herself.[91]

Embodied in Idris, the TARDIS says she originally chose the Doctor, "my thief," to take her from Gallifrey because she wanted to travel, at the same time he wanted to get away with his granddaughter. The Doctor has always known the TARDIS is more than machine, and yet the First Doctor simply calls the TARDIS his "ship." He gives no thought to its sentience until an occasion when the TARDIS attempts to warn him and his companions of danger.[92] Over the centuries, he grows attached to the TARDIS, turning down opportunities to trade it for a better-functioning model. The Fourth Doctor starts calling the TARDIS "old girl" and sometimes expresses concern for her feelings. Calling the TARDIS both *it* and *her* is like the earthly tradition of referring to ships as female, though, and does not confirm how seriously he thinks of the TARDIS as a genuine entity at that point. Nevertheless, the attachment grows. After all, the TARDIS is truly the one enduring companion and partner. The Eleventh Doctor finally gets to speak with her as Idris, then weeps when that time comes to an end.

Three Loves

The Twelfth Doctor commits to guarding Missy in a vault under St. Luke's University. During this time, he sets up office and he lectures on whatever he pleases for over fifty years. In his office, the TARDIS sits by an entrance. On the office desk, facing him whenever he takes his chair, two photographs show Susan and River looking out at him with gentle smiles. He keeps these loved ones with him: the TARDIS, companionate love; River, romantic love; and Susan, family love. Together, they represent the diversity of his love. They also remind him of love of other kinds, such as his love of adventure and his love for the human race. When conflicted over whether to let Bill Potts keep her memories of their first adventure and the fact that he knows this will lead to more, he imagines Susan, River, and the TARDIS all have plenty to say on the matter. He tells them to shut up, "I can't do that anymore. I promised," but then promptly takes the TARDIS outside to reintroduce it to Bill.

Many other loved ones have filled the Doctor's life, many others for whom he cares even if he's rubbish at showing it. His hearts are huge. The Doctor may not have forever with any companion, but they share a powerful *now*.

"Psychology as a science has its limitations, and . . . the ultimate consequence of psychology is love."
—psychoanalyst Erich Fromm[93]

"Love is always wise."
—Twelfth Doctor (Peter Capaldi)[94]

"GRANDFATHER!"
STYLES OF INTERRELATIONS
ACROSS THE GENERATIONS

People relate to their children's children in many ways and for many reasons. One typology of *grandparenting styles* distinguishes them based on the quantity and quality of each grandparent's behavioral interaction with and connection to the grandchild.[95]

The *formal* grandparent follows a traditional role by maintaining a relationship, providing some childcare assistance, but not becoming overly involved. Although the Doctor breaks traditions left and right, the First does seem more formal than subsequent Doctors. This may be the role he plays before becoming her only family.

The *surrogate parent* assumes much responsibility for childrearing. At some point, the Doctor becomes this out of necessity, literally becoming *custodial grandparent*. For how long does he fill that role? The loss of her parents must not be recent for Susan, who has already traveled with her grandfather for years.[96] She neither mentions parents nor shows the kind of behaviors (such as withdrawing or acting out) seen in an adolescent who avoids talking about deceased parents while the loss is fresh.[97] Kids are more resilient than adults, especially regarding events from early in life when everything is new and chaotic. Custodial grandparents may feel disenfranchised from their own grief as they try to stay strong for the grandchild and as the necessities and duties of new roles isolate them from their own peers.[98] This may keep the Doctor from processing grief, thus figuring into why the memories stay so sharply painful centuries later.

The *fun seeker*, playful and informal, wants to do more than simply provide the grandchild with a good experience but wants to have fun together. Fans may find it easier to imagine later Doctors as the fun-seeking type, but the First Doctor can be fun. When later depictions emphasize what a curmudgeon the First Doctor truly can be, they leave out his mischief and mirth. The man chuckles often—and giggles! Susan does not act as though she relates to him as the fun seeker, but she is one serious adolescent and he is, after all, the one who leads her away from Gallifrey in search of fun and adventure. Maybe he has always been her fun-seeking grandparent, or maybe he tries to become that for her, taking her away on travels to escape a world full of unpleasant reminders and to introduce some moments of fun into her tragic life.

The *distant* grandparent, though benevolent, is not around the child much. Contact is infrequent, typically at holidays or specific family gatherings. This is not the Doctor, not even before Susan's parents die. Her familiarity, devotion, and trust toward him suggest that he has been integral throughout the life she remembers. Although, once later Doctors start piloting the TARDIS better, why aren't they seen visiting Susan before they think her lost with the rest of the Gallifreyans?

The grandparent as *reservoir of family wisdom* becomes a source of wisdom, resources, and skills. The Doctor shows many such qualities. "My dear girl," the First Doctor tells Susan, "the one purpose in growing old is to accumulate knowledge and wisdom. And to help other people." Although, he is not as consistently *authoritarian* as that type tends to be. Even at this bossier point in his history, his *anti*authoritarian streak runs strong. He detests blind, unthinking obedience.

Moral foundations underlie a wide range of behavior, sometimes even the acts other people see as villainous. Though the Doctor's views on what's the right thing to do evolves over time, an ethical substrate stays with the traveler who, while seeming aimless, follows a moral path.

3

The Moral Foundations of *Doctor Who*

Deirdre Kelly & Jim Davies

> "Winning? Is that what you think it's about? I'm not trying to win.
> I'm not doing this because I'm trying to beat someone or because I hate someone...
> I do what I do because it's right! Because it's decent! And above all, it's kind."
> —**Twelfth Doctor (Peter Capaldi)**[1]

> "Moral systems are interlocking sets of values, virtues, norms, practices, identities, institutions, technologies, and evolved psychological mechanisms that work together to suppress or regulate self-interest and make cooperative societies possible."
> —**psychologist Jonathan Haidt**[2]

 ocial psychologist Jonathan Haidt proposed a theory of *moral psychology*[3] that helps us make sense of the nature of evil, if it even exists, both in fiction and in our world. His theory holds that people are born with the capacity to develop six foundations that we each care about to varying degrees: care/harm, liberty/oppression, authority/subversion, fairness/cheating, loyalty/betrayal, and sanctity/degradation. The foundations evolved as a result of various adaptive social challenges that humans encountered. For Haidt, a region's history, traditions, and other socioeconomic factors contribute to the moral development of the moral foundations in those groups.

Each person's level of regard for these foundations is like an equalizer that determines their moral profile, and the various antagonists within *Doctor Who* exemplify moral profiles as varied as their cultures. When one or more of these moral intuitions goes too high or too low, a creature can start to believe things to be right that most others will find morally repugnant—it's true for humans, and it's true for the villains of *Doctor Who*.

The Moral Foundations of Villainy?

Doctor Who is full of fascinating villains who vary not only in species but in their fundamental moral outlooks on the universe. Rather than being black-hatted, hand-wringing evildoers, bent on spreading chaos and destruction, many of them think they are doing the right thing. Their morals just conflict with the Doctor's—and ours.

Care and Harm

The foundation of *care/harm* may have developed as a response to our need to care for children and protect them from harm.[4] This foundation originally emerged in response to suffering or distress in children, but can now more broadly be when things we perceive as less powerful are attacked by something more powerful. For example, seeing someone innocent get hurt would generate a response from this foundation.

The human condition is rife with emotion. By the Cybermen's reasoning, there could be no better life than one free of suffering, so the best and morally right thing to do is to remove these emotional bonds from people. The Cybermen offer humans two choices: to be upgraded, like them, or to be deleted. When the Tenth Doctor confronts a Cyberman who explains that they are humans 2.0, it is clear that this Cyberman believes that what they are offering is a genuine gift and opportunity for humans.[5]

Offering someone a life of logic, free from pain and free from worry about death, can be seen as the purest form of altruism within the context of Cybermen's underlying moral foundations.[6] Such a care/harm foundation appears to be the only moral foundation that Cybermen have. As such, they are willing to sacrifice all other moral foundations—such as liberty, fairness, and sanctity—in service of it.

In contrast, Sontaran morality is characterized by its complete *lack* of care—certainly to those who are not Sontaran: They do not mind causing harm to others, and they have a high disregard for those in their society who care for the sick or injured. The Sontarans inflict a lot of harm and are, from our current human perspective, acting immorally. Some human cultures have exhibited similar militaristic values. For example, the Greek Spartans believed that being a good citizen required being a good soldier.[7] Spartan values left little room for compassion or kindness in others, especially when it came to enemies of the state. Based on the Sontarans' moral underpinnings, their actions not only make sense but also are morally appropriate to some degree.

Liberty and Oppression

The *liberty/oppression* foundation is concerned with how much freedom people have and can exercise. Viewing bullies or people trying to dominate others can activate this foundation. It serves as the moral center for those with Libertarian political leanings who want the state to have very little authority over their lives. The Cybermen completely lack the liberty foundation—they are examples of quintessential paternalists. They believe they know what is best for all other species and will upgrade all others for their own benefit. This has also been shown to be the main motivation of the Cybermen in the twenty-first-century *Doctor Who* episodes.

Authority and Subversion

The *authority/subversion* foundation holds that it is morally good to obey those who have authority over you. This foundation developed in the face of having to form societal relationships within a hierarchical group. Interactions with bosses and other superiors or watching others interact with them (*observational learning*) may activate this foundation. We can see signs of authority among nonhuman animals, too, such as chickens, chimpanzees, and dogs, and many other animals that live in groups. Subversive behavior often gets punished in groups of animals, human and otherwise.[8] Our leaders demand things of us, but we also expect benefits from them (such as protection) in return. We are creatures innately predisposed to hierarchical power arrangements.

When Davros creates the Daleks, mutations of his own species, he removes all traits that he perceives as potential weaknesses, such as compassion and love, and gives his Daleks an incredible loyalty to their cause, that of exterminating outsiders.[9] Human beings have been found to be very obedient, too—the shocking experiments of Stanley Milgram in the 1960s showed that a surprising number of people were willing to deliver severe electric shocks simply because they were told to do so by someone wearing a white lab coat.[10] This suggests that the authority foundation is present and can be activated in all of us, to some degree.

When the Fourth Doctor beseeches Davros to stop the development of the Daleks with their evil minds, Davros fails to see the Daleks' desires as evil and insists, "When all other lifeforms are suppressed, when the Daleks are the supreme rulers of the universe, then you will have peace. Wars will end. They are the power not of evil, but of good."[11] As psychologist Erich Fromm noted, many people will tolerate great atrocities for the sake of security, stability, and order.[12] The Daleks never question the order or whether becoming the dominant species is the right thing to do, but instead arrange their lives to conform to it.

The Sontarans, too, adhere to the authority foundation. As in all militaristic cultures, the Sontaran Empire presents with a high respect for hierarchy and authority. We see this in human military culture as well. For example, people who join the military tend to be more obedient to authority and more inclined to follow rules.[13] The Sontaran High Command issues orders downward to the rest of the Empire. Each Sontaran has a rank and acts accordingly. When authority figures call for harm to be done, those who don't have enough of the care/harm foundation may not stop and question the ethics of what they're doing.

Fairness and Cheating

The *fairness/cheating* foundation (based on justness and equitable rewards without taking undue advantage of others[14]) developed out of a need for people to get what they deserve—good things as well as bad. It can be triggered by instances of cheating and cooperation. Violation of this foundation leads to people feeling morally outraged at perceived injustice and unfair benefits. This feeling can be triggered by someone free-riding, where they are getting some benefit they are not entitled to, or when someone doesn't get the credit they deserve, or when someone is unfairly punished.

The person who cheats on a test is deriving an unfair benefit that rule abiders do not receive. This kind of free-riding undermines group cooperation and cohesiveness. Additionally, if the cheater is not punished, this can lead to further feelings of resentment and breakdown of group cohesion.[15]

The Judoon, a rhino-headed lot who strictly enforce justice (for hire), quickly punish any who cheat the system as they see it. They are so focused on adherence to their goals and rules that they are willing to blow up a whole hospital to punish a criminal or destroy the town of Gloucester to find the Fugitive Doctor.[16] This focus on punishing cheaters and disregarding the well-being of those who get in their way demonstrates the danger of having an overly sensitive fairness/cheating foundation.

Loyalty and Betrayal

Loyalty is about staying true to others with whom you have a coalition, those who share your land, heritage, biology, history, values, and other traits to create a consistent group or *ingroup*. These traits are used not only to define those with whom we are connected but, by extension, also those who are outside of the group, the *outgroup*. Because humans are a social species who rely on each other for survival and reproduction, we can see how loyalty would have been an asset for our ancestors. This loyalty can be directed toward a specific person (as is more common among females) or in groups and teams (more common among males).[17] Groups of humans have always competed with groups of other humans, putting an adaptive pressure on preferential treatment to ingroup members.[18]

Identifying with an ingroup and seeing other groups as outsiders may be inherent to the *loyalty/betrayal* foundation.[19] An example of this kind of loyalty to one's group is seen in the Sontarans' willingness to fight only for their own species. Those who would fight for others are seen as traitors. This moral foundation underpins a strong sense of loyalty to those they serve with and to the species as a whole. Contributing to this militaristic culture is their high respect for ingroup loyalty. The loyalty/betrayal moral foundation developed to promote group support and can currently be seen among fans of sports teams when they rally behind their team. This kind of loyalty is also evinced in humans' choices to serve their country through military and other public service.[20]

While they are not an overly aggressive species, the Silurians have entered into combat with humans on a few occasions when threatened, including their first appearance in *Doctor Who*.[21] When revived by underground drilling,[22] they interpret that as an attack and retaliate. The violence comes to a head when the sister of the military leader of the Silurians, Restac, is murdered by humans. In revenge, Restac wants to wipe out all humans. This demonstrates the close nature of the loyalty foundation the Silurians feel to their own species. As a group, they are fiercely loyal to one another to the point of being willing to wipe out another species to avenge a fallen sister.

Sanctity and Degradation

The *sanctity/degradation* foundation evolved to feel disgust in the presence of dangerous pathogens in people or objects, such as corpses, excrement, and visible disease.[23] But now cultures can differ in what triggers disgust, and often find outgroups disgusting for one reason or another. (For example, bloody injuries tend to evoke greater disgust in some cultures than in others.[24]) The opposite is purity or sanctity, which is what makes people feel moral outrage when something sacred to them (e.g., a Bible, a flag, a picture of the Dalai Lama) is treated poorly—such as getting burned as a part of an art project or political statement.[25] (Many atrocities have been committed in the history of our world in the name of racial purity, including forced sterilization[26] and acts of genocide.[27])

Daleks use species purity to set themselves apart from impure Daleks and from other species: The way in which the Daleks view their species as superior to others can be seen as a form of *speciesism*. Daleks consider only themselves to have value. Even those with similar genetics seem dispensable to them, as the Doctor knows well. Facing a

Dalek attack, the Thirteenth Doctor informs a Dalek death squad of the presence of mutant Daleks. Perceiving a purity conflict, the death squad exterminates the mutants and thus saves Earth from them.[28]

Understanding the Morality of the Master

"And so it came to pass that the human race fell, and the Earth was no more. And I looked down upon my new dominion as Master of all, and I thought it good."

—The Master (John Simm)[29]

How then do we as viewers interpret the motivations of someone who does not demonstrate a developed moral sense, a person who seems to place no importance whatsoever on moral foundations? Before Missy accepts incarceration in the vault, the Masters do what they want, when they want. If it makes them happy to do so, then they will be the Doctor's greatest archenemy and attempt to kill their lifelong frenemy at every turn. At other times, they will claim to be a best friend and fight to save the Doctor's life.[30] Is the Master devoid of any moral sense or is there another explanation for the character's amorality? In the purest sense, Missy is an ethical egoist. *Ethical egoism* is the view that the right thing to do is whatever promotes one's self-interest.[31] She can act good when it is in her best interest to do so, but when villainy better suits her ends (and she tends to believe it does), that is the path she takes.[32]

The degree to which humans are inherently motivated by selfish or egoistic reasons remains a question of wide interest. While the research continues to evolve, there is evidence to suggest that human motivations and reasons for ethical behavior are varied. There are times when we are more inclined toward selfishness, but we are also capable of acting incredibly prosocial and in service of others in our family, community, and even complete strangers. Unlike the Master, who seems to act merely from their own self-interest, human morality tends to be much more complex and contextual, influenced by many factors including cognitive biases, our current stress levels, or the people with whom we spend our time.[33]

While the Masters take no issue with lying when it serves them, they do take issue when others lie to or withhold information from them. The Spymaster or "O" Master tells the Thirteenth Doctor he discovered they had been lied to about the nature of Gallifreyan regeneration. In anger, the Master attacks their home planet and all its inhabitants.[34] While many of us see the Master's actions as hypocritical, an ethical egoist could argue that the actions align with maximization of self-interest and, by that logic, are ethically consistent and justified.

The Masters' incredible commitment to self-interest makes them a Dorian Gray–like mirror to the Doctors' continued commitment to acting with kindness throughout all of space and time.

The Moral Foundations of Villainy Explained

> "Evil? No! No, I will not accept that. They are conditioned simply to survive.
> They can survive only by becoming the dominant species."
> —**Davros (Michael Wisher), the Daleks' creator**[35]

The full spectrum of moral foundations can be found in the various villains of *Doctor Who*. Moral development involves a range of views, and morality itself becomes increasingly complex for many individuals. Some of the most heinous acts are committed on the grounds of moral superiority. By understanding moral psychology, we can see how the goals of villains, whether fictional or real, make sense in light of their disparate moral foundations—or, as in the case of the Master/Mistress, lack of moral foundation beyond self-interest.

Jim Davies, PhD, is a cognitive scientist at Carleton University in Ottawa, where he conducts research on computer modeling of human imagination. He authored the book *Riveted: The Science of Why Jokes Make Us Laugh, Movies Make Us Cry and Religion Makes Us Feel One with the Universe,* and has chapters in *Star Wars Psychology: The Dark Side of the Mind, Westworld Psychology: Violent Delights, Daredevil Psychology: The Devil You Know* and *Star Trek Psychology: The Mental Frontier.*

Deirdre Kelly, PhD, is a cognitive scientist who applies her expertise in human decision-making and user experience design to help people, teams, and organizations find novel and innovative solutions to complex challenges. She is currently leading research in the design of healthy and effective organizations and sustainable organizational culture at NAV CANADA. As a neurodiversity advocate, she and her collaborators recently launched a tool to empower people with ADHD to make sustainable and goal-aligned choices.

A MOMENT WITH MICHELLE GOMEZ: MISSY, THE "GOOD LITTLE PSYCHOPATH"

Jenna Busch & Travis Langley

Actor Michelle Gomez, who plays Missy, told us she doesn't think deceptive, destructive Missy is necessarily a villain. "She has no boundaries. It's just various shades of darkness to Missy. It can get into a sort of morass of blackness. There's a weird sort of perverse justice coming from her. Like any good little psychopath, she believes she's doing the right thing, and, for her, the right thing is to annihilate the universe."[36]

Psychopathy is a condition characterized by a lifelong lack of empathy or remorse, missing emotional foundations of morality. Despite its exclusion from the *Diagnostic and Statistical Manual of Mental Disorders* as a separate diagnosis,[37] numerous professionals consider the concept clinically more useful than *antisocial personality disorder*.[38] Whereas antisocial personality disorder's diagnostic criteria depend mainly on antisocial actions, psychopathy is more about the internal qualities that might lead to such actions.

Gomez said that the Doctor and Missy are really the same, except that Missy doesn't mind killing for the greater good, and her greater good is to make the universe disappear. According to her, the Doctor and the Master/Missy are sort of "frenemies." The Third Doctor himself introduces the Master to Sarah Jane Smith as "my best enemy."[39]

Which of us would make a good Dalek?

Can we know that we aren't already?

4

Exterminate!
The Mentality of a Master Race:
Are You a Dalek?

Daniel Hand

"For the purposes of this article, orders to commit genocide or crimes against humanity are
manifestly unlawful."
—Rome Statute of the International Criminal Court, Article 33.2[1]

"Here's my New Year's resolution: I'm coming for you, Dalek!"
—Thirteenth Doctor (Jodie Whittaker)[2]

A re you a Dalek?
       Strange question, I know, but hear me out.
    Because, bizarre as it sounds, the world is
actually full of Daleks. Everywhere you look—
on the telly, on the Internet, on the front pages,
on the streets—there they are, barging through
life, strutting around like they own the place (which, let's face it, is
an entirely Dalek thing to do). Indeed, it may be said that, in many
ways, the Daleks have long since achieved their obsessive aim of
conquering the Earth. Doctor or no Doctor, they're here, and they
mean to stay.

And they certainly aren't averse to the odd extermination.

What a Dalek Is Not

By now, you'll probably have cottoned onto the fact that I'm not talking about *actual* Daleks. It would be pretty hard to miss a bunch of miniature tanks rolling along the pavement! But, quite frankly, I might as well be. Because humans, whom the Daleks have expended so much time and effort in trying to subjugate, think like Daleks all the time. We frequently see ourselves as part of a greater collective rather than as individuals within a wider society, we're good at doing what we're told without stopping to question the orders we've been given, and, yes, we're capable of delivering great evils upon those we perceive as beneath us. Perhaps the reason (or, at least, one of them) the Daleks have always been so terrifying to behold is that, in many ways, they're so much like us.

But why? What about us makes us so similar to those scary robot aliens that used to have us all hiding behind our settees as children? And how do we allow ourselves to fall so easily into the same reprehensible modes of thought that we so despise in these creatures?

Let's play a game of Doctor and take a look.

First and foremost, though, let's get the obvious disclaimer out of the way. For the purposes of an exercise such as this, in which humans in the real world are to be scrutinized, it is important to acknowledge that there are two things which the Daleks most assuredly are not: (1) They are not human, and (2) they are not, um, real. This, of course, means that any discussion here is by its very nature purely speculative. Any attempt to analyze their mentality may only be done through the prism of human understanding. For our purposes, though, that should be enough.

What a Dalek Is

So, if we know what the Daleks are *not*, the obvious question is: What exactly *are* they? How does one *define* a Dalek? Or rather, how does one define the *mindset* of a Dalek? The *psychology* of a Dalek?

This is difficult, not just because of the reasons stated earlier but because, in many ways, a Dalek's mental workings can only be viewed as part of a greater collective: the so-called Pathweb or command network, the literal shared intelligence of their entire species.[5] A single Dalek, psychologically, is virtually indistinguishable from the plural Daleks. *Groupthink*, the practice of group decision-making that discourages creativity and individual responsibility, defines their entire being.[6] Indeed, on the rare occasions that we do get to see a Dalek separated from the rest of their kin, their predominant response is a feeling of hopeless loss and confusion.[7]

Seen in this way, a Dalek becomes the prefect case study for the phenomenon that is crowd mentality: an individual entity, sure, but ultimately one that has become almost mindlessly devoted to the wider group of which it is a part. And this, I suspect, is where you begin to see what I mean when I say that the world is full of Daleks.

Crowd mentality (or group mentality, or mob mentality) has been a topic of discussion for as long as psychology as a discipline has existed. Le Bon, Freud, Jung,[8] social psychologists, personality theorists, and many others have, over the course of the past century and a half, all tried their hands at explaining how and why individuals in a crowd think and behave the way they do. As with any discourse, these august individuals frequently disagree. (Of course, the Daleks were still on Skaro while they were positing their various theories.) What they all agree on, however, is that an individual's *individuality* is impacted as they merge with a wider group. An individual's perceptions and behaviors give way (to a greater or lesser extent, depending on the proponent) to a more consistent, homogeneous set of values that conform to those of the group as a whole.

This *deindividuation* (reduced sense of oneself as individual) is the Daleks' gold medal event—and they've held the title ever since they first trundled[9] onto the world's screens in the early 1960s. More than simply providing a feeling of anonymity, deindividuation sees the individual lose a sense of their own self-awareness, reducing ability to differentiate their thoughts, feelings, responsibilities, goals, and behaviors from those of an amorphous "everyone else." (Anonymity is a part of it only inasmuch as it provides an ideal environment for the remainder of the process.) Outside observers aren't the only ones who lose these individuals in the crowd. The individuals lose *themselves* in the crowd.[10]

Deindividuation is coercively seductive. Becoming a part of something "bigger," of feeling accepted by our peers and free from the internalized restraints we all place on ourselves when we would otherwise be unsure about how our ideas might be received, can result in an intoxicating sense of belonging.[11] But it can also lead to *polarization,* whereby individuals become more extreme in their ways of thinking as a direct result of being part of a group. Put simplistically, when all you hear is what you want to hear, you'll want to hear more of it; and the more of it you hear, the more of it you'll believe.[12]

The Dalek, then, embodies deindividuation taken to its absolute extreme: They typically have no individuating tendencies whatsoever. Their entire existence is caught up with the remainder of their group, and they exult in their group's preeminence. Even physically, they abandon all pretense to individuality. Their appearances are almost always (with a few notable exceptions) entirely indistinguishable from one another. Their literal linking of minds mean that they are never *not* part of their wider collective, with all the fraternity, affirmation, and disinhibition that connection entails.

It all sounds rather exhausting, if you ask me!

Dalek Life

"There is only one form of life that matters: Dalek life!"
—a Dalek to Edward Waterfield[13]

Perhaps the most terrifying aspect of the Daleks, though, is their seemingly limitless capacity for what we would call evil: carrying out innumerable acts of moral reprehensibility, for no better reason than that they can.[14] Throughout their appearances and regardless of whom they encounter or what they hope to achieve, they demonstrate precisely zero compunction in killing anything and everything that offers itself up as a target, enslaving entire planets to carry out their plans, indulging in wanton destruction, or using a situation not just to their advantage but purely to inflict suffering upon "inferior" beings.

Unfortunately, this, too, is a common characteristic of both group-think and crowd psychology more generally.[15] Whereas all the previously mentioned symptoms might be perceived as relatively harmless, affecting the individual and the group but generally leaving outsiders to their own devices, they are laying the groundwork for much more insidious, dangerous, horrifyingly violent ways of behaving. After all, if the Daleks want to take the view that they are the most superior of superior races in the universe, then that's fine and all power to them. That can be their truth. Where it becomes a problem—and where our favorite blue-boxed, secret-named face-changer has their best (or worst, depending on how you look at it) adventures—is when they start trying to impose that belief onto the universe's remaining occupants.

If deindividuation is the process of an individual conforming to the overriding mood of a wider group, it follows that when that overriding mood is one of superiority over and hostility toward "outsiders," this will inevitably result in the individual condoning and even performing actions that, under any other circumstances, they would normally condemn.[16] As the individual becomes subsumed within the group, growing ever more polarized in their beliefs, they become desensitized to the "excesses" of their more extreme fellow group members (you know, little things like looting, destruction, rape, and murder). This, in turn, lowers their own inhibitions, making it all the more likely that sooner or later they, too, will indulge themselves in those excesses.

Such *diffusion of responsibility*, or moral disengagement as a responsibility shared by many, feels meaningless in an individual portion[17] and the individual is essentially able to absolve themselves of any blame for their actions, no matter how inconsiderate or reprehensible. After all, *they* aren't the ones committing the act, *everyone* is. Which makes it all okay, obviously—or so it may feel.[18]

And just ask any Dalek: The "victims" deserved it anyway.

Because it's the smallest of steps to go from "We are superior" to not just "Everyone else is inferior" but also to "Everyone else is *subfe-*

rior" (beneath consideration) and, ultimately, "Everyone else is so inconsequential that they are a hindrance to our superiority." Dissenting views, from without or within, may not be tolerated. Indeed, they must be eradicated. Exterminated, one might say.[19]

This is where that whole pesky genocide thing comes in. The moment a group starts to see another individual (or group of individuals) as a problem that needs to be removed, and its members have become sufficiently willing to carry out the necessary actions, it will have no qualms about "removing" said problem.[20] If you're the master race, sooner or later it's likely to occur to you that there must be a final solution.

In this regard, there are simply far too many examples of the Daleks' behavior to refer to. Turn on any given episode, and it's right there. From using a rare mineral to blackmail an intergalactic community riven by plague[21] to unthinkingly destroying "impure" creatures even of their own kind,[22] there's nothing they won't do to further their aims.

To any third party—victim, bystander, observer—these acts are unquestionably evil,[23] and yet, to this riled-up group of self-professed superiors, they are simply a means to an end—not even a necessary evil; merely an obvious, even tiresome, next step. Certainly nothing to regret. After all, Daleks are never sorry for their actions.[24]

The Dalek Inside

> "You would make a good Dalek."
>
> **—a Dalek to the Ninth Doctor**[25]

So now let's go all the way back to that first, unusual question:

Are you a Dalek?

After everything you've read, you'll probably instinctively say, "No!" without a moment's hesitation. Because *of course* you're not a Dalek. You think for yourself, right? You think things through before you act or speak, you take responsibility for your own actions, and you'd certainly never proselytize against an entire group of individuals just because they happen to be different from you in some way (be it physically, mentally, or socially). Right?

Right??

Alas, I hate to break it to you, but you could lose your sense of self in the moment. Not always, of course, but at some point, you have. Have you committed the same atrocities as those mono-eyed machine-mutants? Probably not, but the fact that I have to qualify that answer just goes to show that, no matter how altruistic we may think ourselves to be, none of us are immune to the processes of thought that, taken to their ultimate conclusion, lead to horrific crimes against humanity.

It is no secret that, in the black-and-white days of 1963, Terry Nation conceived of the Daleks as an analog for the Nazis, whose depravations still hung over a traumatized world.[26] And, like their fictional counterparts, the Nazis provide a perfect example of crowd psychology in action: an entire nation, with a vanishingly small number of exceptions, succumbing to an intoxicating blend of comradeship, inflated self-importance (it must feel pretty good to know that you are categorically the greatest beings in the world), and utter contemptuous hostility toward everyone outside of that exclusive little club. There are, of course, upsettingly numerous other examples throughout history (many of them having been visited—and frequently challenged—by a certain madperson in a blue box), from the Akkadian Empire to the Wild West, from the Social War to the Cold War, from ancient tribal conflicts to modern party politics, from Papal declarations to social media. Humans have always banded together against perceived "outsiders."

In fact, this huddling in groups is why you and I are here, right now. Without that instinct to stay close to one another, our ancient ancestors would have been hunted into extinction. The old adage "There's safety in numbers" derives from the very instinct that has kept our species alive. Those who became isolated or excluded from their group didn't tend to last long on their own.[27] The mindset of those early humans was one of "The world is out to get us, so we have to get it first"—because it *was*, and they *did*.

Now, though, not so much, but that lifesaving instinct is still there, constantly on alert to keep us safe from a danger that no longer really exists. And, like all defense mechanisms that have outstayed their usefulness, this one is frustratingly proficient at causing more harm than good. The wolves are no longer prowling around us in the dark, but we're still ready to fight for our survival.

But what does all of this mean for us, almost a quarter of the way through the twenty-first century? For decades, the Daleks have demonstrated just how dangerous it can be to lose one's individuality. Sadly, too few of us have learned enough from their terrible example. It doesn't matter who we are, what we stand for, with whom we associate. The moment we take that step of believing our stance is indisputable, and that anyone who does try to dispute it needs to be silenced, deplatformed, or worse, we are guilty of behaving like a Dalek: We are superior; those who disagree with us are subferior. From there, no matter how often we tell ourselves that we would never do such a thing, we're on the slippery slope toward "master race" thinking.

It would be too easy, at this point, to wander into the realm of modern world politics and social commentary because it is in these arenas that crowd mentality, deindividuation, and groupthink most frequently make themselves known. However, providing specific examples here would likely only end up putting people's backs up. (You see? Even writing this, I'm concerned about inadvertently triggering Dalek-like behaviors. We all know how a Dalek responds to having their "problematic" behavior pointed out to them.) Instead, try a little thought experiment: Have a go at thinking of a few recent examples where a group of people's behavior, in your opinion, went too far.

The episodes that will first come to mind are of the behavior of *other* groups, such as people you disagree with politically, for example, those who support a different team, or those who simply read a different newspaper. That line of thought may lead to scary chanting at rallies, violence in the streets, suppression of people's voices.

That's the easy part, though.

If you're able to be honest with yourself, and to really scrutinize your own actions, sooner or later you'll come to the conclusion that certain people with whom you agree—and even you yourself—have engaged in these behaviors too. But just because you agreed with the sentiment of a particular event doesn't mean that you should turn a blind eye to the violence that happened to take place there. Even on the lower end of the scale: If you've ever complained about the youth of today or sneered, "Okay, boomer!" or booed at a match, that's you thinking as part of your group, happy in the knowledge that you are probably superior to those others.

And don't lie to yourself: You've fallen into the trap of devaluing your opponents' morals, values, or cognitive abilities perhaps as often and as much as they've devalued yours. Just because you believe you're "right" and they're "wrong" doesn't excuse the behavior. Indeed, it kind of proves the point. The moment you start to dehumanize[28] the people with whom you disagree (anything from "They're just idiots" to "The world would be better off without people like them"), you're already a worrying distance down the road to full-on Dalekism.

Don't panic! Assuming you want to, you've still got time to pull yourself back. You want to, don't you?

The Real Solution

> "I see beauty."
>
> —Rusty, a Dalek with a conscience[29]

So what's the solution to all this apocalyptic portentousness?

In a word: *empathy*. Not with our own groups—that's easy. No, the key to defeating our inner Dalek is to try and see the world from our *adversaries'* (for want of a better term) point of view and having the humility to acknowledge that maybe they may have valid reasons for feeling the way they do. That doesn't mean agreeing with them. It just means trying to understand them—and understanding our adversaries means mutating into something new.[30]

Give it a try. Take a step back and ask yourself, "What would someone on the other side of the argument say, and"—more importantly—"why would they say it?" (And if your answer to that last part equates to "Because they're idiots," you're not trying hard enough.)

In this respect, once again the Daleks can provide some guidance. After all, let's not forget the fact that, whenever the Doctor or a companion has ever interacted with an individual Dalek, be it in a planetary asylum or (for an episode, at least) the last of its kind, that

Dalek has proven to be much more—in a word—*human* than when it is engulfed by the wider collective of its brethren.[31] The same goes for you: When you think for yourself as an individual, detachedly, rationally, objectively, you become able to acknowledge not only the good in others but also the potential evil in ourselves (and our comrades) and act accordingly. It's only when you allow yourself to be subsumed by groupthink and polarization—like, say, as part of an online "discussion," on a march, or at a political rally—that you should start to worry. Remember, no matter which side of a particular divide you happen to be on, you are not altogether different—in thought, in word, in deed— from the people on the other. This means you *must* put in the work, or you'll continue to make the same mistakes as them.

So, one last time…

Question: Are you a Dalek?

Answer: At times, yes. Yes, you are. But you can try not to be—and that makes all the difference.

 **Daniel Hand, MBACP,** is an author, historian, illustrator, game designer, and integrative counsellor in private practice. His latest book is *Role-Playing Games in Psychotherapy: A Practitioner's Guide* (Palgrave Macmillan). For more information on RPG therapy or to get in touch, see www.monomythcounselling. co.uk.

Openness, extraversion, emotional stability, and other sets of correlated traits form constellations of characteristics within each person, as certain qualities tend to emerge as companions to each other. But why do observers differ in the shapes they perceive among those stars?

5

The Five Factors and Company: Constellations of Personality

Travis Langley

"A person is a fluid process, not a fixed and static entity; a flowing river of change, not a block of solid material; a continually changing constellation of potentialities . . ."
—humanistic psychologist Carl Rogers[1]

"I would suggest, Peri, that you wait a little before criticizing my new persona."
—Sixth Doctor (Colin Baker)[2]

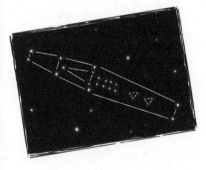

As opposed to *physical traits* (our specific bodily characteristics), *personality traits* are specific psychological characteristics or predispositions to behave in certain ways. Because the Doctor is regularly curious, for example, we see strong curiosity as one of the Time Lord's enduring personality traits, not simply a momentary state. *Trait theorists* are primarily interested in studying human personality by measuring habitual patterns of actions, thoughts, and feelings—in other words, by measuring personality traits.

Gordon Allport, often called the father of personality psychology, identified thousands of terms to describe personality.[3] Personality psychologists trying to detect some order in the chaos observed that certain traits tend to group together in *trait clusters,* constellations of characteristics that are commonly correlated with each other among many people.[4] Sometimes, though, we are simply "seeing patterns in things that aren't there,"[5] as the Eighth Doctor put it—*illusory correlations*, variables we mistakenly perceive as related even though they really are not. The Doctor, who looks for "the threads that join the universe together,"[6] would likely appreciate psychologists' search for these coinciding characteristics, up to a point: "Never ignore a coincidence—unless, of course, you're busy. In which case, always ignore coincidence."[7]

Coincidental Characteristics

One reason to ignore some coincidences is because *correlation*, the mere fact that variables are related, does not reveal *why* they are related. Even though outgoing people tend to be less fearful than others, that could mean that developing an outgoing nature reduces fear, but the reverse—that fearfulness makes a person less outgoing—is possible too. In many cases, some other variable (say, brain cell activity levels) causes both with no causal relationship between the things we see as correlated. The Doctor often falls under suspicion for murder, espionage, and a long list of other crimes simply because the TARDIS tends to deliver its occupant into crisis situations. Just as there is a *positive correlation* between outgoing and fearless traits, there is a positive correlation between the Doctors' arrival and states of crisis: As one becomes more likely, so does the other. From a different point of view, though, a *negative correlation* exists between outgoing and *fearful* traits or between the Doctors' arrival and levels of tranquility while they are around: As one becomes more likely, the other becomes less likely.

Stars do not float through the galaxy independently of one another. Gravity tugs stars into clusters and galaxies into superclusters, forming relationships we barely see because we cannot watch them through all of time and space. From our sliver of time and our viewpoint bound to one planet's location, we gaze. Detecting relationships among large groups of anything—whether interstellar bodies or personality traits—can take a long time, and understanding the relationships we observe even longer.

Trait clusters are groups of characteristics that correlate together in both positive and negative directions, better known as *personality factors* because *factor analysis* identifies the groupings. Sometimes these clusters only show up in certain research samples. That is, the group of people surveyed in those cases show a lot of correlations that other people don't. Just because the Doctor's companions tend to be curious and assertive doesn't mean curiosity and assertiveness will consistently correlate among all other people. Personality researchers sought to identify which personality factors are fairly universal (meaning the traits will cluster together in any group of people measured) and *orthogonal* (statistically unrelated to each other).

Two Factors: Extraversion and Neuroticism

Two of the earliest factors to emerge as universal and orthogonal were the dimensions of extraversion/introversion and neuroticism/emotional stability.

Extraversion

The dimension of extraversion/introversion was first identified and popularized by Swiss psychiatrist Carl Gustav Jung,[8] although he viewed it a little differently than the modern perspective. He saw *extraversion* as a focus on the external world, attending to the environment outside oneself, and *introversion* as an inward focus, paying more attention to one's own internal mental life. Unlike some views that treat people as either extraverts or introverts, Jung believed that we all have both types of traits within ourselves, even if we tend to emphasize one more often than the other. Despite the Doctors' amazing ability to spot details, they can also become oblivious to surroundings when lost in thought. Factor analyses have shown that many other traits tend to accompany the kind of qualities Jung observed.[9]

Examples of Extraversion Traits

✓	Assertiveness	✓	Low Arousal
✓	Boldness	✓	Outgoing Nature
✓	Boredom If Alone	✓	Risk-Taking
✓	External Focus	✓	Social Interaction
✓	Gregariousness	✓	Talkativeness

Chapter 9 elaborates on extraversion/introversion as part of a popular personality test. Note, though, that the test dichotomizes those qualities, splitting people into either this end or that end without distinguishing nuances. We express mixtures of extraverted and introverted traits, depending on the situation, even among those of us who are more prone to one extreme or the other. Some people, *ambiverts*, simply don't tend to go to either extreme.[10] The Doctor and companions demonstrate many extraverted traits (especially those that lead to adventure), but not all. In their more introverted incarnations, the Doctors need others to help them come out of their own head, and sometimes—such as when they become War Doctor—they prefer to be alone.[11]

Neuroticism

Psychologist Hans Eysenck, one of the earliest researchers to study trait clusters, proposed a *two-factor theory* of personality, looking at extraversion and neuroticism as the key personality factors for explaining human behavior.[12] People with characteristic *neuroticism* handle stress poorly, find minor frustrations hopelessly difficult, feel threatened in everyday situations, and are at risk for many nonpsychotic mental illnesses.[13] Named after the term *neurosis*, which refers to nonpsychotic mental difficulties, neuroticism is the personality factor most consistently associated with having unpleasant, negative feelings.[14] However neurotic the Doctors might seem at times, they normally function well under pressure and do not let lesser frustrations get in the way of focusing on higher priorities.

Examples of Neuroticism Traits

✓	Anger Proneness	✓	Instability
✓	Angst	✓	Negative Emotion
✓	Characteristic Depression	✓	Obsessiveness
✓	Emotional Expressiveness	✓	Poor Emotion Regulation
✓	Envy	✓	Vulnerability to Stress
✓	Insecurity	✓	Worry to Excess

Professionals who focus on the more positive-sounding aspects of these personality factors often call this one by the dimension's less neurotic end, *emotional stability*.[15] Emotionally stable people are healthier both physically and mentally, and yet it is possible to be too stable. Other Time Lords try to make themselves and their society stable to the point of stagnation, resisting change and suppressing emotional life. Given their history of suffering when an unstable tyrant like Rassilon takes charge, wreaking such chaos as to endanger all of reality,[16] their reluctance to indulge in a bit of chaos makes some sense.

Theory Regeneration

As different researchers keep proposing their own personality factor theories, some version of extraversion and neuroticism keeps showing up in theory after theory. Despite their persistence, these factors, named after Jungian and Freudian concepts, are not enough. Eventually, even Eysenck agreed that his theory left out a substantial number of personality traits.[17] When he saw the need to add a third factor, the time came for his theory to regenerate into a form both familiar and new.

The Three Factors: Add Psychoticism or Openness?

When psychologist Hans Eysenck's two-factor theory fell short of describing personality thoroughly enough, personality psychologists persisted in trying to identify which constellations of traits would best sum us up. Eysenck's own view underwent renewal and became his *three-factor theory*.[18] Simply identifying that some traits go together does not reveal what ties them together, and therefore, different researchers looking at the same personality factors interpret them differently and give them different names. Compare it to people creating a club: They already share something that brought them together, but they may disagree on the meaning of whatever ties them together and what name the club should have. How long does it take the handful of people investigating the mysterious Doctor to name their group the London Investigation 'N' Detective Agency, a.k.a. LINDA?[19] Scrutinizing the third collection of traits he detected through factor analysis, Eysenck came to interpret it as a set that he believed suggested proneness to developing a *psychosis*, severe detachment from reality, and so he named the cluster *psychoticism*. Other researchers who looked at the same findings, though, would view them in other ways and thus name the same factor differently.

Psychoticism

Once he expanded his views to make room for another major personality factor, Eysenck equated the third factor with psychotic potential because the factor included several traits involving creativity and he believed creativity and madness went hand in hand. "Creativity has from the earliest times been thought to be related to psychosis or 'madness,'" he noted.[20] The Doctor and Amy see the artist Vincent van Gogh suffer from his inner demons,[21] and the real Vincent's multiple maladies remain the subject of diagnostic debate to this day.[22] The Doctor's own creative, divergent way of thinking and tendency to question the status quo likely figure into why some Time Lords call the Doctor "a madman."[23]

Examples of Psychoticism Traits

✓	Aggressiveness	✓	Impersonal Nature
✓	Antisociality	✓	Impulsivity
✓	Creativity	✓	Lack of Empathy
✓	Egocentrism	✓	Toughmindedness

Openness

Other three-factor theories emerged as different researchers ran their own factor analyses and inferred different meanings from what they found. Among the best known was the *NEO* model proposed by personality researchers Robert McCrae and Paul Costa: neuroticism, extraversion, openness. *Openness* (also called *openness to experience*) involves curiosity, ingenuity, analysis, intellectual pursuit, appreciation of things others deem impractical, and readiness for new and unusual experiences.[24] Few fictional characters are more up for new experience than the Doctor, who leaves Gallifrey and rarely slows down while rushing from one adventure to the next. At the dimension's opposite end would be *closedness*.

Examples of Openness Traits

✓	Abstract Thinking	✓	Independent Thinking
✓	Active Imagination	✓	Intellectual Flexibility
✓	Appreciation of Culture and Intelligence	✓	Interest in Adventure
✓	Challenging Norms	✓	Originality
✓	Curiosity	✓	Preference for Variety
✓	Insightfulness	✓	Unconventional Beliefs

Counting Constellations

Though the Time Lord wears many faces and behaves in different ways, common features connect all the Doctor's lives and distinguish them from everybody else. Despite the differences between different theorists' personality factor models, some common features connect them and distinguish them from other theories of who we are. One way or another, each view describes personality in terms of traits, each combines traits into broad dimensions, and the extraversion/introversion dimension runs through them all.

So Eysenck had his three factors while McCrae and Costa had theirs. Should psychoticism or openness be added to the list? Psychoticism included numerous traits that openness omitted. After conducting an extensive review of all personality factor research, looking at the many personality disorder lists identified by different researchers,[25] McCrae and Costa added two plus two and got five.[26]

The Five Factors: Adventures in the OCEAN

Different people, focusing on different details and patterns in how the Doctor acts, refer to the Doctor as Professor, Spaceman, Old One, Skipper, Oncoming Storm, Destroyer of Worlds, Fancy Pants, Grandad, Pops, or Doc[27] and they can all be right. A single version of the Doctor may be Caretaker, Proconsul, Predator, Mad Monk, and Raggedy Man all in one,[28] and a single individual can relate to the Doctor as both her sweetie and her damsel in distress.[29] Each epithet is based on a relatively small number of characteristics and experiences. Finding a single word that perfectly encompasses every single trait in a specific person or within one personality factor might not be possible. Even when researchers agree on how many global factors exist, they call the overall list of factors by an assortment of names: OCEAN, Pentagon, five-factor model, and most commonly "the Big Five."[30]

The Power of Five

Over the course of many studies to determine how many factors best sum up individual personality, the number that turned up most often was five.[31] In an extensive review of the published research, personality researchers McCrae and Costa concluded that this number best fit all the available evidence.[32] They gave their version of the *five-factor model* the acronym *OCEAN* for the names they assigned the factors: openness, conscientiousness, extraversion, agreeableness, neuroticism. Analyzing the constellation of traits that Eysenck had called psychoticism,[33] McCrae and Costa saw not a single factor but instead identified two separate factors within it, conscientiousness and agreeableness.[34]

Conscientiousness

Information bombards us. Our brains filter much of it out, and then whatever reaches our awareness, we sort in different ways. So much information assaults the Doctor's senses that the Ninth Doctor fears it might drive him mad.[35] At one extreme is the person who obsesses over every detail and strives to be orderly, organized, and efficient in dealing with every item, even if attention to detail might mean missing the big picture. At the other extreme is the reckless, disorganized person who takes shortcuts and hopes for the best. The Eleventh Doctor prefers to "talk very fast, hope something good happens, take the credit—that's usually how it works."[36]

The cognitive abilities to receive and store information (*crystallized intelligence*) or make use of it (*fluid intelligence*) are not the same thing as personality traits. Despite attention to some details, the Doctor is oblivious to many others. "The Doctor has no idea of time," says the First Doctor's companion, Dodo Chaplet. This strikes her as paradoxical and "rather funny" for such an experienced time traveler.[37] Fellow Time Lord Romana similarly tells the Fourth Doctor that he's always getting the time wrong,[38] and Tegan calls the Fifth Doctor less accurate than a broken clock.[39] Spontaneity, haste, inattention, annoyance with perfectionism, unreliability in a number of areas, and lack of thoroughness or long-term goals suggest someone low in conscientiousness.

Regardless of many signs of carelessness, though, the Doctor perseveres. Persistence and determination are aspects of conscientiousness. Even though a disheartened Eighth Doctor loses sight of his vow to "never give up, never give in"[40] when he chooses to regenerate as a warrior and be the "Doctor no more,"[41] this act of giving up is an exception in his personality, not his typical characteristic. *Personality* refers to behaviors typical of us, rather than the aberrations. In time the Doctor rediscovers hope[42] and then shows greater commitment and persistence than ever before when the Eleventh stays on Trenzalore for nearly a millennium, rather than giving in.[43] Throughout most regenerations, despite a lack of conscientiousness in many other ways, the Doctors' resolve remains one of their most enduring features.

Examples of Conscientiousness Traits

✓	Achievement Motivation	✓	Perfectionism
✓	Attention to Detail	✓	Perseverance
✓	Competitiveness	✓	Reliability
✓	Controlling Nature	✓	Self-Control
✓	Lack of Spontaneity	✓	Thoroughness
✓	Organization	✓	Time Awareness

Agreeableness

A person may be outgoing, assertive, talkative, and lively without being nice at all. The First, Sixth, and Twelfth Doctors strike many people they encounter as disagreeable, and every Doctor may rub some the wrong way. Agreeable individuals want to help others and feel great compassion and concern for them, qualities that often drive the Doctor, but the Time Lord sometimes regenerates more argumentative, sarcastic, insulting, and indifferent to how many others feel. The most extremely agreeable person wants peace at any price and prioritizes getting along with others above all else. The Doctor stays ready to ruffle feathers.

Examples of Agreeableness Traits

✓	Compliance	✓	Need to Get Along
✓	Cooperation	✓	Optimism about People
✓	Modesty	✓	Sympathy
✓	Need to Be Liked	✓	Trust

The five-factor model of personality has become one of the best-known tenets of personality psychology. The Big Five carry big clout. Even so, researchers continue to examine our constellations of traits to try to account for all the mind's dark matter, the parts of us that the five-factor map of known mental space may have left out. Some say that it overlooked one of the most important dimensions of human behavior and history—good and evil. For example, a highly agreeable person might do many good things to earn someone's approval, but then again, so might an evil minion.

The Six Factors—Adding a Continuum from Good to Evil

Many professionals in psychology examine how we develop our morals,[44] but what are good and evil in the first place? The recently regenerated Twelfth Doctor asks Clara if he's a good man, unsure of the answer himself.[45] The previous Doctor does not think of himself as a good man, telling enemies who abducted pregnant Amy, "Good men don't need rules. Today is not the day to find out why I have so many."[46] Can a person, not just their actions, be good or evil? In terms of individual personality, what do these primal concepts really mean?

HEXACO

The trait lists associated with the Big Five left out terms related to selflessness or selfishness, areas that people might judge as good or bad. Focusing on the positive side of the dimension, later researchers added *Honesty–Humility* (factor H) to give their six-factor theory a name that reads like an alien planet or a spell-casting company, HEXACO.[47]

> HEXACO = *H*onesty–Humility, *E*motionality (essentially the other side of Neuroticism), e*X*traversion, *A*greeableness, *C*onscientiousness, *O*penness.

Good: Honesty–Humility

A person scoring high in this factor is unlikely to be boastful, deceitful, hypocritical, pompous, or sly. The Doctor seeks truth and yet tells many lies. Even a person with good intentions may end up on the not-so-good end of the scale. Long before Clara Oswald has no answer when the Twelfth Doctor asks her if he's good, Jamie McCrimmon questions the Second Doctor's priorities: "People have died. The Daleks are all over the place, fit to murder the lot of us, and all you can say is you've had a good night's work."[48]

Examples of Honesty-Humility Traits

✓	Faithfulness	✓	Loyalty
✓	Generosity	✓	Modesty
✓	Honesty	✓	Sincerity
✓	Lack of Pretense	✓	Trustworthiness

Evil: The Dark Triad/Tetrad

The *dark triad* of psychopathy, narcissism, and Machiavellianism is a model of variables that, when combined, strike people as selfish and on the evil side—more so when combined with a fourth trait, sadism, to form a dark *tetrad*. These constructs tend to go unrepresented in the Big Five, partially correlating with disagreeableness but not completely. All four selfish, overlapping parts of the dark tetrad correlate with the low end of factor H.[49]

For more on the dark triad, see chapter 10.

Gray Areas

Factor H for good and the dark tetrad for evil both remain controversial, with plenty of researchers debating their validity as empirically testable constructs.[50] If good and evil themselves were easy to define, members of the human race would not have spent thousands of years arguing over them. We do not stop contemplating them, nor do the Doctors come up with a clear opinion of how they fit themselves, but their intangible nature does not make them any less important in our lives. Dismissively saying, "We can't define them," does not make them go away.

The Seven Factors: Both Good and Bad

As opposed to the six-factor model, which adds one dimension that runs from good to evil, a seven-factor model treats good and evil as separate things. Early trait researchers left out evaluative terms like *good, evil, worthy,* and *unworthy* on the grounds that they were ambiguous or that they judged quality instead of describing specific personality characteristics.[51] Others, though, argued that these omissions neglected key areas of individual differences.[52] Some versions of the Doctor and Master may be strikingly similar in Big Five traits and yet differ in their motivation to do good or evil. If the Doctors' friends betray them, the Time Lord tries to fix whatever has gone wrong for them,[53] but if any Master's companions turn on him, he tries to kill them and tends to succeed.[54] Two manifestations of the Master even kill each other.[55] Which traits did the Big Five miss that might help identify which is the good man? The HEXACO model offers one answer. The Big Seven model offers another one, a different seven-factor model based less on morality and more on the individual's evaluation of self-worth.[56] We tend to commend ourselves and condemn others.

The Good: Positive Valence

Not everyone sees goodness in terms of morality. A person may be held in great esteem and have many admirable qualities for a range of reasons. Several Doctor speaks highly of their own intelligence, impressiveness, and worth.[57]

Examples of Positive Valence Traits

✓	Admirable	✓	Outstanding
✓	Exceptional	✓	Smart
✓	Important	✓	Unconventional
✓	Impressive	✓	Unusual

The positive and negative valence factors are largely distinct from each other. People with high opinions of themselves might or might not see themselves as also having negative valence traits. Some, especially later Doctors, both recognize their own personal strengths such as exceptional intelligence and yet rate themselves negatively as people.

The Bad: Negative Valence

Characteristics in the negative valence factor come closer to addressing views of oneself as good or evil. After the Time War, the Doctors begin to evaluate themselves more harshly and do not see themselves as good.[58] The Eleventh Doctor tells the Dream Lord, "There's only one person in the universe who hates me as much as you do," showing that his own self-loathing reveals the Dream Lord to be some aspect of the Doctor's own psyche.[59]

Examples of Negative Valence Traits

✓	Awful	✓	Evil
✓	Cruel	✓	Undeserving
✓	Dangerous to Others	✓	Vicious
✓	Depraved	✓	Wicked
✓	Disgusting	✓	Worthless

Even individuals who may be full of self-hatred or who believe themselves to be bad may still value goodness and strive to do the right thing. "Never be cruel, never be cowardly," the Twelfth Doctor repeats his personal promise to Clara before they part ways, this time adding, "and if you ever are, always make amends."[60]

The Further Factors: Infinite Possibilities?

How many personality factors are there? How many distinct clusters of traits that mostly describe who we are? Three, five, six, sixteen . . . ? How many Doctors can there be? When the showrunners conceived the Doctor's first renewal to solve the immediate problem of actor William Hartnell's health difficulties, they did not know two Doctors would become three, five, thirteen, seventeen . . . Doctors without end? Each way of looking at the array of personality factors may be analogous to looking at the variety of Doctors, or at the many versions of ourselves, both of whom can each be the same person. The different configurations may all share truth, while none may capture the truth in its entirety. No single description, no one way of looking at things ever can. There may be other ways to interpret those arrays.

Every cluster both changes and retains some recognizability over time. The person you are at age four both is and is not who you are at age forty. Is the Curator who meets the Eleventh Doctor in a museum really the Fourth Doctor or the Fortieth? "Perhaps I was you, of course, or perhaps you are me," he says regarding the nature of their shared identity, whatever it may be, "or perhaps it doesn't matter either way."[61]

We are who we are.

II.

DEEP BREADTH

To those who believe we hide the most powerful pieces of our minds, even from ourselves, the unconscious seems deep and vast and difficult to explore.

"But if you do start ferreting about in your subconscious, aren't you going to turn up all sorts of nasties? I mean, complexes, phobias, and what have you?"

—Sarah Jane Smith (Elisabeth Sladen)[1]

Universal themes, the unconscious mind, and a personality test based on related assumptions—does psychological science have room for them? Would a true scientist value any of them? And would a scientist not of this world rate them better or worse than any other human theories?

6

Dream Lords:
Would the Doctor Run with
Freud, Jung, Myers, and Briggs?

Travis Langley

"Once, a man fell asleep and dreamt he was a frog. When he woke up, he didn't know if he
was a man who dreamt he was a frog, or a frog who was now dreaming he was a man."
—**Fifth Doctor (Peter Davison)**[1]

"Who looks outside, dreams; who looks inside, awakes."
—**psychiatrist Carl Jung**[2]

Before trait theorists began to define personality psychology in terms of specific characteristics and personality factors, early personality theory mainly came out of *depth psychology*, as the approaches that look deep into the unconscious to explain why we live as we do are collectively known. Sigmund Freud's *psychodynamic* (*psychoanalytic*) approach remains the best known of these areas, with Carl Gustav Jung's closely related *analytical psychology* achieving fame of its own. Their talk-based methods aimed at revealing what's in the unconscious mind include hypnosis, free association, and interpretation of dreams. Freud considered *dream analysis* a royal road to understanding the unconscious.[3] Other professionals would later develop psychological tests based on depth psychologists' ideas, from *projective tests* (like Rorschach's *inkblot*

test[4]), whose developers assume people will project unconscious desires, needs, and values into ambiguous stimuli,[5] to *personality tests* such as the *Myers-Briggs Type Indicator*,[6] which sorts people into types based on how Jung viewed human nature.[7]

Controversy surrounds depth psychology. Its harshest critics call it all unscientific, unsupported, and unworthy of serious consideration.[8] So wouldn't a person of science like the Doctor, with so many centuries of experience and wisdom, reject it all outright? Maybe. Maybe not.

Freud

Many who refute Freud's theories still recognize his creativity and genius, although some go as far as personality psychologist Hans Eysenck did in asserting that Freud was "a genius, not of science but of propaganda, not of rigorous proof but of persuasion, not of the design of experiments but of literary art."[9] The Doctor, a Time Lord who values personal qualities such as genius and creativity, also eschews dogmatic assertion of poor science. Why, then, does the Eighth Doctor say that when he and Freud met, they "got on very well"?[10]

Unconscious

The foundation of Sigmund Freud's theory and all depth psychology is the idea that the unconscious mind exerts powerful influence upon us.[11] Although the term *subconscious* litters popular culture, Freud usually spoke of it as the *unconscious,* the vast portion of the mind outside consciousness. He grew dismissive of the original term, *subconscious,* once its originator, psychotherapist Pierre Janet, offended him by remarking that Freud lifted his ideas from other people.[12] Strax, the Sontaran nurse/warrior/butler, reports that his medical device lets him view Clara Oswald's subconscious mind, revealing "deflected narcissism, traces of passive aggressive, and lots of muscular young men doing sport."[13] Strax may be no better at describing mental phenomena than he is at identifying human organs or gender. Then again, living in Victorian London sometime since Vastra eliminated Jack the Ripper, Strax happens to be saying this after Janet introduced the term *subcon-*

scious and likely before Freud's *unconscious* usurped it. Regardless, the Doctor has a many-layered mind that fits key aspects of Janet's and Freud's theories.

One area where Freud's views receive more favorable reception in psychology is that of the *defense mechanisms,* coping behaviors we use to protect ourselves from stress. These behaviors vary and may be healthy (e.g., altruism), unhealthy (e.g., withdrawing from others), immature (e.g., *regression,* reverting to behavior the person has outgrown), or pathological (e.g., *denial,* refusing to recognize an unnerving truth).[14] Daughter Anna Freud catalogued the defense mechanisms he had described. She named most of them and identified more.[15] Sigmund Freud considered the most important defense mechanism to be repression,[16] and yet it remains the most controversial with the least solid evidence to support it, according to many professionals.[17]

Tenth Doctor (to War Doctor): "All those years, burying you in my memory."

Eleventh Doctor: "Pretending you didn't exist. Keeping you a secret, even from myself."[18]

The Doctor seems to have repressed memories, most notably when forgetting about the War Doctor so thoroughly that the so-called Eleventh Doctor on several occasions thinks he can still regenerate.[19] Only after they save Gallifrey, instead of destroying it, does the Eleventh Doctor come to terms with the War Doctor and admit he has run out of regenerations.[20] Whether this is truly *repression* (in which the conscious mind simply cannot summon a thought that's locked away in the unconscious) or *thought suppression* (consciously blocking a thought that would be unpleasant or distracting[21]), either would fit into Freud's view that we play tricks on ourselves in order to reduce potential anxiety.

An argument against repression playing part in this is the fact that extended lifespan will alter the brain's potential memory capacity, making memories harder to retrieve. How often do people, when asked for their age, stop to think, "Okay, what year is this?" For a Time Lord, keeping track of their own regenerations may resemble that. The longer a person lives, the more files there are in the memory cabinet. The Second Doctor can remember his family but only with effort: "I can when I want to, and that's the point, really. I have to really want to, to bring them back in front of my eyes. The rest of the time, they sleep in my mind and I forget."[22] Whereas physiological psychologists might attribute this to the brain's sheer memory capacity, a Freudian would more likely credit the Doctor with repression or suppression of these memories from easy conscious access.

The Thirteenth Doctor, on the other hand, has learned that actively remembering offers healthier coping.

Yasmin "Yaz" Khan (Mandip Gill): Have you got family?

Thirteenth Doctor (Jodie Whittaker): No. Lost them a long time ago.

Ryan Sinclair (Tosin Cole): How d'you cope with that?

Doctor: I carry them with me—what they would have thought and said and done, make them a part of who I am. So even though they're gone from the world, they're never gone from me.[23]

Methods

Among his earliest methods for delving into the unconscious, Freud used hypnosis. Eventually he came to distrust it, though, suspecting that suggestible, hypnotized patients were sometimes reporting dreams and fantasies as if they had really happened.[24] The Doctor uses hypnosis at times (e.g., to make friend Dodo sleep and forget,[25] to help Sarah Jane recover information,[26] or to free various people from mind control[27]). The Tenth Doctor also shows that hypnosis can fail[28] and knows it has limits: "You can hypnotize someone to walk like a chicken or sing like Elvis. You can't hypnotize them to death. Survival instinct's too strong."[29]

Early depth psychologists often used dream analysis to seek clues as to what lurks in the unconscious. They disagreed on what specific dreams could mean and sometimes about how to study them, and yet they agreed that dreams hold great value and reveal much about the unconscious.[30] The Fifth Doctor sees significance in dreams as well: "Dreams are important, Nyssa. Never underestimate them."[31]

Science

"If Freud had been more of a scientist, he would have pressed no claims to be one. Dogmatism is anti-scientific; and there are reasons to distrust a 'truth' that forms a sect,"[32] psychologist Henry Murray wrote. Despite Freud's influence on him, Murray saw a need for empirical study. He also argued that psychology needed to develop a better understanding of human nature by studying the experiences of normal, everyday people instead of the clinical patients Freud and other therapists often emphasized. The Doctor values science and helps others appreciate it, even the "savage" Leela, who says she used to believe in magic, "but the Doctor has taught me about science. It is better to believe in science."[33]

The Doctor, though, looks at science from a point of view that is millennia more advanced than our own. To some contemporary psychologists, evidence suggests that Freudian theory is wrong far more often than it is right. However, history shows that much of science has been wrong more often than it's been right. The hope is to accumulate ideas that work, weed others out, review, revise, review, revise again, and keep going even though new paradigms may turn it all on its head. To a scientist who cites Einstein, Newton, and other great minds, the Doctor says simply, "You've got a lot to unlearn."[34] He does not treat a scientist like a fool for being wrong, only for clinging to that which is wrong and failing to keep pursuing scientific truth. "A scientist's job is to ask questions," the Fourth Doctor says,[35] and Freudians ask questions aplenty.

Dogma

Existential psychologist Rollo May criticized the psychodynamic ideas spread by both Sigmund Freud and Carl Jung as being too rigid and unable to adapt to different situations.[36] Accusations that Freud and Jung forced facts to fit their theories instead of adapting theories to fit the facts raised questions as to whether either one's views met the scientific standard of *falsifiability*, meaning testability.[37] The Fourth Doctor observes, "You know the very powerful and the very stupid have one thing in common: They don't alter their views to fit the facts. They alter the facts to fit their views—which can be uncomfortable if you happen to be one of the facts that needs altering."[38] Even Jung criticized Freud for inflexibility, calling him dogmatic for rigidly defending his views on how sexuality and the unconscious shape actions and personalities.[39] And yet, the Eighth Doctor later says to someone who does not believe he is a time traveler, "At least Sigmund Freud would have taken me seriously."[40]

Even if Freud's views eventually became dogmatic, psychoanalytic theory did not spring into being as doctrine. Perhaps, then, the Sigmund Freud with whom the Doctor "got on very well" is a younger Freud, exploring the unknown and piecing together new ideas before growing set in his ways.

Jung

Many criticisms of Freud apply to others in depth psychology as well, including Swiss psychiatrist Carl Gustav Jung, so we won't rehash those here. Jung, who by degrees bitterly broke away from Freud intellectually, made his own lasting contributions to psychiatry and psychology. Notable among them were the concepts of archetypes, collective unconscious, and extraversion/introversion.

The Shadow
Chapter 8 describes *archetypes*, themes and patterns that Jung believed we are unconsciously prepared for by heredity, not experience. Among them is one he called the *Shadow*, a representation of one's own hidden qualities, the dark and unrevealed side of each person's nature.[41] To grow as an individual (a process he called *individuation*), Jung believed the person should learn to understand the *Persona* (the outward mask, public face) and other archetypes to descend into the depths of the unconscious and confront the Shadow. Heroic fiction abounds with

heroes facing their own dark sides or fighting enemies who are some-how mirror images of themselves. The Sixth Doctor confronts his own Shadow a bit literally when he faces the Valeyard, a mysterious Time Lord who has somehow been created as a manifestation of every dark thought or impulse the Doctor has ever had.[42] The Eleventh Doctor faces his Shadow again in the form of the Dream Lord, the part of the Doctor that taunts, ridicules, and despises himself the most.[43]

The Collective Unconscious

Beyond the conscious and unconscious mind that Freud popularized, Jung added an additional level to his model of mind: the *collective unconscious*, part of the unconscious that all people inherit and share as members of the same species according to Jung. Archetypes and instincts lurk in the collective unconscious, as he saw it.[44] The Sixth Doctor faces his Shadow inside the Time Lords' sci-fi form of collective unconscious called the Matrix of Time, a computerized reservoir storing the knowledge and personalities of dead and living Time Lords over all their regenerations. Just as Jung felt that the collective unconscious, as a deep pool of the past, could predict humanity's future path, so too can the Time Lords' Matrix predict future events.

Extraversion/Introversion

Carl Jung introduced the concepts of extraversion and introversion. The Doctor feels alone in many ways, perhaps because the hero is unlike everyone else, including fellow Time Lords, and yet the Doctor re-peatedly welcomes new companions. In most incarnations, the Doctor seeks the company of others while still showing that, as Jung expected of each person, the Time Lord has both extraverted and introverted qualities.

Myers and Briggs

The *Myers-Briggs Type Indicator* is both popular and controversial. Its creators' assertions that ESFPs are like this or INTJs are like that may be assertions with poor, if any, support from methodical empirical research. Dichotomizing people as *E*'s or *I*'s (extraverts or introverts) oversimplifies analysis and makes it harder to recognize the complexities of human behavior.

Jung felt no one is purely extraverted or introverted. Each person shows a mix of each, possibly mingled to the point that *ambivert* (both extraverted and introverted) more accurately describes many people.[45] But those who identify themselves by strings of Myers-Briggs letters leave ambiversion out. Seeing all of its problems, would the Doctor, like so many of our world's professionals, reject Myers-Briggs outright? Perhaps, but the Time Lord might very well scoff at all earthly personality tests and the confidence people place in them. An ancient extraterrestrial might consider a personality test's creators as no better or worse than anybody else who created a test of something as difficult to define as personality, and yet might also praise any who at least try. Should a crayon-wielding child be discouraged for drawing a person less realistically than a peer? The one with more creative vision might reveal things the more realistic one might miss. There may be more art than science to how we view people in the first place.

Up from the Depths

Science is flawed—that is a fact. Whether the views of Freud and Jung are more flawed than the views of others remains the subject of ongoing debate, as does the value of the *Myers-Briggs Type Indicator*, which grew out of Jungian ideas. We do not always know why we do the things with do—that is a fact. To many, psychoanalytic ideas about the conscious mind feel like the right way to explain these things. Clearly, the Doctor's personal experiences show that the unconscious mind has power, as when the Twelfth wonders why he unconsciously chose to regenerate with a specific, frowny face[46] and later decides it was to send himself a message about saving people.[47]

A person thousands of years more advanced than us might look at our science the way we look at witch doctors casting spells and ancient physicians draining sick people of blood, thinking that will heal them. The Fourth Doctor looks at us all the same way: "We were just wondering if there were any other scientists . . . You know, witch-wiggler, wangateur. Fortune teller?"[48] Through trial and error, the ancients learned. Superstition could impede progress, but it could also play an important role in bringing progress closer. We're all primitive from an immortal's point of view.

For all the nonsense that fills our dreams, some of the greatest stories and even some amazing scientific achievements come out of them from time to time. That doesn't mean we need to confuse sense with nonsense. It means we need to evaluate and reevaluate the things we call sense and learn sometimes from the nonsense. As the First Doctor put it, "Yes, superstition is a strange thing, my dear, but sometimes it tells the truth."[49]

Travis Langley's bio appears at the beginning of this book.

MODERN ASTROLOGY (BARNUM & BAILEY, MYERS & BRIGGS)

Wind Goodfriend

In spite of its corporate popularity, many psychologists find the Myers-Briggs to be the equivalent of modern astrology. The official survey's website[50] provides descriptions of each personality type—for example, ENTJs pursue improvement and achievement while ESTPs are realistic but adaptable. The difficulty is that this type of vague description can apply to anyone. If your horoscope says, "Your day will be full of opportunity, but watch out for challenges," doesn't this apply to everyone?

Critics have raised many concerns, including these:[51]

> The test forces people into binary categories, ignoring subtle differences that should be measured on a continuum instead.
>
> People's answers to the questions may change from day to day. We all feel sometimes competitive, sometimes cooperative, sometimes optimistic, sometimes pessimistic.

Almost no research studies have successfully linked one's theoretical "type" to any real outcomes or behaviors.

Why, then, is the test so popular? One reason may simply be that it's easy. Unfortunately, another answer may be the *Barnum effect*: When people are given vague descriptions of themselves that could apply to anyone, the descriptions are rated as highly accurate by the individuals themselves.[52] The effect's name comes from a remark about the customers for P. T. Barnum's famous sideshows of "aliens" or "mermaids" (which would become the Barnum & Bailey Circus), a quote widely misattributed to the showman himself: "There's a sucker born every minute."[53] Many psychologists would agree and may even say companies that rely solely on the Myers-Briggs are helping to prove this statement true.

Perhaps the Doctor, when told about the usage of Myers-Briggs, would be skeptical. The Time Lord might even describe it as a big ball of wibbly-wobbly, psychy-wikey . . . stuff.[54]

One of the most famous and most controversial figures in the history of psychology and psychiatry popularized the idea that each of us has a side we do not know, a vast region of our minds hidden away from our own conscious thought.

7

The Unconscious:
What, When, Where, Why,
and of Course Who

William Sharp

> "Funny thing, the subconscious. Takes all sorts of shapes."
> —Tenth Doctor (David Tennant)[1]

> "The laws of unconscious activity differ widely from those of the conscious."
> —psychoanalyst Sigmund Freud[2]

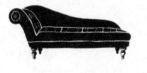

The most significant contribution of Freud's psychoanalysis was his exploration of the unconscious. Freud sought answers to the questions of what dreams signify, what might motivate accidents, and why symptoms present in the way they do. Hard science was not concerned with the significance of a slip of the tongue or a bungled action.[3] Dreams were left to be interpreted by mystics. Freud, however, posited that these occurrences were not merely mental misfires: They each had a point, there was a message, and that message came from the unconscious. Who or what is in the unconscious? Without examining the unconscious, we may be left to believe that forces outside of ourselves, such as luck, are to blame for our history and future.

What Is the Unconscious?

"How does anything get there? I've given up asking."
—Eleventh Doctor (Matt Smith)[4]

The unconscious is everything in our minds of which we are not consciously aware, however it might influence our lives. In the Freudian view, every choice or accident is tinted by each person's unique individual unconscious. Is our unconscious sending us a message to slow down if we trip while running? If we "accidentally" leave our cell phones at home one day, is the unconscious saying we need a break from people, especially those who might call us on the phone? If we forget to set the alarm at night, does the unconscious want us to sleep longer?

How does the unconscious work? What are its qualities and laws? And how does Who fit in with this? Three important elements of the unconscious are reminiscent of the Time Lord's own reality:

It really is bigger (on the inside) than the conscious mind. Rose Tyler and so many others marvel and say the same thing about the Doctor's TARDIS when entering it for the first time.[5]

The unconscious doesn't follow laws of time and space. Elton, the Doctor-obsessed fan whose group studies the Doctor through history, discovers that "the world is so much stranger than that. It's so much darker. And so much madder. And so much better."[6]

There is no "no" in the unconscious. Paradoxes abound, and the way something manifests is only one level of its meaning. As the Fifth Doctor says, "There's always something to look at if you open your eyes!"[7]

Size: Greater on the Inside

Freud believed that the unconscious is infinite and thus far bigger than consciousness. The unconscious affects us far more than we are aware. He considered all the funny and embarrassing errors we make and what message from the unconscious they might contain. Its reach is greater than that of the conscious mind—like the TARDIS, larger on the inside.

Similarly, much like the Doctor's box, what happens in the vortex is affecting our daily lives, and most people never know this. Small choices here and there may seem inconsequential but have a ripple effect on our life events. This concept is important psychoanalytically as analysts work on helping patients see just how much of their experience of the world is created by their own choices. Certainly things happen "to us," but we have to take responsibility for the things we can control. For example, if you find you are dating a cheater and you leave that person, shame on them. If you keep dating people who turn out to be cheaters, shame on you: How are you always finding these people? If you don't ask questions about your choices, you live a life that can seem random and impulsive and without any clear connection between cause and effect. Something as simple as the direction in which the companion Donna Noble turns, either left or right, impacts the future and leads to hugely different outcomes.[8] Consider Donna before, during, and after the Doctor. Before adventuring with the Doctor, she lives a lighthearted but tumultuous life. She is impulsive. She blames family and friends when things don't go her way. She argues and seems immature for her age. During her time with the Doctor, however, she slowly begins to see what her choices have led to, and with that knowledge she decides to start doing things differently. In these ways, Donna before she meets the Doctor is like the unanalyzed patient, as is the post-Doctor Donna once she forgets it all. While she is with the Doctor, however, Donna feels and thinks in new ways, especially about herself and her importance in her world.

Nonlinear Nature

The unconscious does not operate linearly but rather outside time—much as the Doctor says of time itself, "from a nonlinear, non-subjective viewpoint, it's more like a big ball of wibbly-wobbly, timey-wimey stuff."[9] Many patients speak from my version of the TARDIS, the psychoanalytic couch where patients (like the Doctor and companions) explore events from their past although their feelings are in the here and now. Distress from childhood can range from abuse or neglect to getting overlooked by a teacher or breaking a toy from Santa Claus. The feelings are alive and well in the present. The emotion is not locked in the past. It is like a bootstrap paradox or a self-fulfilling prophecy. Often it comes to represent some personal story arc that you are locked into, one of getting mistreated, neglected, alone, or sad. Like the Doctor in the TARDIS, the analyst with a couch is propelled into a strange world often beyond time and space with its own laws and rules that have to be explored.

Layers of Meaning

Freud felt that no "no" can exist: Everything has layers of meaning. The unconscious is always at work—that is, it is always "on." In *Doctor Who*, we are left to consider: How much does the Doctor even sleep? What manifests itself to the conscious eye (*manifest content*) has deeper symbolic meanings (*latent content*). Nothing is a throwaway. This is what led Freud to conclude that dreams are the "royal road" to knowing the unconscious.[10]

Take, for instance, "the crack" in Amelia Pond's wall.[11] It is a crack but is not from the settling of a house. Rather, we find it is a crack in the skin of the universe. The Doctor admits that even if they knock down the wall, the crack will remain. This is true of images in the unconscious as well. Dreams look like something to us, but they are often far more significant than we assume, and we do not take the time to explore them. If ignored, they come back in other places and in other significant ways until they are understood, exactly like Amy's crack.

British analyst Christopher Bollas writes that "unconscious thinking knows no contradictions and opposing ideas easily coexist . . . The analyst is time-warped . . . recurrently confused, wandering in the strange county of even suspension."[12]

The Id, Ego, and Superego of Who

The *id* is primarily unconscious. It works on the *primary process,* which is irrational and interested in immediate gratification of impulses. It functions in accordance with what is called the *pleasure principle* (seeking immediate satisfaction of needs and desires). Think of an infant as the embodiment of the primary process and the pleasure principle:

"Feed me, burp me, hold me NOW!" It could be argued that the newly regenerated Eleventh Doctor is initially id. When Amelia Pond first meets the newly regenerated Doctor and asks who he is, he says, "I don't know yet, I am not done cooking."[13] Like an infant, he arrives and causes upheaval, not fully conscious of the needs of others until his basic needs are met. Amelia, as is true of many of the Doctor's companions, guides him and takes care of him. She offers him every food he asks for, and he "hates" it all until he gets the fish fingers and custard. The id operates on the pleasure principle: It wants what it wants, and it wants it now.[14] At the end of that process, once his needs have been satisfied and a language between the two established, the Doctor pulls out the brilliant interpretation that if all the events that have unfolded in that first night have not scared Amelia, that "must be a hell of a scary crack in your wall."[15] The Doctor is no longer id. He shows another part of himself that is more heroic, the part guided by morality.

The Doctor has a strong desire to help. In that light, this defender of worlds can be viewed as Freud's *superego:* the *super-I.* The superego is the impingement of the social world (rules, mores, our parents' attitudes, etc.) that oppose the id. It is the antithesis to the pleasure principle that guides the id. The superego is ruled by the principle of the *ego ideal:* basically what has been incorporated into personality as the perfect way of behaving and living. The ideal is culturally bound and learned early in life and is full of rules and mores that most of us take for granted as the way we are supposed to behave. Often, it is heard in the back of the mind as a critical voice saying "do this" or "don't do that." This ego ideal[16] and the superego may help explain what drives the Doctor to defend humans and save their Earth over and over. It is what tortures the Doctor for playing part in the supposed destruction of Gallifrey. The superego is mostly in the unconscious part of the mind, but some of it is in the conscious mind. Think of any time you hear the past words of your parents or teachers telling you how to behave in a current situation. That is the superego.

> "The good things don't always soften the bad things, but vice-versa, the bad things don't necessarily spoil the good things or make them unimportant."
>
> —Eleventh Doctor (Matt Smith)[17]

"The group grants the leader superhuman powers. His words are given more weight and imbued with more wisdom than they possess."
—psychiatrist Irvin Yalom[18]

Freud's *ego* is a mediator that emerges to deal with the frustrating
conflicts that ensue between id and superego. It is our "character" or
"personality"—neither all good nor all bad. According to Freud's theory, we need all three: id, ego, and superego. The various Doctors present as generally (as well as literally) all over the place. They have degrees
of impulsive, attention-deficit/hyperactivity disorder (ADHD)-ridden
behaviors that are signs of the id, alternating with self-sacrificing and
morally driven behaviors indicative of the superego. There is little evidence of a functional ego working on the reality principle. There is
little consistent awareness of self. In fact, the Time Lord regenerates
every now and then into someone who is considerably different! That
would make Freud's head spin.

Is the Doctor egoless, then? We can find evidence for the id and
superego of the Doctor but arguably not evidence for an autonomous
ego, at least not within. For that, we need to look at the companions.
It is when the Doctor and companions are working as a group that
things really click for them. The companions in this way function as
the Doctor's ego. It is an externalized ego—which sounds strange, but
what doesn't in the Who universe? Perhaps an externalized ego is the
side effect of too much time in the vortex. Perhaps all the regenerations
lead to difficulty forming an ego. Companions repeatedly implore the
Doctor not to travel alone because the Time Lord does not do well
when alone.[19] The Twelfth Doctor experiences some inability to recognize faces and is perplexed by his own.[20] The companions as externalized ego are what keep the Doctors from destroying themselves while
encouraging them to let the good times roll. Each companion balances
the Doctor in some way. It is with the team—companions and Doctor—holding hands and supporting one another that there is strength
and power to overcome the obstacles before them.

There is more in the unconscious than in the conscious. There is
no linear sense of time, there is no "no," and paradoxes abound. Enter
the Doctor with the big blue box, where paradoxes also abound. An

invitation into the world of Who can be disorienting, to say the least. The main character seems mad (or at least both brilliant and a complete fool), time and space are relative, and there is no obstacle the character seems unable to overcome. The Doctor both talks about rules and then proceeds to break them, dealing with paradoxes that create almost impossible situations. Who is this person exploring the universe?

It takes years to become an analyst and learn the language of the unconscious, but the Doctor, companions, and blue box illustrate some of the basic ideas. All analysts in training start the same way as do new Who fans—ordinary humans who cross over into another person's world. In exploring this, I found that the Doctor's box and my analyst couch are not that different.

Cracks in the Universe and the Unconscious

"... like a nerve tapping the subconscious of the human brain."
—Second Doctor (Patrick Troughton)[21]

Young Amelia Pond has a crack in her bedroom wall. That crack, however, has more significance than it would if it appeared only in a single episode. It appears repetitively through several seasons. Like the Doctor's explorations of that crack, psychoanalysts try to explore the significance of the behaviors of a patient in treatment beyond the reason a behavior emerges in any one session. Like the crack in the skin of the universe, patients' struggles can be seen in much of what they do in their personal universes. The same issues can emerge in all work and play. The Doctor tries to explain the crack to Amelia, but like any interpretation it has to be given at the right time, in the right way, and with the right feeling. If it is not, the interpretation can be *narcissistically wounding* to the patient and useless for treatment and understanding. The artistry of when to make an intervention is part of what makes psychoanalytic treatment different from other forms of treatment. Most non-insight-oriented approaches to therapy are less concerned with the meanings and significances of problems and more focused on treating symptoms and removing behaviors. A *behaviorist* might try to control the behavior with rewards and punishments. A *cognitive therapist* might try to change the way a patient is thinking about something. Both behavioral and cognitive approaches, however, can leave the unconscious and the feeling world untouched. For therapies of depth, insight, and relationship, exploration is the key. What the patient says is unpacked in psychoanalytic technique to reveal the deeper layers of meaning. The Doctor/psychoanalyst invites companions to join, and they do. Together they explore cracks and their many manifestations, eventually getting to the apparent cause.

Why don't more people choose this exploratory and *insight-oriented* type of psychoanalysis as a course of treatment then? Like many of the Doctor's companions, people often have an overpowering curiosity about what makes things tick in the blue box of their unconscious, but there is a cost to pay. Ignorance is bliss, and analysis is anti-ignorance. Socrates said that the unexamined life is not worth living, but it certainly doesn't lead to a happily ever after. Consider the lives of the Doctor's companions after they leave him. People don't choose psychoanalysis out of fear. The freedom from the unconscious enactments we engage in can be overwhelming and too much for many. A lot of people would prefer the quick fix of a pill to cover emotions over the slow fix of a maturational intervention on the couch to deal with them head on.

Freud looked at the common repetitive ways we act to avoid suffering and defend against that which we don't want to know. We get a hint about Amy's repetition: She is always the girl who waits and is let down by others. The Eleventh Doctor encourages Amelia to look for things she is not noticing "from the corner of your eye."[22] He wants her to see what she has been ignoring, but we analysts can't rush the process just because we are in a hurry. If we do, we can get ourselves caught in a patient's repetitions. The Doctor ends up falling into Amy's *transference* narrative. What does he do to let her down? He makes a promise and doesn't keep it. This happens twice at least, and he isn't aware of it either time. He tells Amy he will be back in five minutes but takes 12 years instead. He then does it again even after learning a little about the oh-so-patient Amy, leaving for another two years. A good supervisor might have helped the Doctor avoid that trap.

The Doctor as Psychoanalyst

"In my view, the analyst plays both figures in the transference," British analyst Christopher Bollas writes, "the wise figure who sustains illusions and thereby encourages the patient to speak, and the fool who does not know what is being said to him."[23] This is a tough line to walk. How many times does the Doctor straddle those roles? The Time Lord is famous for claiming to have a plan despite having no such thing. While protecting the town called Christmas and preventing the crack in the universe from falling into the wrong hands, the Eleventh Doctor tells Clara, "I haven't got a plan, but people love it when I say that."[24] He knows his audience loves believing that when he says it. A good analyst does not necessarily know the plan at the start of treatment. Each patient is unique. In their own therapy and supervision (psychoanalysis requires each analyst be in therapy as well), analysts can keep their own neuroses in check. The structure of a treatment can contain both patient and analyst, as does the TARDIS for the Doctor and companion. The blue box and the analyst's couch are the same in that respect.

The First Session

> "If you are a doctor, why does your box say POLICE?"
> —Amelia Pond (Caitlin Blackwood), future companion[25]

The first session of an analysis starts with the analyst asking some variation of "What brings you here?" In asking this, the analyst is inviting the patient to tell the story of their life: the past, present, future, dreams, and even day-to-day happenings. They all reveal something about the character of the person the analyst is with for that hour. Both patient and analyst, when meeting for the first time, need to get their bearings straight and establish a common language.

When we meet the young Amelia (Amy) Pond, she is praying to Santa at Easter because of a worrisome crack in her wall. That scene is rich with paradoxes as are most first sessions with patients on the couch, but the analyst doesn't know all the meanings yet. The initial presenting concern is the crack (the obvious manifestation, or *manifest content*, of her concern as opposed to the deeper, unconscious meaning, or *latent content*, of the matter). The Eleventh

Doctor tells Amy that there can be some immediate relief, but he is going to invite her to a greater character-changing journey aboard his TARDIS/couch.

In a great example of the common ironies analysts ask patients to face at first, we learn that to close the crack, the Doctor must first open it up. Analytic work is replete with evidence of these paradoxes. Many patients come to me and want to be less depressed or less anxious. I need to get them to open up and tell me about their depression and what is making them anxious. They resist. When patients resist, the problem persists. I have to work on their resistance until they are ready to share more. Only after we open the crack can we work on closing it, as the Doctor does with Amy.

Closing it doesn't always solve the problem. It takes the whole course of a treatment (or multiple seasons of a show!) to find all the significances of the crack. And so, the work continues.

Paradoxes: Making a Better Analyst of the Doctor

"Psychoanalysis provides a place for self-exploration for those who are in the midst of cultural shifts, conflicts, and contradictions."
—psychoanalyst Neil Altman[26]

Is the Doctor an analyst or a madperson? I think both. The resurgence in popularity with the modern episodes of the BBC series might speak to a larger cultural trend of thinking of heroes as a mixed bag. Villains likewise (think of the Master) have backstories that cause us to pity them. Things are not all black and white. Psychoanalysis "provides a place for self-exploration for those who are in the midst of cultural shifts, conflicts, and contradictions."[27] I believe the Doctor's tendency to do "wild analysis" results from a lack of personal analysis and supervision.[28] The Doctors travel without a more experienced Time Lord to mentor them (and, in the First Doctor's days as a student, he listens too little to any instructor he has[29]). They have no discernible "professional" ego of the sort that is required for this kind of work. The Doctors have issues around keeping companions as they hate endings and avoid them, even ripping the last pages out of books without reading them.[30] This is why it is hard to know if the Doctor is an analyst or a "madman with a box." The Doctors use companions as egos to stabilize them so that they don't have to develop one themselves. This causes blind spots, and the Doctor is lost in that way. But again, there is hope.

The Eleventh Doctor says that there is one place a Time Lord must never go: the site of that Time Lord's eventual death. But when he finally starts to address his own "most feared place,"[31] he can transform and become more than any previous incarnation of the Doctor that we are aware of. By bravely going and facing what is there, he becomes able to regenerate a thirteenth time even though we have been told that Time Lords regenerate only twelve times.[32] He is able to continue his work. In our Doctor-as-analyst metaphor, now that he is not resisting a place and feelings, he should be able to work with more of his patients' feelings.

The Issue with Time Travel and the Unconscious

Psychoanalysis is the method we use to get a glimpse of the dynamics of the unconscious (hence, *psychodynamics*). *Doctor Who* provides us with a great metaphor of how uncomfortable yet tantalizing it is to delve into the unknown. It shows us that it is also dangerous work but can be life-changing and the best adventure to undertake. The companions jump in with both feet.

The unconscious is messy and uncomfortable.

Studying *Doctor Who* is a great way to begin to think and play with the unconscious world as revealed in psychoanalysis. The Doctor is neither someone to write off as a "madman" nor the consummate professional analyst. With the right support, the Doctor can do remarkable things that change the course of the universe while changing lives along the way. I am not ready to trade in my couch for a TARDIS yet, but maybe one day I will be.

William Sharp, PsyaD, certified psychoanalyst, is an associate teaching professor at Northeastern University in Boston, a practicing psychoanalyst in Brookline, and the director of the Masters in Clinical Mental Health counseling program at the Boston Graduate School of Psychoanalysis. He has contributed to Popular Culture Psychology books on *Stranger Things,* Spider-Man, and Daredevil, and written on psychotherapeutic treatment in *The Joker Psychology: Evil Clowns and the Women Who Love Them.* Follow him on Twitter: **@DrWilliamSharp**.

While a city dreams, the TARDIS sits ready to explore realms unknown. Photo and TARDIS courtesy of Matt Munson.

One well-known and difficult-to-test theory holds that deep in the inherited portion of the unconscious dwell archetypes, universal themes that shape our stories, dreams, and expectations. Could these be part of the reason why some things scare anybody anywhere?

8

Weeping Angels, Archetypes, and the Male Gaze

Miranda Pollock & Wind Goodfriend

"Don't blink. Don't even blink. Blink and you're dead. They are fast. Faster than you can believe. Don't turn your back. Don't look away. And don't blink. Good luck."

—Tenth Doctor (David Tennant)[1]

"Not for a moment dare we succumb to the illusion that an archetype can be finally explained and disposed of . . . The most we can do is dream the myth onwards and give it a modern dress."

—psychiatrist Carl Jung[2]

A hero is born from humble beginnings, finds guidance from a nurturing mentor, discovers special talents, falls in love, and overcomes almost insurmountable challenges to fight evil. If this story sounds familiar, it should. It's been told thousands of times in hundreds of cultures, ranging from King Arthur to Spider-Man to Katniss Everdeen. All that changes are the details—the names of the characters, the gender of the mentor, and the nature of evil. Psychologists over time have noted that throughout literature and legend around the world, there are basic storylines and personas that arise in pervasive and ubiquitous ways. These persistent characters fit *archetypes*, universal patterns that some psychologists argue come from a common and primordial origin of humanity that binds each of us together in a fundamental, but unconscious, manner.

Every story—including *Doctor Who*—provides examples of these archetypes in the fictional characters created for the plotlines and in the ways they interact with each other. Clearly, the Doctor is the hero or protagonist of this story, and there are seemingly endless enemies the Time Lord must confront. One of the most intriguing groups of villains would be the Weeping Angels. How do the angels represent psychological concepts, including archetypes and the psychoanalytic perspective of the unconscious mind?

Angels and Archetypes

In the dark and rain, a lone woman with a camera climbs a wrought iron fence and breaks into an abandoned, derelict house. She notices the letter *B* peeking from behind the fragments of wallpaper and eventually reveals the message, "Beware the Weeping Angels."[3] Why is this first exposure to the idea of Weeping Angels so terror inducing? Why are the Weeping Angels such an iconic enemy, from a psychological viewpoint?

Angels are common visuals in contemporary culture from decorating a holiday tree to collectables and even in our television shows and movies. These heavenly beings often appear as caring, sympathetic, and beautiful creatures (although perhaps less so in some twenty-first-century depictions). The pervasive visual depictions of angels from art have shaped our ideas of the appearance and behavior of angels and in turn shaped the portrayal of angels in popular media. Over time, the angel has become a cultural symbol of the doer of good deeds, the helper, the advisor, and the personal guardian. However, the common heavenly depiction of angels is completely upended in *Doctor Who*, which moves away from the original biblical characterization and instead portrays an almost exactly opposite depiction with the Weeping Angels who are, according to the Tenth Doctor, "the deadliest, most powerful, most malevolent life-form ever produced."[4]

The word *angel* derives from the Greek term *angelos*, meaning "messenger." In the Christian, Islamic, and Kabbalistic traditions, the *an-*

gelos take on roles such as "messenger," "guardian," and "attendant" to God's throne.[5] In the 273 times the Christian Bible references angels, they are never mentioned as winged, they have male names (Gabriel, Michael, and Lucifer), and they are portrayed as weapon-wielding warriors. These images are a far cry from the blond and smiling guardian or the diaper-wearing cherubic archer of love. The original biblical angels are not our friends. They are God's soldiers.

The *Warrior* or *Hero* may be one of the most well-known archetypes coming from the original conceptualization by Carl Jung,[6] the famous psychoanalyst and associate of Freud. Jung believed that humans all share a *collective unconscious,* a "storehouse of archaic remnants from humankind's evolutionary past."[7] This collective unconscious explains why common themes and characters—*archetypes*—continually pop up symbolized in religious traditions and stories, in cultural legends, and in newly created fiction. According to this perspective, we have certain concepts that are so deeply embedded in our psychological heritage (such as the concepts of evil and of an omnipotent higher power) that these characters speak to us on an unconscious but powerful level.

If angels fit the warrior archetype in their biblical depictions, how did they morph into the cute and nurturing mother or guardian figures more likely to be seen in children's toys and Precious Moments figurines? The early Christian church controlled various facets of religious art. It was in 787 CE that the Second Council of Nicaea decided that it was lawful to depict angels in painting and sculpture. This decision allowed artists freedom to explore and alter the visual depictions of angels.[8] By the twelfth century, depictions of angels were popular in religious art and their appearance had gradually changed. Although the Bible mentions male angels, most angels now appeared androgynous with long, flowing hair and soft, feminized features.

It was around the Victorian era (mid-to-late eighteenth century) that the images and roles of angels proliferated popular culture, including everything from mourning angel statues in cemeteries to literary references. Angels no longer solely represented religious scenes. They now also represented the moral and idealistic roles of the women in the household. The "ideal" middle-class woman was compared to an angel in appearance and morality. She was referred to as the "angel in the house."[9] This modern view of an angel fits into a second Jungian archetype called the *Great Mother*. The mother character embodies nurturance, caregiving, empathy, and beauty.[10] Examples of Great Mother symbols throughout history and various cultures include Mother Nature, the Greek goddess Gaea, the Virgin Mary, and even contemporary mother figures such as Mrs. Weasley from *Harry Potter*.

Angels have thus represented, over time, the two very distinct Jungian archetypes: the Warrior and the Great Mother. Perhaps the supernatural aspect of angels allows them to be more subjective and flexible, open to interpretation based on the modern zeitgeist of one's region and era. However, neither of these depictions will fully fit the terrifying Weeping Angels that confront the Doctor time and time again (nor will a simple mix of the two). To truly understand the Weeping Angels, we need a third Jungian archetype: the *Shadow*. According to Jung, the Shadow is the worst, most terrible, darkest form of evil in all of existence. Summarized respectively as "the devil within,"[11] "the embodiment of the unacceptable,"[12] and "the evil side of humankind,"[13] the Weeping Angels represent the most powerfully fearful being imaginable. In some representations, the Shadow is Satan, the Shadow is pure evil.

It can be argued that the Weeping Angels strike fear deep in our hearts and minds (Jung would say in our collective unconscious) for many reasons. First, we are afraid because we have gotten used to the idea of angels as guardians, as gentle feminine beings who want us to be safe. The jarring realization that the Weeping Angels are not the Great Mother, but instead are the Shadow, makes their betrayal of our implicit trust in angelic figures worse. Their entire appearance fools us. They seem to be beautiful and mourning, which brings out human empathy—but this simply makes us lower our guard and approach them, making it easier for them to destroy us.

Finally, we are forced to keep from looking away. This again tears at our unconscious instincts to run and hide from that which we fear. The psychological concept of staring at your enemy requires us to confront it, going against all human tendencies to seek safety and shelter. Carl Jung would be impressed with how the Weeping Angels seem specifically designed to conjure up our unconscious conceptions of evil and force us to confront the evil all around us—even, potentially, the evil in our own shadow.

Other Archetypes

Jung proposed several different archetypes he believed were pervasive across cultures and time periods.[14] Examples include these:

Anima: Our "feminine" side, even as it exists in all men, including beauty, creativity, and demure sexuality. Examples of Anima through history are Helen of Troy, Juliet, and Cinderella. When the Twelfth Doctor regenerates from white-haired Scotsman into blonde-haired woman as the Thirteenth,[15] a Jungian could see this as growth or individuation because the Time Lord is getting to know other aspects of the Doctor's own mind.

Animus: Jung's concept of masculinity, even as it exists in all women, including aggression, a sense of adventure, and physical strength. Examples of Animus include Hercules, Don Juan, Thor, and many aggressive foes the Doctor faces among foes, friends, and allies alike. The War Doctor could be seen as the Doctor's most Animus-like representation when the Eighth Doctor decides the time has come to regenerate into a warrior.[16]

Trickster: A more relatable and amusing version of an antagonist, the Trickster exemplifies intelligence and mischief. Tricksters includes characters such as clowns, Norse god of mischief Loki, Shakespeare's Puck, and a villain called the Trickster who vexes Sarah Jane Smith and her young friends.[17]

Child-God: A combination of innocence, humility, and a fantastic destiny, the Child-God typically has supernatural powers but not physical strength (until possibly later in life or through magic). Examples include leprechauns, dwarves, the Christ child, and *Doctor Who*'s mysterious Timeless Child.[18]

Wise Old Man: The embodiment of age and wisdom, the Wise Old Man is unassuming and humble but provides essential guidance and can often predict the future. Classic representations of this archetype are seen in Tiresias (from *Oedipus Rex*), Merlin, and Gandalf. Though to many the Doctor may be the Fool, the character also strikes many as the Wise Old Man. To the Doctor, mentor figures such as K'anpo and Azmael fit this role.[19]

Angels and the Male Gaze

Although their appearance is somewhat ambiguous (indeed, they are alien), the Weeping Angels appear female. River Song clarifies this when she is grabbed by one of them and then asks the Doctor, "Well, I need a hand back. So which is it going to be? Are you going to break my wrist or hers?"[20] The only way to survive a Weeping Angel is to stare at its female form, unblinkingly. We *must* look at it.[21]

Throughout the history of art, the female form as depicted in paintings and sculpture is constructed almost exclusively for the male viewer. The eye may linger on a hip, breast, or curve. As she is depicted in art, the female's eyes are often turned away demurely. She is frozen in a vulnerable moment and unable to respond to the viewer. This act of viewing a piece of art becomes a voyeuristic activity for the viewer and is one type of *scopophilia*, a term for the sexual pleasure of looking at an object or person in an erotic fashion.[22] The idea that most visual arts are centered around a male view or perspective and that they objectify and sexualize female targets is the so-called *male gaze*.[23]

The Weeping Angels are only seen in their frozen state. As we are initially introduced to them (before we realize what they are), the angels appear as statues—pieces of art—with their eyes covered by their hands. They do not move, they do not respond, and our gaze lingers upon them as much as it pleases us. We become voyeurs, enjoying the power of knowing they are harmless, stone, and submissive to our needs as the viewer. However, this assumption of the male gaze is another reason the Weeping Angels are terrifying: They turn the tables on their prey. We no longer receive pleasure from looking at them once we realize we cannot look away. We *must* not. They suddenly turn the tables and make us utterly powerless.

The Doctor explains these monsters: "They don't exist when they are being observed. The moment they are seen by any other living creature, they freeze into rock . . . And you can't kill a stone. Of course, a stone can't kill you either, but then you turn your head away. Then you blink. Then, oh yes, it can."[24] We are forced to keep our eyes upon her. We are no longer the consumers, the arrogant observers, the ones receiving pleasure by gazing upon a harmless object. We are no longer voyeurs. The Weeping Angel is the one in control. She tortures us with the realization that if we stop looking at her, we will no longer exist. We must do everything we can to keep our eyes open.

The Weeping Angels become even more frightening when we learn that the Angels can harm us even when viewed through a television screen. River Song explains, "Whatever holds the image of an Angel, is an Angel."[25] Not only can they cause harm when we look away or blink, but any image of an Angel—whether it is a drawing, a photograph, or on a screen—can also allow that Angel access to us. The realization dawns on us that we cannot be safe, whether the Angel is in a room or even if we are watching a Weeping Angel on a screen. The lack of any ability to protect ourselves strikes fear in our deepest unconsciousness, as the root of anxiety is lack of control.[26] Cognitive psychologist George Kelly, a practicing psychotherapist, pointed this out when he theorized that we try to have *constructs* or logical frameworks to explain and predict the world, but that fear and anxiety result from failed constructs.[27] The Weeping Angels break all of our ideas about how stone things of beauty cannot hurt us. They prey on our overconfidence.

We must, however, not look *too* closely. The Doctor warns Amy Pond, "Look at the Angel, but don't look at the eyes. The eyes are not the windows of the soul. They are the doors. Beware what may enter there."[28] Pond is now caught in the agonizing trap of being forced to look at her attacker instead of fleeing from it. Any voyeuristic or visually oriented pleasure is turned on its head. As the encounter progresses, we learn that in entering Amy's vision, the image of an Angel inside Amy's visual field allows the Angel to enter her mind.[29] This is perhaps our deepest fear: complete loss of control and identity. Suddenly we realize that the Angels can harm not only if we look away or blink but also if we look in the eyes of an angel, thus allowing it control of our minds and souls. If we look away, we will be transported to another time. If we look at an Angel in the eyes, we will become an Angel. If we cannot look away and cannot look at its eyes, where is it safe for us to look? Where can we be safe? The reasonable response is sheer panic.

To Be "Angelic"

A Weeping Angel is a frightening monster because it challenges our notions of safety and trust, removes any control, and represents a deep-seated archetype of evil. The kind and gentle angels that have graced our lives as guardians, caretakers, and mother figures are now something to be feared. The Great Mother archetype has transformed into the Warrior and the Shadow. Faced with this primordial fear from our collective unconscious, the Weeping Angels represent a foundational concept of fear in psychology. Even more terrifying, we cannot hide from the Shadow archetype, as we would from other monsters, for we must return her gaze. We cannot even look her in the eyes in a moment of brave confrontation, or we will become her. The art that we so willingly consumed with voyeuristic pleasure from "the male gaze" perspective is now unsafe. There is no escape from the Weeping Angels. Only the Doctor can help us.

Miranda Pollock, MFA, is an assistant professor of graphic design and director of the gender and women's studies program at Buena Vista University in Storm Lake, Iowa. She earned her bachelor of fine arts degree and her master of fine arts degree from University of Minnesota Duluth. Pollock is a multidisciplinary artist whose work has been published in various journals and books. She has presented at conferences on the role of interactive design in learning environments. Her research interests include design-user interaction, visual storytelling, and design theory.

Wind Goodfriend, PhD, is a professor of psychology, director of the trauma advocacy program, and Assistant Dean of Graduate Studies at Buena Vista University in Storm Lake, Iowa. She earned her bachelor's degree at Buena Vista University, then earned her Master's and PhD in social psychology from Purdue University. Dr. Goodfriend has won the "Faculty of the Year" award at BVU several times and won the Wythe Award for Excellence in Teaching. She is the principal investigator for the Institute for the Prevention of Relationship Violence.

A popular yet controversial test offers a framework for discussing and comparing personalities along specific dimensions. Though the Doctor retains some heroic traits and quirks through one regeneration after another, striking personality differences between Doctors can emerge.

9

New Face, New Time Lord:
A Personality Perspective

Erin Currie

"Right now, I'm a stranger to myself. There's echoes of who I was and a sort of call towards who I am. And I have to hold my nerve and trust all these new instincts. Shape myself towards them. I'll be fine. In the end. Hopefully."
—**Thirteenth Doctor (Jodie Whittaker)**[1]

"Personality is less a finished product than a transitive process. While it has some stable features, it is at the same time continually undergoing change."
—**personality psychologist Gordon Allport**[2]

What if you could change your personality? What would you change? How would your life be different as a result? Each time a Doctor regenerates, they get to try on a new personality and find out. *Personality* is essentially a pattern of thoughts, feelings, and actions considered typical of an individual. It must be more than a culmination of patterns learned through life experiences. Otherwise, the Doctor's personality would remain much the same after each regeneration. This suggests that there is something essential and internal to the Doctor's personality that exists outside of his or her experiences.

Going a step further, what if each new personality is influenced by the needs of the Doctor? One theory that emphasizes built-in tendencies that incline us to certain personality patterns while leaving space for growth is Carl Jung's theory of psychological types. He and his intellectual successors Katharine Briggs and her daughter, Isabel Briggs Myers, proposed that we have essential orientations toward the world around us that influence our patterns of thought, feeling, and behavior—and therefore our personalities. Their ideas provide a model for looking at the personality variations of the many Doctors featured as the lead characters in the *Doctor Who* TV series and how the experience of each personality could influence the next.

Controversy

Briggs and her daughter used these ideas to create the *Myers-Briggs Type Indicator* (MBTI), a personality assessment based on Jung's personality theory.[3] Within the field of psychology, there is a history of controversy around Jung and the MBTI due to Jung's practice of psychoanalysis and his views on the collective unconscious. The inclusion of spiritual elements in his writings alienated him from many in the scientific community. Such controversy has often overshadowed his contributions, such as the development of the concepts of introversion and extraversion, which are prevalent in modern personality research.[4]

Regardless, there is over half a century of research on the MBTI by Briggs and her daughter, the company that purchased the rights from them, and independent academic researchers showing evidence for the reliability and validity of the basics of this assessment, as well as the areas in which the test needs improvement. Further, consultants and psychologists worldwide use the MBTI as a tool in their practices because it provides a systematic way to think about differences in normal human behavior using non-stigmatizing language.[5]

Personality According to Jung and His Companions

According to Jung's theory, people use two essential processes to manage their lives: decision-making and processing information about the world. Two additional factors—energy focus and environment management style—fine-tune those processes according to Jung. The resulting personality model has four factors, each with two orientations. Similar to handedness, people may use both orientations, but one comes more naturally and is therefore used more often.[6]

Information Processing

The two orientations for processing information are labeled Sensing and Intuition. People who prefer *Sensing* (indicated by the letter S), by definition, are those who focus on experiences from the five senses and the experiences of people they trust to figure out how the world works. A focus on the senses usually involves being close to the information, and so awareness of the immediate consequences for one's actions is common in this group. People who prefer *Intuition* (N) focus on relationships and patterns to understand the world or indeed the universe. This creates a big-picture view of the world and the larger impact of one's actions.[7] After centuries traveling through space and time, it could be assumed that the Doctor would automatically show an Intuitive style. That is a huge picture, after all. However, both information-processing styles are represented.

Decision-Making

The orientation for decision-making is based on the information a person focuses on most when deciding how to act. Some people focus foremost on subjective factors such as needs, values, and feelings of self and others—called *Feeling* (F). The other, *Thinking* (T), focuses on objective factors such as data, logic, and analysis. Each Doctor demonstrates both clever analysis and care, but the weights they hold for the Time Lord and how they manifest fluctuate.[8]

Energy

Jung suggested that there are two orientations for directing energy: *Introversion* (I) and *Extraversion* (E). Jung's ideas on these orientations overlap with but are not identical to modern ideas regarding the personality factors of introversion and extraversion. (See chapter 5.) A person with a preference for Extraversion, as originally defined by Jung, gets the bulk of their inspiration and energy from engaging with the environment and the beings in it. Those with a preference for Introversion, on the other hand, get the bulk of their inspiration and energy from their internal world of thoughts, feelings, and reflections. Both introverted and extraverted Doctors need companions. The difference is that extraverted doctors get more energy from being around their companions.[9]

Environment Management

Briggs and Myers added a fourth factor, pointing out how they person-ally thought people prefer to approach the world. The orientation they labeled Perceiving (P) favors taking in information about the world and what it has to offer before drawing conclusions. Alternatively, some people prefer to use preexisting structures to navigate the world. These structures can take the form of plans, theories, and deeply held values. This preference is labeled Judging (J).

The four factors interact, creating a personality system by which Briggs and Myers believed that individuals manage themselves and the world. The resulting sixteen possible personality styles are denoted by the primary letter for each preferred orientation (e.g., Introversion, iNtuition, Feeling, and Perceiving combine as INFP). Each personal-ity style provides a different foundational framework from which each person can grow through life experience. The Doctor is no different.

The Doctors

First Doctor (originally William Hartnell): INTJ

Individuals with combined preferences for Introversion, Intuition, Thinking, and Judging come in many psychological shapes and sizes, as is true of every combination of characteristics. However, advocates of the Myers-Briggs test see a few common essential personality pat-terns within that diversity. One notable pattern is the tendency toward having strong internalized ideas about how the world should work that drive almost everything people do and how they do it.[10] People who follow a *judicial thinking style* (focused more on analysis than on abstract possibilities or rules) prefer activities that require evaluation, analysis, comparison, and judgment. This fits several versions of the Doctor, beginning with the gruff and intellectual First Doctor. His use of objective facts to define his environment and his attempts to contain the behavior of his companions within that framework are clues to his preference for Thinking and Judging. Take, for instance, his reaction when he encounters ancient Aztecs. His companion Barbara is dismayed by the impending human sacrifice, but the Doctor demands that she not interfere lest doing so alter human history.[11]

People with a combined preference for Introversion and Intuition may be seen as intelligent and insightful, with a far-reaching internal conceptual map they use for insight into the complex workings of the universe. Combine a universe-sized big picture with a strong value placed on objective facts, and the logical result would be high intellectual standards. In times of stress, the First Doctor treats those who fall short of his standards with impatience and even condescension, even if they're his own future selves.[12] If not guarded against, this may be a tendency among those with a combined judicial and thinking style. However, toward the end of this incarnation, the Doctor shows increasing sensitivity to the emotional needs of the people around him,[13] a change that continues to progress into his next incarnation.

Second Doctor (Patrick Troughton): ISFP

The first time one Doctor transforms into the next on screen, personality differences immediately catch his companions' attention.

> **Polly (Anneke Wills):** It is the Doctor. I know it is. I think.

> **Ben (Michael Craze):** It's not only his face that's changed. He doesn't even act like him.[14]

People with a combined preference for Introversion, Sensing, Feeling, and Perceiving supposedly tend to be ready and willing to provide quiet support, often in the background, according to Myers.[15] The extent of help they provide with everyday practical details frequently goes unrecognized until their presence is missed. A focus on details, especially as it relates to prior experience, is a theoretical hallmark for a Sensing preference. Upon initial regeneration, the Second Doctor demonstrates the Sensing preference as he recovers his understanding of himself and the universe by touching mementos and reading the diary of the experiences of his former self. His use of a recorder to play music to help him calm down and think supports an Introverted and Sensing combination.[16]

The Second Doctor is especially sensitive to the needs of his closest companions, experiencing great distress when he is separated from them. He is punished by the Time Lords for meddling in the affairs of Earth without regard for the larger structure of the time stream.[17] This supports a preference for Feeling and runs counter to a Judging approach. In the end, the Time Lords force him to regenerate and exile him to Earth, leaving him stranded there by disabling his TARDIS. This could explain why the next personality is more likely to get energy and fulfillment from interactions with others.

Third Doctor (Jon Pertwee): ENFP

One key pattern for those with preferences for Extraversion, Intuition, Feeling, and Perceiving may be the large amount of energy they get from and give to other people, friends, and strangers alike.[18] Myers believed that the high degree of attention sought from and directed toward people is the hallmark of a combined preference for Extraversion and Feeling, and the Third Doctor enjoys attention. He is flamboyantly yet carefully dressed, and his choice of a car is a vivid yellow Edwardian roadster. He enjoys impressing others with his intelligence and uses charm to convince others to help him save the day.[19]

Individuals with a combined preference for Extraversion, Intuition, and Perceiving appear to be known for their wit and humor. This Doctor's penchant for amusing non sequitur is a great example. It makes theoretical sense. A big picture of the world means greater awareness of the ways in which everything is related. A Perceiving preference means the Doctor is less likely to exclude information as irrelevant.[20] Add the tendency of an Extravert to think out loud, and voilà: non sequitur.

Being emotionally intertwined with people isn't all fun and games. This incarnation of the Doctor experiences guilt for the people he cannot save, even when it's the villain. It is possible that connection to these negative feelings drives him to a more objective and directive personality style.

Fourth Doctor (Tom Baker): ENTJ

Look around a room full of executives and politicians and you might find quite a few people with a combined preference for Extraversion,

Intuition, Thinking, and Judging. This is not surprising considering their penchant for decisive leadership founded on a logical analysis of the bigger picture.[21] When this type of person is not in a position of power, there is a tendency to flout rules not seen as necessary, which could be common for those with a preference for Intuition, Thinking, and Judging. The Fourth Doctor has little patience for ineffective people and arbitrary rules.

Take-charge behavior, as well as a tendency to think out loud, indicates a preference for Extraversion.[22] The Third Doctor is strident, taking charge of difficult situations almost immediately whether he is invited or not. Another example is his response to measured praise by a companion: "I do dislike faint praise. It was astoundingly clever, wasn't it?"[23]

Extraverted Judging brings a lot of intense, dominant energy to each situation. It may be for that reason that the Doctor's next self has a personality style generally known for being a bit more detached.

Fifth Doctor (Peter Davison): INTP

According to Jung's theory, clues to personality style come from the way individuals function when at their best and when under stress. Perhaps because the Fifth Doctor's tenure starts as his physical and psychological regeneration results from the Master's sabotage, much of the Fifth Doctor's personality in his first season seems characteristic of what the INTP personality style may be like under major stress.[24] Myers believed that people with a combined preference for Introversion, Intuition, Thinking, and Feeling exhibit a personality style that features heightened and erratic emotionality during times of chronic or acute stress. For someone with a preference for Introversion and Thinking, high levels of external stress would hinder development of their strongest place for psychological regeneration and decision-making, that internal think tank.[25]

When at their best, people with a combined preference for Introversion, Intuition, Thinking, and Perceiving may thrive in complex situations, quickly perceiving and processing vast amounts of information. Unfortunately for the Doctor, the scope of his understanding is often too big for him to communicate effectively with others. This is shown in the frequency with which his companions say things such as "Why do you always have an incomprehensible answer for everything?"[26] Maybe it's time to get back in touch with the tangible world.

Sixth Doctor (Colin Baker): ESTP

People with a combined preference for Extraversion, Sensing, Thinking, and Perceiving may be seen by others as having an insatiable curiosity about the world and the people around them, sitting still only when required to do so by others—or so Myers believed. It has been noted that social learning and cultural rules temper inborn personality traits, and so we rarely see a "pure" example of any psychological type.[27] The Sixth Doctor may be the exception. He is a caricature of the theoretical ESTP personality type. His demeanor is often highly jovial, and he assumes that others enjoy him as much as he enjoys being himself, indicating a combined preference for Extraversion and Perceiving.[28] Joviality becomes irritability when anyone slows down his pursuit of his schemes and curiosity, and this is a caricature of the Thinking and Perceiving combination. A voracious *joie de vivre* is typical of those with combined Extraversion, Sensing, and Perceiving processes. The Doctor's preference for clothing with many bright primary colors and patterns that he designs by stitching together pieces of old clothes is an expression of his personality.

Toward the end, the over-the-top personality of this Doctor does start to be tempered. Maybe it starts to exhaust him. That could explain why his next personality is more somber.

Seventh Doctor (Sylvester McCoy): INFJ

Individuals who identify with a combined preference for Introversion, Intuition, Feeling, and Judging often report a desire for deep understanding of others and are supposedly fiercely loyal to those they care about. The combined preference for Introversion and Feeling directs interpersonal energy inward, taking time to consider situations quietly in the context of personal values and others' needs.[29] This preference makes the Seventh Doctor different from his predecessor in many ways. First, he is much more subdued. Second, he seems to have an intuitive sense of what motivates people, saving the day by using adversaries' desires against them.[30] This is thought to be a special skill among people with an Intuitive and Feeling orientation. Even though he cares about others, the Doctor has a tendency to be gruff with people who don't live up to his standards, like his predecessor with preferences for Introversion and Judging.[31]

Eighth Doctor (Paul McGann) and War Doctor (John Hurt): ?
We'll come back to them.

Ninth Doctor (Christopher Eccleston): ISTP
According to type theory, people with a combined preference for Introversion, Sensing, Thinking, and Perceiving are likely to be highly creative problem solvers due to their open and imaginative approach to information that is oriented toward practical solutions. They supposedly seek new data about the physical world in response to the problems at hand. You can see this in the Ninth Doctor's practical yet mischievous response to crisis.[32]

Jungian theory holds that extraverts draw energy from interacting with other people whereas introverts get energy from their internal world. When the Ninth Doctor first appears, he has been traveling without a companion. Regardless, he has a grin on his face as he runs around saving the day by himself. This suggests that he doesn't lose energy in prolonged solitude, indicating a preference for Introversion.[33]

When he meets Rose, he finds someone whose drive and bravery he admires. Her bravery is rooted in deep caring for others, and that puts the Doctor's Thinking and Perceiving into stark relief. In the end, the Doctor regenerates after saving Rose from the consequences of her bravery.[34] After that scene, it's no surprise that his next self takes on many of her characteristics.

Tenth Doctor (David Tennant): ENFJ
People with a combination of Extraversion, Intuition, Feeling, and Judging preferences are said to be attentive to the needs and feelings of others and can be fierce champions of human rights. A combined preference for Intuition and Feeling is hypothesized to create a big picture of the world that is focused on the needs of others.[35] The decisions the

Tenth Doctor makes center on a need to alleviate suffering. His habit of rushing into a dangerous situation, taking charge, and rallying the people to save the day indicates a preference for Extraversion and Judging.[36] *Allons-y!* (Let us go!)

Despite an intense concern for the welfare of people, a key to this combined preference for big-picture Intuition and Judging becomes apparent in situations in which the person doesn't save the day. When the Doctor initially refuses to save people of Pompeii from the explosion of Mount Vesuvius, he explains to his companion Donna Noble that he cannot interfere because the destruction of Pompeii is a fixed point in time, a necessary event in the time stream that is sacrosanct to Time Lords. His feeling preference is still there, though, creating inner conflict that is visible in the self-hatred on his face as he nearly leaves people to die.[37] Toward the end, the Tenth Doctor has lost many people he loves deeply for the sake of humanity. That may explain the shift to lightheartedness in his next incarnation.

Eleventh Doctor (Matt Smith): ENTP

Individuals with a combined preference for Extraversion, Intuition, Thinking, and Perceiving seem to thrive on new challenges.[38] For this reason, they are allegedly drawn to entrepreneurship and consulting, specializing in finding new solutions to problems while leaving the drudgery of "dotting *i*'s and crossing *t*'s" to others. In theory, when you combine Intuition, Thinking, and Perceiving and focus on the external world, you can get an open doorway to all the information that the world has to offer and put it together in new ways. The Eleventh Doctor has a universe of information and resources at hand. As a result, he is able to find nearly impossible solutions to mostly impossible situations.[39]

The extravert's need for stimulus from the world, with awareness of the countless possibilities available in a large world, can make it difficult to take day-to-day problems seriously. This Doctor is goofy and lighthearted until there is a problem to solve. Dealing with a crisis in the environment brings out his ability to focus, something that seems common among individuals with a preference for Extraversion and Perceiving.[40] He also doesn't sit still for long. With all of space and time available to him to explore, a person with an ENTP preference would want to see and learn everything. With all the goofiness, it can be easy to overlook the moments in which the Eleventh Doctor shows that he is haunted by past mistakes. His regrets find their way to the front of his mind.[41]

Twelfth Doctor (Peter Capaldi): INTJ

There are only sixteen combinations possible with four personality styles and so we are bound to see repetition within the Doctors' unknown number of regenerations.[42] This is where we get to see how people with the same personality type are both similar and yet also different. A key pattern noted in people with preferences for Introversion, Intuition, Thinking, and Judging as depicted by this Doctor is the awareness and analysis of the potential pitfalls of plans, people, and systems. Myers hypothesized that a judicial approach to analyzing a very big picture requires a high level of discernment.[43] This Doctor brings us back to the INTJ personality previously shown by the First Doctor, as he takes on a face from a man he saved from the volcano in Pompeii[44] and the accent of a friend he couldn't save from Weeping Angels. The INTJ personality style is well suited for scrutiny of self and others. It's all connected to the question on his mind, "Am I a good man?"[45] It seems that the Doctor finally is willing to face his past, and he chooses a personality style well suited to make that judgment.

Placing value on facts seems common in those with a combined preference for Introversion and Thinking. The Twelfth Doctor tells it like it is, focusing on the objective facts of the situation without any sugarcoating. He often is surprised when people react negatively to his approach. This is why he relies so heavily on Clara, Nardole, and Bill to interact with people and convince them to go along with his plans.[46]

Thirteenth Doctor (Jodie Whittaker): ESTP

Few Doctors travel with a whole entourage, much less a "fam" of companions. If there is any question about whether the Thirteenth Doctor is an introvert or an extravert, just watch how often she talks to herself to comfort herself even when no one is around, like when she tells herself bedtime stories out loud while in prison.[47] Her Extraversion directs her Sensing and Perceiving preferences, resulting in a rush toward whatever adventure lies outside the TARDIS door. You can see this excitement for the adventure of the moment in counterpoint to her companions' frustrations when the TARDIS takes them someplace they weren't planning to go. This doesn't slow the Doctor down. Instead, she uses all the sensory information available, even tasting the soil, to figure out where and when they are and to find the mystery that the TARDIS brought them to solve.[48] It also directs her Sensing, Thinking, and Perceiving combination, creating her ability to see and use what is in her environment to manufacture the tools needed to save the day.[49]

Although she cares a great deal for her fam, attending to the feelings of others and communicating what is in her hearts doesn't generally come easily for someone with a Thinking preference, even for an Extravert. However, the Feeling preference aligns with Western female gender roles that promote emotional caretaking as women's primary skill. Meanwhile, the Thinking preference aligns with Western male gender roles that promote analytical problem solving as their primary skill.[50] It can be challenging for women with a Thinking preference to thrive in cultures that prefer women to focus on emotional caretaking. Yaz shows us how a female Doctor, by not conforming to expectations about the female emotional caretaking role, can create misunderstanding and hurt feelings in a way that the Sixth Doctor doesn't experience, not because of anything wrong with her but because of how people are prepared to react.[51]

WAR DOCTOR, FUGITIVE, VALEYARD, EIGHTH, FOURTEENTH, FIFTEENTH, AND MORE?

What about the Eighth Doctor (Paul McGann), War Doctor (John Hurt), or later-revealed Fugitive Doctor (Jo Martin)?[52] Not only do viewers see relatively little of them on screen, the crisis and chaos that surround those appearances may make for atypical experiences not representative of what those characters would act like under other circumstances. Though audio dramas subsequently reveal more about these three along with other variant Doctors such as the Valeyard (Michael Jayston on TV, others in audio),[53] those stories take place off screen, are rarely confirmed as canon to the long-running show, and at times contradict themselves and later TV episodes. Viewers do not get to know the Fourteenth Doctor (David Tennant again) for long,[54] and his entire incarnation centers on the Doctor's situational stress and existential crisis, thus making it difficult to know what he would really be like for a longer term.

It can be tempting to try to figure out someone's character and personality style on first interaction. However, we all can respond flexibly to our environment based on the pressures of the moment and the social rules we've been taught. Trying to identify someone's personality type quickly or during times of great stress can cause incorrect assumptions about the person. These assumptions can result in the implicit bias called the *fundamental attribution error*: when we see the behavior of others and assume that it reflects their personality instead of being caused by the environment or personal circumstances, especially when it's someone we don't know well. This can be harmful when the behavior we see is negative. The interaction between our implicit biases and the tendency to try to figure someone out at first glance is a root of discrimination.[55] So, although we've gotten glimpses of additional Doctors, it is a mistake to make assumptions about their personality styles based on such limited information.

—E. C. & T. L.

Regeneration and Evolution

Although humans do not have the same ability to regenerate, we can learn from the consequences of our behavior and make changes. According to Jung, we each go through a personal crisis in which we are faced with the limitations of the natural strengths of our personalities. We then must choose whether to grow by incorporating the skills and strengths of other personality styles, or to cling to what comes naturally and stagnate. Hopefully like the Doctor, we will take the opportunity to evolve.

The Doctor has had thousands of years to learn from a range of different personality styles, sexes, and genders they can still remember, including the consequences of the behaviors that stemmed from them. Every iteration has given the Doctor the opportunity to try a new approach. Each has new strengths and weaknesses and a new series of lessons to learn.

> "We all change when you think about it."
> —Eleventh Doctor (Matt Smith)[56]

> "My different personalities leave me in peace now."
> —psychoanalyst Anna Freud[57]

Erin Currie, PhD, LP, is a counseling psychologist who is driven to use her psychology superpowers for good. By day, she teaches college students at the University of Portland about how their brains work, why they sometimes don't, and how to develop personal and interpersonal superpowers. By night, she gives her inner geek free reign to write about the psychological factors influencing her favorite characters and adventures. She has written for other Popular Culture Psychology books including *Game of Thrones Psychology*, *Wonder Woman Psychology*, *Supernatural Psychology*, *Westworld Psychology*, and *Stranger Things Psychology*.

III.

HANDS TO HOLD

Social animals that we are, we often identify ourselves by the company we keep. Companions help the Doctor maintain a sense of interpersonal connection and remember what all the running around is really about. It is through the companions that viewers get to know each Doctor and discover the real worlds of *Doctor Who*. It is also through the companions that viewers get to wonder for themselves: What if a blue box appears, a door opens, and an invitation follows . . .?

> "There's a lot of things you need to get across this universe. Warp drive, wormhole refractors. You know the thing you need most of all? You need a hand to hold."
>
> —**Tenth Doctor (David Tennant)**[1]

Physical qualities and personality traits can all be attractive. Circumstances can also heighten a person's appeal. Danger excites us and can make other feelings more exciting as well. So when the Doctor gains a new companion in the course of an adventure, what really makes each person choose to run with the other?

10

Who Makes a Good Companion?

Sarita J. Robinson

"You don't just give up. You don't just let things happen. You make a stand! You say no!
You have the guts to do what's right when everyone else just runs away."

—Rose Tyler (Billie Piper)[1]

"We need each other."
——developmental psychologist Erik Erikson[2]

Psychologists, especially occupational psychologists, have often wondered whether it would be possible to identify whether a person would be a good fit for a job role. For example, is it possible from an interview or an observation to identity someone who has the resilience to be a teacher or the compassion to be a nurse? Identifying selection criterion for different occupational roles is big business because choosing the wrong person can be costly and, in some cases, dangerous. The Doctor has shown the need for companionship, from granddaughter Susan Foreman and her teachers Barbara Wright and Ian Chesterton in 1963 through many dozens of others such as Rose Tyler and Ruby Sunday in the twenty-first century. However, selecting a companion is a difficult task as a good companion will need to have a certain psychological makeup to enjoy traveling with the Doctor.

We know that the Doctor has had many companions. Some have been aliens such as Romana from Gallifrey, Adric from Alzarius, Nyssa from Traken, or Vislor Turlough from Trion. Other companions have been robotic such as dog-like K9, the shape-changing robot Kamelion, the Cyberman head called "Handles," or the humanoid alien-cyborg Nardole. The Doctor tends to choose an Earthling, although not all of them make the grade. For example, both Captain Jack Harkness and Ashildr (also known as "Me") are rejected by the Doctor because they are immortal.[3] The Twelfth Doctor tells Ashildr that companions have to be like "mayflies" so that they can remind him of what is important in life. So how does the Doctor select companions and what other characteristics is the Doctor looking for?

So Who Makes a Good Travel Companion?

Sometimes companions are thrust upon the Doctor. The Time Lords send Romana (or Romanadvoratrelundar to give her full name) to help the Doctor fulfill the White Guardian's mission to find the Key to Time. Some companions, such as Dodo Chaplet or Tegan Jovanka, appear to stumble into the TARDIS believing it to be a genuine police box. Donna Noble tracks down the Tenth Doctor to accept a travel invitation she previously declined, Amy Pond waits patiently for the Eleventh Doctor to take her traveling, and others such as Yaz Khan, Ryan Sinclair, and Graham O'Brien find themselves accidently dragged along.[4] No matter how a potential companion gets aboard the TARDIS, the Doctor has the ultimate power to decide if they are worthy of a TARDIS key.

Although modern selection processes for adventurers can have a psychological basis, historically selection has been a little more hit and miss. Ernest Shackleton, the famous Antarctic explorer, recruited men for his 1914 *Nimrod* expedition. The story goes that he placed an advert in a London newspaper asking for volunteers for the hazardous journey. "Low wages, bitter cold, long hours of complete darkness. Safe return doubtful. Honor and recognition in event of success." Shackleton received five thousand applications, which he divided into three piles labelled *Mad, Hopeless,* and *Possible.*[5] Shackleton's selection criteria for fellow adventurers appeared to include optimism, patience, physical endurance, idealism, and courage. These qualities also appear in many of the Doctor's companions, and so it is possible that the Doctor takes some advice from Shackleton.

Today, the selection criteria for adventurers are thought to be more robust, but it is only recently that detailed psychological screening has been included in astronaut selection procedures.[6] Before psychological screening was commonplace, it was merely an assumption that you could spot who had the "right stuff." People with the "right stuff" were thought to be easy to spot as they would be independent, expressive, and driven to work hard. Whereas people with the "wrong stuff" tended to be competitive, impatient, and irritable. Selectors also want to screen out people with "no stuff," those people who are unassertive with low levels of motivation.[7] Again, the Doctor does not want to select people with the wrong stuff or no stuff.

The Doctor's Selection Process

The Doctor does, on most occasions, select companions who have the "right stuff." All the Doctor's companions tend to be independent and expressive with a strong work ethic. However, the Doctor's selection process is much messier. What other factors does the Doctor take into account?

A number of the Doctor's companions have either medical or academic qualifications. For example, both Martha Jones (who is a medical student when she first meets the Doctor) and Harry Sullivan (a lieutenant surgeon in the Royal Navy) are medically trained. Dr. Grace Holloway is an accomplished cardiologist who inadvertently triggers the Doctor's regeneration after subjecting him to an ill-judged heart operation.[8]

Perhaps the Doctor is selecting companions based on their *intelligence quotient* (IQ). IQ is determined by a set of tests that are designed to measure human intelligence. High IQ levels are thought to be associated with occupations such as medical and academic jobs. It is likely that if archaeologist River Song, astrophysicist Zoe Heriot, and UNIT science officer Dr. Elizabeth Shaw took an IQ test, they would score highly. However, psychologists are now starting to think that IQ alone is not the best predictor of success in occupations such as medicine. Recent research suggests that traits of self-discipline and motivation are also important.[9] In fact, not every companion would have scored well on traditional IQ tests. Jo Grant, for example, who is hired by UNIT to be the Doctor's lab assistant, says she failed her science exams.[10] Many of the Doctor's companions have not had high-powered jobs, with Ace working as a waitress, Rose Tyler in a department store, and Bill Potts in the university canteen. Indeed, when Romana boasts that she graduated from the Time Lord Academy with top honors, the Fourth Doctor is not impressed.[11] He points out that she lacks experience. Therefore, like occupational psychologists, the Doctor knows that academic smarts do not automatically mean that someone is the right fit for a job role.

Intelligence

In fact, some psychologists today suggest that even the traditional IQ view of intelligence is limited and that there is more than one way in which to be clever. The *multiple intelligences model* introduced by developmental psychologist Howard Gardner suggests that people can be smart in different ways:[12]

Linguistic intelligence—good oral communication skills including the ability to express yourself and your point of view. Investigative journalist Sarah Jane Smith, who makes her living through words, would perform well on tests of linguistic intelligence.

Logical-mathematical intelligence—the ability to think logically, see patterns, and deduce solutions from the evidence presented. Adric, the mathematics genius from the planet Alzarius in E-Space, is likely to score highly on tests that tap into this.

Musical intelligence—the ability to make music. There is limited evidence of musical intelligence in the Doctor's companions. Maybe this is a trait the Doctor does not value in them (even though the

Second Doctor plays his recorder regularly to help himself think and the Twelfth Doctor amps up his electric guitar).[13]

Bodily-kinaesthetic intelligence—the ability to carefully control your body in the physical world. Leela demonstrates this quality as a warrior of the Sevateem. However, high levels of bodily-kinaesthetic intelligence do not seem to be a key selection criterion. Companion Ryan Sinclair, for example, has the developmental coordination disorder *dyspraxia,* which makes him struggle with motor skills such as riding a bike.[14]

Spatial intelligence—the ability to recognize and use space around you. One companion to the Fourth Doctor, Harry Sullivan, may score low on this trait as he is well-known for being clumsy.

Intrapersonal intelligence—the ability to understand your own thoughts and feelings and how they affect your behavior. Many of the Doctor's companions have high levels of this type of intelligence. For example, companions such as River Song, Clara Oswald, and Bill Potts all help the Doctor to understand how his behavior impacts others.

Interpersonal intelligence—the ability to understand other people's needs and motivations. All of the Doctor's companions show high levels of this, such as Dan Lewis who volunteers at a food bank and notes, "What is the point of being alive if it is not to make others happy?"[15] Each Doctor may feel they need the companions because the Time Lord may not always understand the life-forms they meet while the companions are more likely to grasp the essence of any crisis and make the personal connection.

Gardner's *interpersonal intelligence* is similar to another concept, emotional intelligence. *Emotional intelligence (EI)*[16] comprises of skills that allow people to do the following:

• Understand and express their own emotions as well as the emotions of others.

- Regulate their own emotions and the emotions of others.
- Use their abilities to motivate, plan, and achieve their goals.

Only a few of the Doctor's companions appear to be low in EI. The Brigadier and maybe his daughter Kate could do well to improve their EI abilities. For example, Kate Stewart does not want to negotiate with the Zygons and feels that bombing them would be a better approach (twice).[17] Perhaps for this reason, neither of them regularly joins the Doctor in the TARDIS, though. In fact, Kate seems surprised when the Thirteenth Doctor invites her along for one ride.[18]

In most cases, the Doctor's companions care passionately about all the life-forms whom they meet while they journey through time and space. Many companions even put themselves in harm's way to help life-forms they have only just met. Rose, for example, takes pity on the Dalek who has been tormented by Henry van Statten and pleads with the Doctor for the Dalek's life.[19] Donna Noble insists the Doctor save Lobus Caecilius and family from the volcanic eruption[20] (and the Twelfth Doctor later suspects that he has regenerated with Caecilius's face as a reminder to himself to save people). Graham and Ryan act as birth partners for Yoss Inkl onboard the medical evacuation spaceship.[21] They often help despite great risk to themselves, a defining aspect of altruism.[22]

However, although intelligence testing (whether IQ, multiple intelligences, or EI) can tell us about some of the characteristics of a person, they cannot tell us everything we need to know to determine if someone would be good in a certain role (such as being a good traveling companion). In addition to intelligence tests, psychologists can also use personality measures to see if people are a good fit for a certain job role. For example, having a high IQ might make you good at math, but you're not going to make a good math teacher if you don't like people!

Personality

Psychologists have identified five main personality factors (the Big Five) that are universally present in both Western and non-Western cultures.[23] And from what we have seen, these personality types also seem to be present across the Who universe. It is thought that most people fall between two extreme points on a scale for each of the five factors (as opposed to sitting completely at one end or the other).

The previous chapter looks at how different Doctors manifest traits across these and other personality factors, but what about the Doctor's companions?

Openness to Experience

People range from very curious to very cautious. It is a fair assumption to say that all of the Doctor's companions are very curious. Ace, for example, with her homemade science lab, has already managed to find her way to the planet Svartos before joining the Seventh Doctor on his travels. Then there is Clara Oswald, who replies to the Eleventh Doctor's questions about where she would like to go by requesting to see "something awesome."[24] A companion expelled from the TARDIS by the Doctor, Adam Mitchell, shows a low level of openness. In fact, he does not cope well with his travels, fainting the first time he sees Earth from space and acting reluctant to try the beef-flavored slushy that Rose offers him.[25]

Conscientiousness

People may be organized and effective or disorganized and spontaneous. The Doctor's companions tend to demonstrate a high level of conscientiousness, attentive to detail. Clara Oswald organizes her work as a teacher around her travels with the Doctor.[26]

Extraversion

Some people are outgoing and revel in social interactions, whereas others act more reserved and prefer their own company. The Doctor's companions tend to be quite outgoing and show a high degree of extraversion. Ace in particular stands out as a companion who has a highly extraverted nature. As evidenced by the job she has taken as a waitress in the Iceworld's ice cream parlor, she enjoys being around people (even if she does not always tolerate their behavior).[27] Ace, hefting her boombox about and quick to make friends, really is the "life and soul" of the party. These skills and interests doubtless help her found her organization, A Charitable Earth.[28]

Agreeableness

The Doctor's companions tend to have a high degree of agreeableness: being caring, cooperative, and considerate. People who are less agreeable possess low levels of empathy and little concern for the health and well-being of others. One of the key characteristics of all the Doctor's companions is their caring nature. After the Daleks murder Victoria Waterfield's father, the Second Doctor's companion Jamie McCrimmon becomes protective of her.[29] Companions also look out for the people they encounter. Donna, for example, helps the Tenth Doctor to free the Ood from slavery,[30] and Nardole (companion first to River, then to the Twelfth Doctor) devotes his life to helping to keep a group of people safe from Cybermen.[31]

Neuroticism

People range from nervous to confident. Generally, the Doctor's companions appear to have low levels of nervousness and have the ability to deal with even the most stressful of situations. Tegan, for example, refuses to stay safe in the TARDIS with the Watcher but goes to help the Doctor even though the planet is falling apart.[32] In most adventures, the Doctor's companions show remarkable ability to stay cool, calm, and collected. Psychological research into the ways in which people react to emergency situations suggests that only about 10 to 25 percent of people will have the ability to stay mentally alert and carry out prompt and well-thought-out responses.[33] The vast majority of the population do not respond well to life-threatening events and can suffer from *cognitive paralysis* in which they fail to undertake any actions at all. Obviously this would not be helpful for the Doctor's companions, who need to be able to work well under pressure. Most of them excel under pressure. Martha Jones, for example, independently travels around spreading the word of the Doctor in a world controlled by the Master and the Toclafane.[34]

In addition to having the "right stuff" in terms of intelligence and personality, companions often have a range of past experiences, which means that they are able to cope with the adventures that the Doctor thrusts on them. For example, Yasmin Khan's training and experiences as a police officer help her to deal with tricky situations. When dealing with the Master's attempts to mess with her mind, she notes that she has "heard worse on a Friday night in Sheffield."[35]

The Dark Triad:
Psychopathy, Machiavellianism, and Narcissism

The Doctor rarely errs in choosing companions, but one exception is Adam Mitchell. (Although Adam essentially comes along as Rose's date, the Ninth Doctor lets him.) As well as suffering from time sickness, Adam has some of the personality characteristics that fall within the *dark triad*. The dark triad refers to three personality traits that appear to be typical of people who are manipulative and exploitative.

Narcissism: Narcissists show low empathy and have a high level of entitlement. People with narcissist personalities do not make good companions. They are not team players and are simply out for themselves.[36] Adam displays some narcissist characteristics, as he only seems interested in how he can profit from his travels. For example, he tries to download advances in technology with no consideration for the impact of his actions.

Machiavellianism: People with Machiavellian personality traits tend to be manipulative and are willing to exploit others.[37] People with this trait generally lack a moral code and have a high level of self-interest and deception. We can see that Adam is self-interested, as he does not actively help the residents of Satellite Five.

Psychopathy: People with psychopathic traits lack empathy and are reckless, feeling little to no remorse for their behavior.[38] Adam displays some of these traits. He is reckless, opting for major brain surgery to download information about technological advances. When he gets caught, he does not appear guilty or apologetic. He simply tries to justify his actions.

What are the Benefits for the Doctor of a Travel Companion?

Whereas the Master simply wants a companion so that they can bask in his brilliance or function as pawns toward some other goal (on the rare occasions when the Master has a companion at all), the Doctor's reasons for wanting a companion relate to maintaining well-being. There are many psychological advantages of having a good social support network. Without a friend or family member to turn to, humans can feel lost and alone. When the Ninth Doctor meets Rose, we know that he has been traveling without a companion for some time[39] and this has impacted negatively on his happiness. Having a traveling companion has many advantages for the Doctor:

Help with moral decisions. The Doctor draws on the experiences of companions and relies on them at times as a moral compass. When weighing whether he has the right to destroy the entire Dalek race, the Fourth Doctor asks Sarah Jane.[40] By calling on the help of companions such as Sarah Jane, the Doctor can get a new perspective on important decisions.

Emotional support. Psychologists know that friendships are extremely important for remaining mentally healthy.[41] The Doctor appears to have strong emotional ties to the companions and sometimes appears devastated when companions leave. Missy (the Master) suggests that the Doctor's relationship with the companions is not 100 percent equal and that the Doctor sees them more as faithful pets. However, even if this is the case, psychologists have found that having a pet can also be beneficial to your mental well-being.[42]

Physical benefits. The Doctor's companions can help the Time Lord remain physically healthy by also saving the Time Lord from other dangers. Melanie Bush, for example, puts the Sixth Doctor on a regimen of carrot juice and exercise.[43] Psychologists know that people who feel lonely can have health problems and that exercise is much easier if you have a friend to help you out.[44]

After the Doctor?

Traveling with the Doctor has a profound effect on many of the Doctor's companions. Some are forced to leave the TARDIS, but some decide that it is time for them to move on and stop their travels. For example, as he chooses to return home, Ian Chesterton tells the First Doctor that he misses sitting in a pub and drinking a pint of beer,[45] and Martha Jones later chooses to stop traveling with the Tenth Doctor after she decides that their relationship is not healthy for her.[46]

The Doctor becomes emotionally attached to the companions but does want the best outcome for them. For example, even though the Tenth Doctor wipes Donna's memory of their travels together, he returns on her wedding day and gives her a mysterious lottery ticket as a wedding gift.[47] Even when companions cannot be saved, the Doctor does try to do right by them. After River Song dies in the Library, saving the people trapped by its computer, the Doctor uploads her to the Library's mainframe so that a version of her can continue to live on.[48] A number of companions who are returned to Earth, such as Sarah Jane or Tegan, feel abandoned by the Doctor. When the Third Doctor's companion Jo meets the Eighth Doctor, she learns that he has checked on them all "and I was so proud," and when Tegan meets the Thirteenth Doctor after thirty-eight years, the Fifth Doctor (as A.I. interface) assures her, "I never forget any of you."[49]

On a positive note, most of the companions seem to grow from the traumas that they have witnessed on their adventures. For example, shortly after witnessing Adric's death, Nyssa chooses to remain on the hospital ship *Terminus* to help develop a cure for Lazar's disease.[50] And Amy and Rory appear to lead a happy life after getting catapulted back to 1938, adopting a son and publishing Amy's books.[51] Psychologists refer to such positive outcomes after trauma as *posttraumatic growth* (PTG).[52]

Readjusting to life on Earth after traveling with the Doctor can be challenging. Companions such as Sarah Jane Smith, Martha Jones, Tegan Jovanka, Ace, Graham O'Brien, and more use the skills and experience gained during their travels with the Doctor to become freelancers for UNIT (United Nations Intelligence Taskforce, later

UNified Intelligence Taskforce[53]). After his return to Earth, Graham O'Brien finds it especially difficult to readjust to everyday life, noting that he has no one to talk to about his adventures with the Doctor. He therefore sets up a peer support group for ex-companions so that they can share their stories and experiences.[54] Peer support has been found helpful for survivors of traumatic events, increasing well-being and promoting PTG. Being around people who have had similar experiences has been found to encourage people to talk more openly about what has happened.[55]

Selecting the Perfect Companion

Selecting anyone for a job role is difficult. Occupational psychologists have researched for many years how different traits can fit with different occupations. Although not one who subjects companions to psychometric testing, the Doctor does appear to know who will make a good companion. The Doctor selects those who are mortal, moral, motivated, emotionally intelligent, extraverted, agreeable, conscientious, and above all able to deal with a stressful situation. Rarely does he give someone undeserving the TARDIS key.[56]

"Through others we become ourselves."
—developmental psychologist Lev Vygotsky[57]

Sarita J. Robinson, PhD, is the Associate Dean of the School for Psychology and Humanities at the University of Central Lancashire, England. Over the last seventeen years, Sarita has investigated the psychobiology of behavior, specifically focusing on how the brain functions (or doesn't) when we face life-threatening events. Sarita's research frequently means she finds herself in high-pressure environments, working with firefighters, people undergoing helicopter underwater evacuation training, and other stress-inducing survival courses. Sarita is a life-long *Doctor Who* fan who enjoys combining her passion for *Doctor Who* with her love of psychology. In her spare time, Sarita enjoys doing stand-up comedy and public engagement talks.

RELATIONSHIP STAGES AND THE POWER OF THREE

Erin Currie[58]

Each classic Doctor up through the Fifth travels with a group of companions for at least part of his journey. After that, though, the Doctor usually travels with one companion at a time, only briefly including a second one here and there. The Eleventh and Thirteenth Doctors become unusual in the modern series by traveling with more than one for long periods. The Eleventh Doctor presents a particular exception in that a married couple accompanies him.

When you go beyond the *dyad*, the social grouping of two who interact sheerly one-on-one, group dynamics come into play.[59] In addition to the personality interplay between the Doctor and one companion, a group involves personality dynamics playing out among pairs, trios, and more.

Group dynamics theorist Bruce Tuckman developed a theory of how groups develop and evolve.[60] Take the married couple and their Doctor for example.

Stage 1: Forming. People in the group start to get to know each other. Although Amy knows both Rory and the Doctor, they all learn more about each other in the context of the group.[61]

Stage 2: Storming. Tension arises as people vie for roles in the group. The Doctor is accustomed to being in charge, but he often cedes that role to Amy while Rory struggles to figure out where he fits.[62]

Stage 3: Norming. Everyone settles into their roles in the group. Amy is the leader who unites them as a group, Rory is the caretaker, and the Doctor is the brains.[63]

Stage 4: Performing. People are comfortable in their relationships and group roles, so they start trying new growth behaviors. The Doctor slows down and becomes more relational while Rory becomes fiercer and more confident. Amy, meanwhile, learns to rely on others.[64]

Stage 5: Adjourning. The group disbands, preferably when the members have grown as individuals. Amy and Rory start to talk about fully participating in their life on Earth.[65] Although they experience grief when they're finally separated from the Doctor, they move on to have separate adventures.[66]

Compassion offers advantages for its recipient, but what about the one who shows it? What does science reveal about the benefits for the compassionate person? Who cares . . .

11

The Compassionate Doctor: Caring for Self by Caring for Others

Janina Scarlet, Travis Langley, & Alan Kistler

> "I'm not sure any of that matters—friends, enemies—
> so long as there's mercy. Always mercy."
> —**Twelfth Doctor (Peter Capaldi)**[1]

> "Compassion may have ensured our survival because of its tremendous benefits for both physical and mental health and overall well-being."
> —**psychology researcher Emma Seppälä**[2]

Throughout centuries and many lives, the Doctor displays endless compassion toward companions and those they are trying to save. The Doctor's many enemies—in particular Davros, creator of the Daleks[3]—argue that compassion makes the Time Lord weak. Are they blinded by their own cynicism, or might they sometimes be right? Is compassion a human flaw or a source of strength? What role does compassion play in people's physical and emotional health?

Compassion and Survival

Compassion involves witnessing the suffering of another being, feeling empathy toward that being, and experiencing the desire to alleviate that suffering.[4] From an evolutionary standpoint, compassion seems to be necessary for survival. Specifically, compassionate parenting will result in the best care for the offspring, ensuring the best chances of survival for the child. Compassionate caregiving provides physical and emotional stability for the child, ensuring that he or she will grow up and reach the age of reproductive maturity.[5] Compassion is also necessary for marital satisfaction, as well as the overall survival of others. When she travels to the year 1938, River Song intends to kill both Hitler and the Eleventh Doctor, but is then impressed by the Time Lord's compassion. Convinced to be compassionate herself, she saves the Doctor's life even though she only recently met him (from her perspective) and, in doing so, sacrifices her ability to regenerate.[6] This is a powerful act of *altruism* on River's part, possibly *heroism,* helping another person without expectation of personal benefit despite incurring great cost.

When people see strangers suffering, they are less likely to display compassion than they would toward people they care about, like family members and friends.[7] This can be especially problematic if the observers, such as Kaleds like Davros, do not view those who are suffering as true people. The Kaleds reject and banish any who are biologically and physically "inferior," arguing that they "must keep the Kaled race pure."[8] In fact, the less people view others as similar to themselves, the less likely they are to help them.[9]

However, by recognizing similarities between the observer and the sufferer, such as shared food or music preferences, the observers are more likely to cultivate compassion for the sufferers. The Eleventh Doctor teaches wealthy mogul Kazran Sardick compassion for people of lower classes partly by using time travel to alter the man's childhood, adding experiences that teach Sardick to see them as fellow human beings rather than replaceable resources.[10] These added experiences by themselves do not change Sardick's mind and behavior, but they provide a strong push in that direction. The rest is up to him.

Compassion and Health

Compassion practice helps individuals manage their physical and mental health.[11] Practicing compassion can involve reaching out to others as well as engaging in meditation, such as *loving-kindness meditation*

(LKM).[12] Such compassion practice can lower symptoms of depression, anxiety, posttraumatic stress disorder (PTSD), and chronic pain.[13] In addition, compassion practice can improve the quality of social interactions,[14] increase positive emotions,[15] and benefit physical health.[16]

People who experience as much loss and trauma as the Doctor may sometimes develop mental health disorders, such as PTSD, anxiety, or depression. Unsure of how to cope, some of these people engage in avoidance behaviors by disconnecting from their emotions or not talking.[17] When Rose tries to get any answers about who the Ninth Doctor is or where he comes from, he becomes defensive, angrily shouting, "This is who I am! Right here, right now! All right? All that counts is here and now, and this is me!"[18]

When experiencing that rage and avoiding talking about personal tragedies, the Doctor may be struggling with at least some symptoms of PTSD. During and right after the Time War, the Doctor's experiences are similar to what many combat veterans undergo after exposure to battle. This is especially true when it comes to anger and aggression when encountering a reminder of the war (a Dalek, for example).[19] In addition to PTSD, many veterans and other war survivors experience depression.[20] However, when veterans who struggled with these disorders received a twelve-week compassion training course, they demonstrated significant reductions in PTSD and depression symptoms. During the compassion training, the veterans were taught loving-kindness meditation, which assisted the veterans in cultivating compassionate wishes for themselves, for their loved ones, for strangers, and eventually, even for their enemies.[21]

After the Ninth Doctor is first introduced, he willingly watches Lady Cassandra die, evidently thinking this a just punishment for her crimes. However, after he spends time connecting with Rose, who shows compassion toward friends and enemies alike, he changes. When the Dalek Emperor later threatens all of Earth, this Doctor chooses instead to risk death at the hands of several Daleks (regeneration is unlikely from multiple hits by Dalek weapons) rather than defeat them by committing genocide. This effectively indicates that, through Rose's compassion toward him and others, he grows from the person who ended the Time War.[22]

Core Values and Happiness

Many people can find happiness of some kind even in the most difficult of circumstances by following their core values.[23] Adhering to one's values without losing sight of the things that matter most to them provides a different kind of satisfaction. Whether they do so naturally or by making themselves stay mindful or by inviting companions they believe will help them stay on track, those who live a *values-driven life* stay more conscious of their core values and live better lives.[24] The Doctor may be going through many difficult lives, enduring much pain and heartache, but ultimately stays true to the core value of what it means to be the Doctor—showing compassion and helping people.

Although happiness resulting from *instant gratification* (immediate fulfillment of needs and desires), such as the Master or Missy will gain from destructive actions, may bring some pleasure-based satisfaction (*hedonic happiness*), the effects would be temporary. On the other hand, meaning-based happiness (*eudaimonic happiness*)—which the Doctor experiences when achieving a moral victory and spending time with friends—has long-term benefits. Pursuing eudaimonic happiness is physiologically and psychologically healthier than seeking hedonic happiness.[25]

Doing the right thing can hurt. The Doctor must make difficult choices for the sake of what is right, for the sake of that which she values most. When the Thirteenth Doctor and companions watch Rosa Parks stand up for civil rights by staying seated, the Doctor knows this must happen. The experience is difficult and it hurts, but the Doctor is not only supporting her own values regarding what must happen in history, she is also supporting Rosa's priorities as well. Seeing the pain but also the adoration the Doctor has for Rosa is important. Holding back to let Rosa assert herself can achieve only eudaimonic happiness, not hedonic, because there is nothing pleasant about that moment.[26]

When companions such as Jo Grant and Sarah Jane Smith end their travels with, respectively, the Third then Fourth Doctor and leave, he is sad to see them go but also proud that they have grown into heroes. Jo and Sarah Jane may feel somewhat abandoned when the Doctor does not continue to visit or check on them. The Eleventh Doctor explains that this is partly out of faith that they will continue to do good work on their own, no longer needing his help, and admits to admiring their achievements from afar.[27] Whereas people actively pursuing hedonic happiness may have certain health problems, people leading a *meaning-based life* are more likely to have better health.[28] Meaning means more to us.

Compassion Fatigue or Empathic Distress

Witnessing or experiencing death and destruction, such as the events of 9/11 or what the Doctor witnesses during the Last Great Time War, could negatively affect anyone. After enduring such tragedies, even the most compassionate people might occasionally find themselves incapable of empathizing with others (*compassion fatigue*) or oversensitized to the point of feeling stressed by it (*empathic distress*). This usually occurs when someone's mental health or physical resources are depleted, leaving them unable to care for others.[29]

The Seventh Doctor decides that too many good people have died and continue to die at the hands of evil forces, and so he becomes proactive, now hunting monsters and setting up traps to destroy or imprison them. These traps sometimes involve lying to his companions or hurting them emotionally (most overtly the companion known as Ace).[30] Though scolded for becoming too harsh and manipulative during this time, he believes he is doing what's best. He voices a fear that his next incarnation won't be willing to do everything necessary to stop evil, even if it means alienating himself from his core principles and companions who once trusted him.[31] By his eighth known life, he realizes that he had lost some of his principles during that time, as well as some compassion. The Eighth Doctor gives up master plans and schemes in order to embrace compassion and fun once more.

"I knew a man . . . a man who became obsessed with the future, with predicting and planning for every variable, who lost himself in the big picture. But the more he planned, the more he gained, the more he realized that he was losing the one thing most precious to him . . .

He only wanted to be more human."

—Eighth Doctor (Paul McGann),
recalling the Seventh (Sylvester McCoy)[32]

There are many reasons why someone might experience compassion fatigue or empathic distress—like a stressful job, personal trauma, difficult work or home environment, or lack of self-compassion.[33] Studies that focus on teaching participants to cultivate compassion for themselves or others find that, after developing and practicing compassion skills, participants experience less compassion fatigue, stress, and worry, and more resilience against work-related burnout.[34] Some compassion researchers suggest that the term *compassion fatigue* is not accurate and should instead be called *empathic distress* because compassion appears to build resilience while empathy without self-support can lead to burnout.[35] (Consider, for example, the toll taken on healthcare workers during lockdown.)

Empathy, the ability to experience someone else's emotional state, may diminish when an individual is in distress and lacks resources to cope with their own struggles. On the other hand, actively practicing compassion for oneself and others might actually aid the observer in coping with their suffering as well as the suffering of others.[36] Soon after the Last Great Time War, the Ninth Doctor is reluctant to speak about the loss of his people and even struggles to talk about this loss with those who are aware that the Time Lords are gone. But after Rose witnesses the Earth's destruction in the far future and explains what that means to her, this Doctor sees that they now have some common ground. They have each lost a home and know their species is gone, so he is finally able to say out loud, "My planet's gone. It's dead . . . They're all gone. I'm the only survivor."[37] Thus begins a journey toward healing and acceptance.

Alleviating Empathic Distress

Every Doctor who initially seems less sympathetic or empathetic toward others grows more caring over the course of that incarnation. Even though the First Doctor chooses the name Doctor out of concern for others,[38] he seems more distant and curmudgeonly by the time his granddaughter's schoolteachers discover him inside the TARDIS.[39] He has been hiding on Earth, which further suggests that he has emotionally needed time off from previous suffering. Freshly after regeneration, the Sixth and Twelfth Doctors each come across as aloof, arrogant, and uncaring, and yet they grow to become some of the most ardent advocates for justice, the most appalled by anyone's mistreatment of others. Even though the Twelfth Doctor once calls Clara "my carer—she cares so I don't have to," he is also the version who shows the First Doctor that it's all right to rewrite a few lines of history to save some lives, and he's the one whose final advice to the oncoming Thirteenth Doctor is to "be kind."[40] The crankiest Doctors still care, even if they must remind themselves and consciously reconnect with those feelings over time.

Active compassion practice may reduce compassion fatigue for multiple reasons. First, active compassion practice lowers the distress that occurs when individuals see their loved ones suffer. Specifically, compassion practice activates the empathy centers of the brain. Although the Nestene Consciousness is his enemy, the Ninth Doctor apologizes with great remorse that he couldn't save the creature's home planet during the Time War.[41] When the Tenth Doctor realizes that he has inadvertently caused a Cyberman to experience human memory and pain again, he apologizes for causing the Cyberman any suffering.[42]

Second, this practice reduces the negative effect of stress on the body, typically present when seeing another person suffer. Some negative effects of stress include an increase in the stress hormone cortisol. Prolonged exposure to this hormone can lead to poor health, weight gain, and heart disease.[43] Active compassion practice allows the observer to experience both empathy and soothing for the sufferer, reversing the negative effects of stress.[44] For instance, after finding different ways to cheat her death, the villainous Lady Cassandra inhabits the body of a person who has accepted that he will die soon and she finds herself finally understanding such a perspective and making peace with her own mortality. The Tenth Doctor then shows compassion to a dying enemy by bringing Cassandra into her own past so she can see her younger self one last time, an experience that brings her happiness before she dies.[45]

Integration Between Past and Present Selves

"From the past!"

—Seventh Doctor (Sylvester McCoy) to Thirteenth (Jodie Whittaker)[46]

In seeing the Doctor remember past selves and yet sometimes avoid thinking about them, we see some of what humans go through in terms of *fragmentation*, when the person "divides traits and feelings and groups them into smaller sections, keeping some of them hidden until a safe space for expression is provided."[47] A more extreme breakdown of self could be viewed as *personality disintegration*.[48] People who undergo severe trauma sometimes close mental doors to parts of themselves, *dissociating* or separating active parts of themselves without sharing information between the parts. They may try to avoid remembering certain pieces of their lives that might be too painful, and it is for survival's sake that this happens until they are ready to open those metaphorical doors into themselves. Given the opportunity to remember missing portions of her own history simply by opening a watch, the Thirteenth Doctor instead drops it into the TARDIS, telling the TARDIS to keep it safe somewhere deep, "somewhere I can never find it—unless I really ask for it."[49] She is not ready to confront that part of her past or self, not that she has to. She has the freedom to do it on her own schedule when the time suits her, if at all.

True healing may happen when *integration* becomes possible, when the past and present selves can work together to feel and show compassion for different pieces of themselves. The Thirteenth Doctor chooses not to open herself to part of her history that may supplant her self-concept, changing how she sees herself as drastically as when the Tenth Doctor previously opened a watch that made him remember he is a Time Lord and not a human schoolteacher.[50] It is a sign of self-acceptance that she does not feel compelled to open that door and thus risk altering the person she has become. Nevertheless, the Thirteenth Doctor works on healthy integration of self by working with her past selves more dramatically than any previously known Doctor. It is she who activates the *artificial intelligence* (A.I.) with interfaces that can represent her or her past selves, notably the Fifth and Seventh Doctors but also showing glimpses of others. She is also the Doctor who revisits past selves within her own mind rather than passively accept a forced regeneration.[51]

By interacting with past companions Tegan and Ace, the A.I. interfaces reveal something of how the Thirteenth Doctor has integrated parts of her past into her current self. An A.I.-based hologram of the Seventh Doctor shows how that part of the Thirteenth Doctor's mind feels about the fact that the Seventh's Machiavellian ways once led companion Ace to part company with him. One person's healing can also assist another's. Decades after leaving the Seventh Doctor, Ace comes to make her own peace with his memory.

> **Ace (Sophie Alred):** You never failed me, Professor. You made me the person I am today. I'm sorry we fell out. I'm sorry I judged you. I didn't understand the burden you carried.

> **Seventh Doctor hologram (Sylvester McCoy):** All children leave home sooner or later. The joy is to watch them fly.

> **Ace:** So we're good?

> **Seventh Doctor:** Oh, we're more than good. We're ace.[52]

Though the Seventh Doctor does not physically appear within the scene, the hologram operates on an advanced artificial intelligence that the Thirteenth Doctor has based on her own psyche. The A.I.'s regrets and the compassion finally shown in this moment come from within the Doctor herself and how the Seventh Doctor portion of her psyche now feels.

Having conversations with past versions of ourselves can be therapeutic, which is why some therapists ask clients to try doing so in therapy. We can imagine ourselves from earlier days, look at pictures of our younger selves, and consider what that part of who we are now might say or need to hear. The A.I. versions of the Fifth and Seventh Doctors not only help Tegan and Ace, but they also reveal consideration that the Thirteenth Doctor, in programming those interfaces, feels regarding those parts of herself. Demonstrating compassion toward one's younger self is monumental in treating complicated grief and heartbreak. Simply by mentioning Adric, a companion killed by Cybermen,[53] the Fifth Doctor shows Tegan that she is not alone in bearing that pain. By showing compassion to Tegan and Ace, the Thirteenth Doctor reveals compassion toward her selves.

The Compassionate Way

Ultimately, compassion seems to be necessary for survival, allowing for better care of the young, as well as social support.[54] In addition, compassion practices that encourage social connection and meditation promote better physiological and psychological functioning.[55] Specifically, compassion practice can help improve people's mood, reduce inflammation, as well as reduce symptoms of depression and potentially help them recover from traumatic events,[56] such as some of those the Doctor experiences. Although Davros has repeatedly told the Doctor that compassion is a weakness, compassion is one of the Time Lord's greatest strengths. Throughout many adventures and incarnations, the Doctor has found that acting compassionately means more in the long run than failing to act with compassion, distinguishing every Doctor from their enemies and providing the peace of mind that genocidal maniacs will likely never find. In fact, helping people and living life according to one's own moral code is more likely to result in eudaimonic happiness, leading to a more meaningful and satisfactory life, compared to a life based on immediate gratification and hatred.[57] It is not an easy path, but it is the right one.

"Laugh hard. Run fast. Be kind."

—Twelfth Doctor (Peter Capaldi)[58]

Janina Scarlet, PhD, is a licensed clinical psychologist, author, and a full-time geek. The United Nations Association awarded Scarlet the Eleanor Roosevelt Human Rights Award for her work on superhero therapy. She regularly consults on books and television shows including *Young Justice*. Scarlet authored *Superhero Therapy, Super-Women, Dark Agents,* and *Harry Potter Therapy,* plus chapters throughout this Popular Culture Psychology series. She can be reached via her website at www.superhero-therapy.com or on Twitter: **@shadowquill**.

 **Alan Kistler** authored the *New York Times* best-seller *Doctor Who: A History.* He is an actor, writer, podcast creator, story consultant, and popular culture historian focusing on science fiction and American superheroes. His contributions to the Popular Culture Psychology series include editorial assistance and chapter co-authorship in *The Walking Dead Psychology, Star Trek Psychology, Wonder Woman Psychology,* and *Daredevil Psychology.*

Travis Langley's bio appears at the beginning of this book.

IV.

LOST THINGS

Anything we have can potentially become part of how we see ourselves and how others see us too. So can all things we have lost.

> "Lost. Shh! Perhaps. Things do get lost, you know."
> —The Curator (Tom Baker)[1]

How we face death inherently plays a role in how we face life. We are mortals who can imagine immortality, dread our own demise, and fear for the loss of others. We all outlive some of those who matter to us. Which is healthier—running from mortality or coming to terms with its inevitability?

12

Death and the Doctor: Interview on How Immortals Face Mortality

Janina Scarlet & Aaron Sagers

"I have lost things you will never understand."
—Eleventh Doctor (Matt Smith)[1]

"The more unlived your life, the greater your death anxiety. The more you fail to experience your life fully, the more you will fear death."
—psychiatrist Irvin Yalom[2]

 Death is inevitable. Fear of death is universal, usually beginning at an early age when children first observe the impermanence of living things. Most often, when they question their parents about death, they receive little guidance and are often asked simply not to think about death.[3] Death can be a taboo topic about which some people may be afraid to speak out loud or at all.[4] Although the Doctor is able to regenerate, which may prolong life, different Doctors seem at times to fear for their own life and act uncomfortable with the subject of their companions' mortality.[5] Is this fear of death natural and healthy, and if so, what are some ways in which a person may be able to reduce mortality fears?

Fear of Death

Fear of death can manifest in different ways, from feeling overwhelming anxiety to taking extreme risks. For some people, trying to overcome the fear of death may involve watching scary movies or playing violent video games. For others, it may involve engaging in potentially life-threatening sports such as skydiving.[6] In addition, after experiencing the death of a loved one, an individual may no longer wish to risk getting into situations that could lead to witnessing the death of another being. This may result in the individual's avoidance of people or animals who are nearing death or avoidance of talking about death. Both forms of avoidance, though seemingly helpful in the short term, may lead to added emotional suffering in the long term.[7] For the Doctor, who has both experienced death in the form of regeneration and lost many people to death, this is an especially painful topic.

Change is stressful. Regeneration migrates the Doctor from one personal world to another every time. Immigration can feel very much like you have died and been reborn. For the Doctor, it is like a death. As the Tenth Doctor puts it, "It feels like dying. Everything I am dies. Some new man goes sauntering away, and I'm dead."[8] Whether you compare it to immigration or changing jobs or new relationships (and each Doctor does form new relationships), it is a kind of stress but also a kind of growth, and so the Doctor illustrates what many of us go through during our lives. The Doctor's changes speak to ours.

When a terrified man threatens to kill him, the Twelfth Doctor says, "Don't. You will only make me angry."[9] Though he wants the man to keep his weapon aimed at the Doctor, not the companions, the Time Lord does not wish to get shot and regenerate that day. (Admittedly, this happens to be the story that leads to his regeneration anyway.) Most people know they will not regenerate, which may make this attitude seem less relatable to ours. Not everyone worries about their own demise, though, and the majority who do don't worry about it all the same way. Exposure to trauma, for instance, turns some people fearful and yet gives others an *illusion of invulnerability* or *illusion of immortality* for having survived. Many adolescents tend not to worry about death because it seems remote; some among the elderly accept its inevitably while feeling good about the lives they've led; and many other factors make death concerns vary.[10] A *sense of immortality* and corresponding reduction in death anxiety can even be healthy when the person feels a sense of personal integrity about where they are in life or feel *existential comfort* that they will continue to exist in one way or another, whether through personal accomplishments, contributions to the world, spiritual afterlife, or kin and companions.[11] Those who do live the longest lives tend to grow conscious of the fact that they have outlived the majority of people they have ever known.

We asked actors who played the Doctor and River, two characters who can regenerate and outlive those around them, how their characters face mortality.

Aaron Sagers: How does the Doctor view death?

David Tennant (Tenth Doctor): He's running away from the mortality of the people he spends time with. I don't think he likes it when he has to face up to it. I thought that was really well done in Toby Whithouse's script with the "School Reunion" story.[12] I thought it was a really clever thing to do, to have a companion who had got a bit older—and for Rose to see that.[13] The interview between those two characters where she's looking [at Sarah Jane] and goes, "Oh, I see what happens; I get dumped because you can't face up to the fact that we get old and you don't." It is a great thing to play as a character note.

The types of therapeutic interventions that are best suited to help people overcome the fear of death include existential therapy and humanistic therapy. Whereas *existential therapy* seeks to resolve the conflict many humans have about their mortality and the meaning of their lives, *humanistic therapy* focuses on acceptance of unchangeable struggles in order to foster personal growth.[14] Psychiatrist Irvin Yalom, known for his work in both existential psychology and humanistic psychology, suggests that for most people it is not easy to live with a constant awareness of death. He adds that as an individual goes through each stage of life, they may experience a new surge of death anxiety.[15]

As the average human life span grows longer and the species gets closer to perpetuating its members through cybernetics or replication via artificial intelligence, perspectives on death may change and each period as human, cyborg, or artificial intelligence (A.I.) may be seen as a different stage in life. However, every transition or form of renewal may be as dreaded as death by some because the previous version will still die. By this account, regenerations may be thought of as different stages of the character's life, with each one possibly affecting their struggle with death. How will these characters change?

> **Matt Smith (Eleventh Doctor):** When one person dies and another person comes along, you're not changing. It is just the same bloke getting a new face. So I don't know. I always compare it to Hamlet, weirdly enough. I think the actor basically brings all his own makeup. All his own foibles, all his own humors, all his own silliness, really.

> **Sagers:** How did River change over time and through her own regeneration?

> **Alex Kingston (River Song/Melody Pond):** I don't know if she did change over time. She has shown different facets of her personality over the years. You certainly got to see a bad side of her, and then you see a vulnerable side. I don't think she necessarily changed. It's just that the audience has gotten more opportunity to learn more about her.

When asked about the saddest Doctor regeneration, Matt Smith voiced an opinion similar to that of many viewers:[16] "Definitely David's."

Grief

Perhaps even more than their own death, the Doctor fears the deaths of those closest to them. In particular, the Doctor fears losing friends and companions.[17] In fact, when one or more friends are taken from the Doctor, the Time Lord may go through years of isolation and grief, as the Eleventh Doctor does when he loses longtime companions Amy and Rory.[18] Such prolonged grief, if untreated, may lead to individuals' withdrawal from their support groups. This isolation often exacerbates the effects of grief. In addition, failure to process a loss one has experienced may lead to several mental and physical problems, such as depression, chronic pain, sleep disorders, and other illnesses.[19]

People's grief reactions can often be predicted by their functioning before they experience loss. For example, mothers who reported fearing for their own deaths and the premature deaths of others were more likely to experience prolonged or *complicated grief* (grief lasting more than six months that causes significant impairment in a person's functioning and does not naturally lessen over time).[20] In addition, pre-loss dependency on the individual is more likely to lead to prolonged grief as opposed to acceptance of death, which may lead to *death resilience*.[21] Finally, guilt over the deaths of others and avoidance of processing that guilt may prolong an individual's grief.[22]

> **Smith:** I think that's very interesting. I think there is so much about that. One of the things I really gravitated toward, actually, was the blood on his hands and the guilt he carries. That is sort of why, for me anyway, there was always the sense of joviality—of him being upward and spritely. Because he is sort of fighting this undercurrent of darkness constantly.

A MODEL OF GRIEF

In 1969, Swiss psychiatrist Dr. Elisabeth Kübler-Ross published a book, *On Death and Dying*, based on her work with patients with terminal illnesses.[23] In that book, Kübler-Ross identified the five *stages of grief* that she observed:

Denial—refusing to believe that an individual or a loved one is going to die or has passed away. Often people believe that someone has made a mistake and that the situation will resolve itself. For example, after River's death, the Eleventh Doctor ignores her virtual presence because he seems to be in denial about the fact that she is dead.[24]

Anger—blaming someone for the loss. After Clara dies, the Twelfth Doctor grows furious and issues threats to other Time Lords.[25]

Bargaining—making an offer to reduce the likelihood of the tragic outcome, such as when the Tenth Doctor downloads the deceased River into a computer[26] or the Twelfth Doctor tries to trick the universe into letting Clara continue her life.[27]

Depression—feeling tremendous loss or sadness after the realization that the death cannot be prevented. The Doctor sulks for a time in nineteenth-century century London after losing Amy and Rory.[28]

Acceptance—making peace with the inevitable loss, such as when the Doctor finally tells River good-bye.[29]

—T. L.

Acceptance and Meaning

Some research studies suggest that the age at death and the specific circumstances surrounding it are most responsible for the way loved ones will cope with loss.[30] On the other hand, other studies suggest that acceptance of death and finding meaning in the tragedy are most predictive of resilience.[31] In fact, *terror management theory* explains how a person may overcome inner conflict when faced with the fear of death, suggesting that close friendships may serve as a buffer against death terror.[32] Specifically, scientists suggest that humans' fear of their own mortality may encourage them to maintain close friendships, which may make an individual feel less anxious about their own death.[33] Other studies find that close friendships, such as those the Doctor maintains with companions, may actually reduce the risk of stress-related deaths, possibly because of the physical and emotional benefits of social connection.[34] It is possible that the Doctors may be trying to manage their death-related fears by maintaining close friendships.

Sagers: Does he view human life as precious?

Smith: Yeah, but he is always sort of leaving people behind. With David's Doctor, when he lost Rose, it was a complete nightmare for Martha. Rose felt, to a viewer, like such a sort of linchpin for Number Ten. And it is weird why he admires humanity so much, because people do spend all of their lives together and he never really gets to do that with anyone.

Kingston: [The Doctor] loves humankind. He doesn't know exactly why he has this affinity with human beings, but he does. He wants to save them, and that's very powerful.

The Doctor seemingly struggles with establishing close connections with companions, and this may be the reason for the Time Lord's struggle with death acceptance. In fact, death acceptance and death fears appear to be related in that both depend on one's perceived life meaning.[35] Whereas some people may have uncompleted life missions or the perception of an unfulfilled life, people who believe that they have lived a meaningful life are more likely to accept their death.[36] This is the case for the Face of Boe. The Face of Boe appears to be an eons-older version of Captain Jack Harkness. After eons of life, the Face of Boe greets his final fate and passes with acceptance.[37]

Scientists have identified different types of death acceptance, including neutral, approach, and escape.[38] The *neutral acceptance* of death appears to be the healthiest approach and entails not fearing death but instead allowing it to happen as and when it should, as does the Face of Boe. The *approach acceptance* is one in which an individual is happy to die/regenerate, often as a result of a belief in an afterlife. This seems to be how the War Doctor greets his own regeneration into the Ninth Doctor when he says he is "wearing a bit thin" and allows the regeneration to take place.[39] With *escape acceptance*, an individual wishes to die to escape the pain and suffering he or she is enduring. For example, Vincent van Gogh wishes to die and takes his own life to escape the deep emotional suffering he experiences.[40] Overall, death acceptance, especially *neutral or approach acceptance*, appears to be related to better coping with death. In contrast, the fear of death is more closely related to depression and poorer coping with mortality.[41]

Conquering the Fear of Death

The interviews, the episodes, and the research studies all seem to suggest the same message: Making meaning of one's life is most important in reducing one's fear of one's own death as well as allowing the individual to cope with the deaths of others.[42] When someone, such as the Doctor, avoids getting close to people for fear of losing them, they are more likely to experience prolonged grief and depression after a loss.[43] In contrast, acceptance of one's mortality and the mortality of others, as demonstrated by the War Doctor,[44] is more likely to allow a person to cope better with a loss.[45]

Bio for Aaron Sagers appears in chapter 1; Janina Scarlet's, in chapter 11.

A MOMENT WITH PETER CAPALDI: "EVEN AT 2,000 YEARS OLD, LIFE IS SHORT"

Jenna Busch & Travis Langley

Actor Peter Capaldi played the Twelfth Doctor, the first Doctor to appear after the Time Lords grant their runaway Gallifreyan a new cycle of regenerations (before the Thirteenth Doctor's discoveries about the Timeless Child raise questions about that).[46] As such, having spent centuries clinging to his existence as the Eleventh Doctor, the Twelfth may gain new perspective on his own mortality. He would, in fact, come to resist regenerating again, feeling the weight and weariness of all his years. Capaldi offered us his thoughts on how the Doctor views life and mortality.

Peter Capaldi (Twelfth Doctor): He has a different perspective from other people. I think he's always on the side of good, but he doesn't have time to be nice about it. He knows that, in order to save the universe, he has to run over there and fix that bit. "Can't chat. I have to fix that." I think when you regenerate, you have to get to know yourself. The Doctor has a lot of complications. I think he's got to know himself better and recognize that even at two thousand years old, life is short. He's in a fabulous position. He has all of time and space. Running toward adventure and challenging himself and being almost reckless, he knows that at some point he'll be taken to a very dark place. At some point, he'll have to fight the good fight the way no one else has been able to do it.

Posttraumatic stress disorder differs from common conceptions about it. Not every trauma produces posttraumatic stress, and not everyone who suffers it suffers the same way. When does a person who has experienced many traumas hurt the most? Which straw breaks them?

13

Post-Time War Stress Disorder

Kristin Erickson & Matt Munson,
with Travis Langley & Stephen Prescott

> "Everyone lost. They're all gone now. My family. My friends."
> —Tenth Doctor (David Tennant)[1]

> "Guilt is perhaps the most painful companion of death."
> —psychiatrist Elisabeth Kübler-Ross[2]

A person can experience trauma without developing posttraumatic stress disorder (PTSD). In fact, soldiers, first responders, and people living in war zones can experience many traumatic events without developing it, although their odds certainly increase.[3] When the television program *Doctor Who* returned after a long period of cancellation, the Doctor returns as a man suffering a deep psychological wound after a great trauma. The mere suggestion of the Time War nearly brings the Ninth Doctor to tears.[4] Avoiding or getting upset by a topic or a stimulus can indicate many different difficulties with or without PTSD.[5] Actual diagnosis requires much more information. Details emerge over time, but it is not until the War Doctor, the incarnation of the Doctor who participates in the Time War, appears that viewers learn how he once decided he would have to destroy all Daleks and Time Lords to end the war and save the universe,[6] and it is this cataclysmic event that ultimately shapes the modern Doctor into the person each incarnation becomes from the Ninth Doctor onward.

Diagnostic Criteria: Who Suffers from PTSD?

Myths and misconceptions about PTSD abound. Despite the volume of available information, many people misunderstand what posttraumatic stress disorder is, along with the when, where, why, who, and how of it.[7] For one thing, the majority of people exposed to events that qualify as severe trauma do not develop it, and not all traumas affect people equally. Tragedy of human design (e.g., murder, rape, war) leads to PTSD more often than do other traumatic events (e.g., accidents, natural disasters).[8] *Survivor guilt* (feeling guilt for surviving when others did not) and other forms of trauma-related guilt make PTSD more likely and complicates its treatment,[9] although guilt can help some individuals experience *posttraumatic growth* in that they find purpose, grow as people, and accomplish good things.[10] Impressed by how well the Tenth and Eleventh Doctors handle a UNIT/Zygon conflict, the War Doctor speculates that guilt may make the Doctor a better man and save many lives.[11]

The American Psychiatric Association's *Diagnostic and Statistical Manual of Mental Disorders* (a.k.a. DSM, DSM-5, or DSM-5-TR for versions of its fifth edition[12]) lists a specific set of criteria that must be met for a person to qualify as having PTSD. The event that ends the Time War is clearly traumatic (meeting criterion A), but so are many other events in the Doctor's millennia-long life. Whether the Doctor then has PTSD therefore depends on personal reactions in terms of how often, how severely, and how many of the other criteria (listed as B through H in the DSM) the character meets.

A. Trauma

The DSM lists qualifiers for this criterion: The individual faced death or serious physical injury, whether actual or threatened, whether directly or vicariously through someone else, and felt intense fear, horror, or helplessness in response. War is undisputedly traumatic. Combat, carnage, and potential catastrophe for the entire cosmos[13] ultimately push the War Doctor to make a decision to end the war, seemingly with the result of wiping both sides from existence.[14]

B. Reliving the Trauma

For a PTSD diagnosis to apply, the DSM requires that the patient relive the event repeatedly in at least one of a set of specific ways. The Doctor experiences at least two of them: flashbacks and intrusive, distressing recollections. A *flashback* consists of mentally reliving trauma, however briefly, so vividly that the individual feels that the traumatic event is recurring.[15] According to Clara Oswald, the Eleventh Doctor talks about the Time War "all the time,"[16] indicating that the version of the Doctor who tries hardest to forget actually has frequent recollections. Deliberately trying to avoid thinking about something can paradoxically make an individual think about aspects of it even more at times, while keeping that person from finding a healthy way to process distress.[17]

Combined, the facts that the Doctor has occasional flashbacks and recollections about the Time War "all the time" meet this criterion for PTSD.

C. Avoiding Reminders

Avoiding trauma-related reminders is practically a core competency for several Doctors, such as the Ninth. When a representative of the Forest of Cheem expresses her sorrow because she knows that the Ninth Doctor is the last of his people, he shows only a flash of sadness before he snaps back to the task at hand of saving the station.[18] This Doctor, more than any other, tries to live in the moment. Present-focused people experience less depression than do those who ruminate over the past and less anxiety than do those who fret about the future.[19] For some people who are trying to avoid depression and anxiety without distorting reality, focusing on the present can be a coping strategy.[20] Focusing on the present while refusing to think about a prior trauma may provide some short-term relief, but it can worsen symptoms in the long term when an individual has avoided facing stressful facts and feelings—as is seen in too many combat veterans.[21]

In the Ninth Doctor's first line of dialogue on screen, he tells Rose to run. Running from the past and from things that bother him has been a consistent part of the Doctor's behavior to the point that it is a *central trait,* a defining quality that affects much of an individual's behavior.[22] In childhood, he runs from secrets he learns in the Time Lords' Matrix[23] and from "the raw power of time and space" he beholds in the Untempered Schism at age eight. "I never stopped."[24] The theme of running via the physical action of running or the Doctor's suggestion to run can be interpreted as an indication of an ongoing desire to avoid trauma-related reminders. While a preexisting avoidant trait would not be a posttraumatic symptom, avoidant behavior could make the person prone to experience severe stress reactions to specific trauma.

Avoidance can take numerous forms and can even involve lying to avoid an uncomfortable truth. When the Tenth Doctor explains to Martha some of the nature of the war and its effects on him, he acknowledges that he has been lying about his people so that he "could pretend, just for a bit. I could imagine they were still alive underneath the burnt orange sky." The Doctor has not been *delusional* about them because he does not convince himself of a falsehood that is grossly inconsistent with his reality, nor does he experience a psychotic degree of *denial*[25] because he admits the truth to himself and knows when he is pretending.[26]

After the Thirteenth Doctor learns that the Master has converted other Time Lords into Cybermen, she withholds this information from others. She does not want to talk about it. So she avoids topics, diverts discussions, and misleads her companions more frequently than she already has.

D. Negative Changes in Thought and Mood

The DSM provides a list of items related to negative alterations in cognitions and mood associated with the traumatic event, two of which must be present to satisfy this criterion. The Doctor easily satisfies at least that many.

Detachment or isolation. Perhaps the most prevalent of the seven possible conditions, this pertains to feeing distant and disconnected from other people, one of the most frequently reported symptoms among combat veterans with PTSD.[27] The Doctor makes a choice at times to stay detached and isolated in an attempt at self-preservation. The Tenth, Eleventh, and Twelfth Doctors all spend long periods traveling by themselves, more so than any pre–Time War Doctors.

Negative self-evaluation. PTSD sufferers may hold persistent, exaggerated beliefs or expectations about themselves. Before he enters the Time War, "the Doctor" and "the good man" are the same thing in the Eighth Doctor's mind.[28] Later, though, the Eleventh Doctor hates himself[29] and believes he is not a good man.[30] When negative self-evaluation becomes ingrained in a person's self-concept, it does not easily subside. Even after rectifying the things he has done as the War Doctor,[31] the Twelfth Doctor doubts that he is good but he still tries.[32]

E. Elevated Arousal

The criterion of *hyperarousal* (excessive arousal inappropriate for current circumstances, markedly increased from pre-trauma levels) can be satisfied with two of the six specifiers listed in the DSM. Of those six, the Doctor meets several. Whether they show posttraumatic *changes*, demonstrating them to a degree not present before the trauma, may be open for debate.

Irritable behavior and angry outbursts. Anger intensification has become one of the most widely recognized adjustment problems for many war veterans.[33] The Doctor has some angry outbursts or episodes of irritability, such as when the Ninth Doctor succumbs to the weight of his Time War experiences and yells, "The Daleks have failed. Why don't you finish the job and make the Daleks extinct? Rid the universe of your filth! Why don't you just die!"[34] Earlier Doctors, even the crankier ones, do not explode as readily into upset, shouting rants. Arguably, though, these examples might not meet this qualifier because provocation is apparent in every instance.

Reckless or self-destructive behavior. People who have suffered trauma may engage in risky or harmful behavior,[35] particularly if they feel self-loathing or guilt for having survived when others did not (survivor guilt).[36] Exhibiting reckless or self-destructive behavior is almost the hallmark of any Doctor adventure. Typically, the

Doctor's regeneration is prefaced by a choice to self-sacrifice by entering willingly into a deadly situation.

Before the Time War, the Doctor regenerates eight times—as far as the character can recall—over the course of many centuries, but in a mere six years after the war,[37] he burns through what should be his final four regenerations (War Doctor to Ninth, Ninth to Tenth, Tenth's Metacrisis, Tenth to Eleventh[38]).

Hypervigilance. Extreme alertness to danger can be appropriate for people in dangerous professions. Nearly one-third of Vietnam War veterans eventually experienced PTSD, and many felt an ongoing sense of threat.[39] The Doctor is alert to the possibility of danger but does not tend to show excessive vigilance given the Doctor's lifestyle and therefore does not satisfy the requirements for this qualifier.

Problems with concentration. Posttraumatic difficulties with concentration and attention are visible not only in combat participants but also in people living in war-torn environments.[40] War can make it hard for people to think straight. Although distractibility seems common among Doctors, it worsens after the Time War. While building a makeshift TARDIS, the Eleventh Doctor exhibits acute poor concentration as he pauses to argue with Idris (the personification of his own TARDIS) while work needs to be done with no time to spare.[41]

Sleep disturbance. *Insomnia* (a pattern of frequent and extreme difficulty falling or staying asleep) or restless sleep is common among PTSD sufferers. When companions Amy and Rory sleep, the Eleventh Doctor steps out on extra adventures. This may be because the Gallifreyan species simply requires less sleep, and so the greater issue is whether the Doctor's sleep is notably poorer after the Time War than before. For each of these qualifiers and criteria, there must be alterations from previous behavior. To be posttraumatic, they must differ dramatically after the trauma. Long before the War Doctor ends the Time War, the Fourth Doctor says, "Sleep is for tortoises."[42]

Comparing pre-trauma functioning with post-trauma functioning is essential. In the Doctor's case, not every arousal disturbance is new after the trauma. Showing at least two of the criteria in ways clearly different from before the trauma, though, is sufficient for a diagnostic assessment of this qualifier.

F. Duration

Symptoms must persist for more than one month to qualify as PTSD. The duration of the symptoms is difficult to quantify, as many of the Doctor's adventures happen off screen, the Time Lord's age is reported inconsistently, and the post–Time War Doctors never indicate which world's years they mean when referring to their age. Nevertheless, more than a month does go by.

G. Impaired Functioning

With PTSD, the disturbance causes impairment in social, occupational, or other areas that are important to the individual.[43] The Doctor's lack of social grace and awareness worsens in the Twelfth Doctor, whose social deficiency is so pronounced that he takes to using apology cue cards with prewritten phrases and expressions to help him navigate the murky waters of social interaction. When he uses a card that reads, "I'm very sorry for your loss. I'll do all I can to solve the death of your friend/family member/pet,"[44] he is effectively using the kind of social cue card that has helped some children with autism spectrum disorders improve and maintain social skills.[45] This becomes necessary as a method of compensating for the Doctor's impairments.

H. Disturbance Not Attributable to Substance Abuse or Other Medical Condition

Victims of PTSD suffer a high rates of substance abuse as a symptom attributable to external agent.[46] For so many, alcoholism and other substance disorders are consequences, not the cause, of their PTSD symptoms. Substance abuse has never been the Doctor's forte, though. The Doctor rarely drinks. Over the course of the Time Lord's centuries, different Doctors are known to have a glass of mead or brandy, and the Tenth takes credit for inventing the banana daiquiri. The Doctor drinks wine so rarely that the Eleventh spits a sip out, uncertain whether he has ever tasted wine before. (He has, but it's been a few centuries.) The First Doctor's bottle of brandy sits unconsumed for more than a thousand years until the Twelfth Doctor serves it to a soldier from World War I.[47] Though the Doctor is not quite a teetotaler, the Time Lord tends to decline drinks people offer.[48] Nothing suggests that the Doctor consumes alcohol often, certainly not more often after the Time War than before. In fact, when the Ninth Doctor mentions a prime minister who "used to drink me under the table," he is most likely referring to a less recent, pre–Time War Doctor.[49]

Specifiers

To reach a full diagnosis, we must consider specifiers as set forth in the DSM.[50] Does the individual show any dissociative symptoms, signs of splitting portions of mental contents away from conscious awareness? Examples include feeling a sense of unreality of self or body, of time moving slowly, or as though one were in a dream. Whether or not the Doctor sometimes shows the forms of dissociation specified in the DSM's description of PTSD (*depersonalization* or *derealization*) not attributable to circumstances, the Eleventh Doctor does sequester portions of mental contents away from conscious awareness when he lies to himself about the War Doctor—a clear example of dissociation.

The Diagnosis

Based on these considerations and the various criteria exhibited by the Doctor, we can conclude that the Time Lord suffers from *chronic post–traumatic stress disorder with dissociative symptoms*. We view this PTSD as *chronic* because the individual has suffered from it for a long time. The kind of duality, avoidance, thought and mood changes, and social impairment that some people may use to evade their suffering in the short term can prolong it in the long term by keeping them from developing other ways of coping and managing distress. The Doctor has never been one to share past pains easily, rarely even discussing loved ones, and so when the weight of trauma bears down, the Doctor does not know how to express the pain. Soldiers and others who experience so much trauma may suffer silently, keeping their painful stories locked inside.

Kristin Erickson is a marriage and family therapist. She received her master's degree in counseling psychology in 2011. Kristin has served various populations, including children and adolescents in school settings, individuals on the autism spectrum, trauma sufferers, and adult clients in a drug and alcohol detox/treatment center. Her counseling interests includes a holistic approach to therapy, mindfulness, play therapy, CBT, and solution-focused therapy.

Matt Munson can often be found spending time with his local group of fellow Whovians, "Team TARDIS." His earliest memory in life is of watching a Tom Baker episode of *Doctor Who* from behind the couch, spawning a lifelong love of all things science fiction. His love for the show culminated in the completion of a year-long project to reproduce a full-sized replica of the Eleventh Doctor's TARDIS shown below.

Stephen Prescott, curator and host of the *A Madman with a Box* podcast, brings together Whovians from all walks of life to discuss and dissect their favorite *Doctor Who* stories. With a penchant for minutiae, he possesses an almost encyclopedic knowledge of the modern show. An avid cosplayer, he prides himself on his Eleventh and Twelfth Doctor costume collection.

Matt Munson, contributor to this chapter, shows his replica TARDIS to Neil Gaiman, who authored the episodes "The Doctor's Wife" and "Nightmare in Silver."

COMPLEX PTSD

Travis Langley

Times change. People change. Diagnostic standards change, too, as professionals learn more and come to understand mental disorders better. A growing number of clinicians now apply the term *complex PTSD* (C-PTSD) in cases when posttraumatic stress is complicated by repeated or prolonged trauma.[51] Soldiers, first responders, abuse victims, people living in war zones, and others develop different reactions to trauma compared to those who experience one traumatic event, no matter how severe. Not everyone develops PTSD from such experiences. Contributing factors that influence who will or will not develop PTSD or C-PTSD include genes, environment, learning, resilience, family dynamics, and the intensity, duration, or timing of traumatic events.[52]

The Doctor regularly faces danger and death. Between the regularity of threat and Time Lord immortality, the Doctor sometimes forgets how hard these things hit mortal people and needs companions to point that out. Depictions of modern Doctors differ from those in the classic episodes in ways that fit PTSD almost symptom by symptom, and storywise it is the Time War that separates them. What happens, though, when personal losses keep happening—when the companions die or get stranded elsewhere in space and time, when the Doctor's friends die, or Gallifrey seemingly falls once more?

In the classic (twentieth century) episodes, only one of the Doctor's long-term companions dies: Adric. During the First Doctor's tenure, Trojan War survivor Katarina joins him in one adventure and dies in the next.[53] Soon after, fortieth-century security officer Sara Kingdom dies in the same twelve-part serial that introduces her.[54] Horrific as it is when Sara Kingdom enters a "time field" that makes her abruptly age, die, and crumble to dust, her passing does not haunt the Doctor the same way Adric's will.[55] After stowing away from another universe,[56] Adric travels with both the Fourth and Fifth Doctors until a fateful encounter with Cybermen. An escape shuttle explosion kills him in the only classic *Doctor Who* episode to end with no music, only silence through the closing credits.[57] Fellow companion Tegan Jovanka witnesses this explosion. One of the longest-running companions on *Doctor Who,* Tegan shows her own signs of C-PTSD. Horrors accumulate, and in time she reaches a breaking point. "A lot of good people have died today. I'm sick of it," she tells the Doctor after a battle with Daleks leaves many fallen. "I just don't think I can go on." He tries to talk her out of it, but Tegan runs off. After the TARDIS dematerializes, Tegan looks back and murmurs the words she wishes the Doctor would have said: "'Brave heart, Tegan. I will miss you.'"[58] Decades will pass before a Fifth Doctor interface gives her that "Brave heart" and each admits they've missed the other.[59]

Modern Doctors suffer personal losses more frequently. The Ninth through Twelfth Doctors all see companions die[60] or people they invite to join their travels get killed before they can.[61] The Twelfth Doctor loses everyone.[62] Although Martha Jones chooses when the time has come to stop traveling with the Tenth Doctor and all the Thirteenth Doctor's companions also depart by their own volition,[63] modern companions tend to complete their travels in the TARDIS involuntarily and under tragic circumstances. With some exceptions such as the Doctor's own granddaughter Susan, whom the First Doctor leaves behind so she can live her own life,[64] or his best friend Sarah Jane Smith, who cannot accompany the Fourth Doctor when he's summoned back to Gallifrey,[65] classic companions each choose when it's time to leave him. So while the Time War divides classic and modern Doctors, it is the fates of the companions that wear the Doctor down, to the point that the Twelfth Doctor so strongly wants rest and resists regenerating.[66] Even though his successor keeps her companions alive, it is the Thirteenth Doctor who sees that the Master has ransacked Gallifrey and turned the other Time Lords into Cybermen, the so-called CyberMasters.[67]

Complex Assessment

How do clinicians assess C-PTSD when it's not in the DSM? The American Psychiatric Association left complex PTSD out of its fifth edition.[68] Despite the DSM's dominance as the primary diagnostic system in North America, though, it is not this planet's only classification manual. The World Health Organization (WHO) publishes the *International Classification of Diseases* (ICD or ICD-11 for its eleventh edition), with a section on mental disorders.[69] That section includes C-PTSD as an official diagnostic option, outlining diagnostic requirements and associated features.

For the person who has been exposed to situations "of an extremely threatening or horrific nature, most commonly prolonged or repetitive events from which escape is difficult or impossible,"[70] several core elements determine whether they qualify for a C-PTSD diagnosis. These include standard PTSD symptoms such as hypervigilance and reliving trauma vividly through flashbacks, intrusive memories, or nightmares, typically feeling strong emotions at the time. More people with C-PTSD show angry outbursts, negative self-evaluation, survivor guilt, and avoidance of other people—all of which turn up more in the post–Time War Doctors.

Unlike classic Doctors who rarely travel without a companion, modern Doctors go through many spells of journeying by themselves. During those periods, people keep telling the Doctor to stop spending so much time alone, especially at Christmas.[71] Sometimes the Doctor travels alone out of fear for companions' safety, but sometimes the Time Lord simply feels undeserving. When the Judoon imprison the Thirteenth Doctor for decades, she uncharacteristically shows no sign of forming her own escape plan, accepting this fate in resignation until Jack Harness breaks her out.[72]

Complex posttraumatic stress disorder may compound the impact made by discovering both the Fugitive Doctor and the fact that the Doctor's own memory has gaps in her personal history. Together, these may account for why the Thirteenth Doctor regenerates into a version of a past self, the Fourteenth Doctor with the face of the Doctor who didn't want to go.[73] She manifests the posttraumatic symptom of reliving her past somewhat literally by turning back into the one who, on some level, hopes to fix unresolved issues such as Donna Noble's fate. Events that frustrate because we still feel a need to complete them in a better way burn hotter in our memories (the *Zeigarnik effect*).[74] Such task interruption or failure also prepares us to seek opportunities to try again to complete them or achieve completion in a more satisfying way (the *Ovsiankina effect*).[75]

The Doctor has unresolved conflicts, unfinished business, and always will because that is how life works. Ruminating over the *counterfactual* thought, "If only things had gone another way," can contribute to depression[76] in one person or push another person to force a situation to fulfill the wish in an inappropriate way. Sometimes closure is an impossible wish and people must find peace in other ways, but sometimes some broken things can be repaired. Complex PTSD is not an all-or-nothing problem, and it does not go away with a flick of the switch, but it also does not mean the person can never find any joy. Just as Tegan Jovanka achieves some closure with her Doctor and Donna Noble can rediscover hers, the Doctor will find a bit of peace here and there too.

Enduring one loss after another can wear a person down. Some people may avoid potentially satisfying experiences as one way to avoid loss at the end. Experiencing the best things in life means taking risks and making ourselves vulnerable.

14

Behind Two Hearts:
Grief and Vulnerability

Janina Scarlet and Jenna Busch

"He was different once, a long time ago. Kind, yes. A hero, even. A saver of worlds. But he suffered losses which hurt him. Now he prefers isolation to the possibility of pain's return."

—Madame Vastra (Neve McIntosh), Silurian detective[1]

"Vulnerability sounds like truth and feels like courage. Truth and courage aren't always comfortable, but they're never weakness."

—social work researcher Brené Brown[2]

 It is a sad fact that most people experience numerous losses throughout their lives.[3] After experiencing losses, some people shut down and avoid interacting with others,[4] while others might thrive and demonstrate extreme resilience.[5] Having lived for over two thousand years, the Doctor has arguably experienced more losses than most, carrying two hearts undoubtedly broken by the many deaths endured.

Between the deaths of several companions and countless people and other beings whose lives they have touched in some way, the Doctor has had more than their share of grief and guilt. After devastating losses, such as those the Doctor endured, some people cope by committing to their work, others by communicating with people, and still others by trying to avoid feeling anything at all.[6] What, then, is the most effective way of coping with loss and past heartache?

Grief

Grief is the typical reaction one may experience after a painful loss due to death, a breakup, a job change, or a change in one's health status.[7] In turn, grief that results from a sudden traumatic loss, called *traumatic grief,* can negatively affect a person's psychological and physiological health. For example, after Clara's death, the Twelfth Doctor spends two billion years in an energy loop, dealing with his grief.[8]

When a group of researchers interviewed people whose spouses were diagnosed with terminal illnesses, they found that even the impending eventuality of such a traumatic loss had significant health effects on the partners. Specifically, spouses of people diagnosed with life-threatening conditions were more likely to develop high blood pressure and heart problems, demonstrate poorer eating habits, consider committing suicide, and eventually develop cancer, compared to people whose spouses did not face such difficulties.[9] After losing the Brigadier, saying good-bye to River Song, losing Amy and Rory, and witnessing the first two deaths of versions of Clara,[10] the Eleventh Doctor feels the weight of so many years and so much loss, and so he becomes more withdrawn. The Twelfth Doctor's subsequent losses surely compound those feelings and contribute to his decision to resist regenerating, his wish to rest and find peace.[11]

Experiential Avoidance

One of the common ways people try to deal with grief is to suppress any painful thoughts or emotions that arise after the loss.[12] Avoiding or suppressing painful experiences is called *experiential avoidance.*[13] Experiential avoidance may sometimes provide temporary relief because the individual is temporarily able to escape painful emotions. However, in the long run, experiential avoidance may lead to worsening symptoms.[14]

The consequences of such avoidance vary. Overall, experiential avoidance after a traumatic loss is likely to result in prolonged grief, depression, and painful catastrophic thoughts about the loss. For instance, after losing Rose and then Donna, the Tenth Doctor doesn't take on an ongoing companion again.[15]

Social Isolation

In addition to worsening psychological symptoms, experiential avoidance can bring on potentially serious health conditions. Specifically, avoidance in the form of social isolation can lead to inflammation, which in turn can trigger several physiological and psychological conditions, including chronic pain and depression.[16] In addition, chronic social isolation can also cause neurological changes, such as a reduction in the brain's white matter. White matter consists of specific structures responsible for sending and delivering messages between the different structures of the brain and the rest of the nervous system. If the white matter is reduced, then the brain and the body might not function properly.[17] For example, multiple sclerosis (MS) is a disease caused by inflammation that destroys white matter and affects the person's ability to regulate how the body functions.[18]

Sometimes people might blame themselves for a traumatic loss, even when they had nothing to do with the tragedy. When the Eleventh Doctor loses Amy and Rory, he is devastated. He retreats to Victorian England and retires for some time. Though his friends Vastra, Jenny, and Strax try to entice him with mysteries to solve, he refuses to participate (that is, until one with an alien menace comes along).[19]

Shame and Guilt

When people blame themselves for a tragic loss, they might experience guilt or shame. *Guilt* is regret for a specific action, whereas *shame* refers to feeling bad about oneself as a whole. Overall, people who experience shame are more likely to struggle with grief than individuals who experience guilt, and men are more likely to be affected by shame than women.[20] Thoughts that might arise from shame or guilt after losing a loved one are likely to prompt people to struggle with prolonged grief and depression.[21]

There are numerous instances where the Doctor expresses regret, guilt, and shame about having been the sole survivor of the Time War, which has seemingly destroyed the entire Gallifreyan race along with the Daleks.[22] It affects him throughout his so-called Ninth, Tenth, and Eleventh versions. Only after he realizes that Gallifrey still exists in a pocket universe can the Doctor begin to loosen that tight grip on the guilt.[23]

The Wholehearted Way

Vulnerability researcher Brené Brown has found that people who reported living the most fulfilling lives were ones who were open to vulnerability. She refers to these individuals as *wholehearted*. Wholehearted individuals embrace vulnerability by opening themselves to both success and failure, love and heartbreak, as well as creativity, play, and laughter.[24] Wholehearted individuals seem to possess qualities such as these:

Authenticity—staying true to oneself, rather than responding to other people's expectations. After living for so many years, the Doctors do not do what others think they should do. Each follows their own directions, their own rules, and their own moral values.

Self-compassion—letting go of perfectionism and practicing self-acceptance and self-support. The Doctor has difficulty with this, especially since the Time War.

Resilience—letting go of numbing through connection: Connecting to others helps the Doctor avoid growing numb to experience and emotions, which helps the Time Lord keep going.

Gratitude—practicing appreciation for what one already has. For instance, when the Eleventh Doctor meets a "human" incarnation of the TARDIS, Idris, he celebrates her life and expresses gratitude to her.[25]

Trust—letting go of the need for certainty. The Doctor trusts the companions, even allowing some to operate the TARDIS.

Creativity—letting go of comparison and instead following one's own creative process. The Doctor often uses a creative mind to solve problems, defying what one is "supposed" to do and coming up with solutions no one would expect. For instance, the Tenth Doctor sends a message to Sally Sparrow from 1969 to warn her about the Weeping Angels,[26] and the Twelfth uses a hologram of himself to confuse a ghost.[27]

Play and rest—releasing oneself from the idea of exhaustion and achievement to raise one's self-worth. On many adventures, the Doctor finds the time to laugh and enjoy the experiences. For example, when the Tenth and Rose find out about encountering potential werewolves, they are both excited about this venture.[28]

Practicing mindfulness—slowing down enough to notice the present moment. The Twelfth Doctor, knowing this is going to be the last outing with his wife, River Song, shows her the Singing Towers of Darillium and spends time with her, allowing himself to weep and take in every moment.[29]

Meaningful work—letting go of self-doubt and doing what matters, rather than what one is "supposed to." Despite knowing the havoc his longtime enemy Davros will cause himself and the universe, the Twelfth Doctor goes back to save Davros as a young boy, stating that it doesn't matter what side one is on, as long as there is mercy.[30]

Laughter and dance—letting go of being in control.[31] Instead of retreating into himself when the Twelfth Doctor believes he's facing his final day of existence, he travels to the Middle Ages and puts on a show, playing guitar for the crowd.[32]

Vulnerability

The opposite of experiential avoidance is vulnerability. *Vulnerability* refers to the willingness to face uncertainty, risk, and emotional exposure. Instead of avoiding situations that might result in heartache, vulnerability refers to taking chances even in the face of uncertainty. Some examples of vulnerability include love, trust, creativity, and joy.[33] The Doctor knows that his wife, River Song, is going to die because their timelines are running in opposite directions. When the Tenth Doctor first meets her, he learns that they've known each other for many years and then he sees her perish.[34] Even knowing the tragic end she'll face, the Doctor continues to meet River throughout time and space and develops a relationship with her.

Vulnerability and Resilience

Connecting with one's core values and engaging in meaningful activities may reflect vulnerability, but it also seems to be helpful. Connecting with people and activities may have profound effects on psychological resilience. In fact, research on this topic suggests that when people who struggle with depression connect with their core values and perform meaningful deeds, their depression symptoms abate.[35]

Connecting with others can also increase positive emotions, extend lifespan, and prompt the release of *oxytocin*, the body's own stress-protecting hormone.[36] In addition, the willingness and the ability to experience and focus on positive emotions boost human resilience. For example, people who are more likely to practice vulnerability in terms of connecting with positive emotions are more likely to recover from stress quickly, as well as have improved cardiovascular (heart) recovery after getting exposed to a stressful situation. Such recovery could lead to improved heart health and serve to protect the individual against the potentially damaging effects of stress.[37]

Healing Broken Hearts

As counterintuitive as it may seem, embracing their vulnerability allows people to be more resilient. In some ways, vulnerability can be a strength. For the Doctors, it is arguably their best asset. Though they experience some of the negative reactions to grief, like guilt and isolation, the Doctor moves through them. The choice to travel with companions who will eventually leave and die shows their willingness to experience grief and move through it.

Jenna Busch is a host and writer, covering entertainment. She writes for /Film and Vital Thrills, and Story Attic, a division of The Third Floor. She co-hosted *Cocktails with Stan* with Spider-Man co-creator Stan Lee and hosted *Most Craved*. Busch has appeared in the documentary *She Makes Comics* and as a guest on various news programs and *Tabletop with Wil Wheaton*. Busch co-authored chapters in most books in this Popular Culture Psychology series, beginning with *Star Wars Psychology: Dark Side of the Mind*. Her Twitter handle is **@JennaBusch.**

Bio for Janina Scarlet appears in chapter 11.

How much humanity do we give up

before we stop being human at all?

15

From Human to Machine: At What Point Do You Lose Your Soul?

Jim Davies & Daniel Saunders

"Your species has the most amazing capacity for self-deception, matched only by its ingenuity when trying to destroy itself."

—**Seventh Doctor (Sylvester McCoy)**[1]

"The idea of machinery with a conscious mental inner life frightens or enrages some people . . . It will soon be our honor to welcome some of it to the land of the living, however upsetting that may be to our traditional categories."

—**robotics expert Hans Moravec**[2]

 In our world, technology-savvy people line up for the latest model of smartphone and look forward to new features and bug fixes in new versions of software. Not everyone welcomes new tech, though,[3] and some people suffer extreme fears regarding both technology and change.[4] What does the Doctor have against upgrades? For an expert in technology and a being who has upgraded their body at least a dozen times (and sonic screwdriver almost as often), it may seem like a surprising position.

It could stem from the fact that, in the Doctor's universe, alluring technology for augmenting human performance often turns out to be a Trojan horse for evil agendas—such as when Ear Pods, which provide communication and direct brain downloads of news and other current information, are revealed to be a mind control device that causes the entire population to march into the factory where they are to be processed into Cybermen.[5] The Doctor seems to reserve special distaste for technology that replaces significant parts of sentient creatures with cybernetic components. The Fourth Doctor, for example, calls the typical Dalek "a machine creature, a monster"[6] and the Cybermen "a pathetic bunch of tin soldiers."[7] Given the potential advantages of having a body made of durable, replaceable parts, or a mind that can draw on computing power to guide one's actions, are there sound reasons from psychological science to share such a fear? Do cybernetic features pose a threat to our morality?

Cybermorality

One feature of the Daleks or the Cybermen is that they all look like each other, with little or no visible individuality. People are more likely to do selfish acts when they feel they are anonymous.[8] This is true when people are wearing sunglasses,[9] and also when they're wearing masks. In one experiment conducted around Halloween, children were asked to take only two pieces of candy from a bowl. Masked children took more candy than they were supposed to (seemingly feeling more comfortable breaking the rules when in costume).[10]

What about the fact that the Daleks have no face, and that the Cybermen have faces that can't express any emotion? It could be that this affects their moral attitudes by reducing their overall ability to feel empathy. A study of people who had some of their facial muscles disabled found that those who were less able to smile developed more depressive symptoms.[11]

Maybe the fact that the Daleks are working through machinery makes it easier for them to act in an evil way. Studies show that, sometimes, interacting with people through a technological medium reduces empathy. For example, it's easier to "flame" people online, berating them from a distance, because you don't have to face the consequences of their facial expressions and retaliatory anger.[12] Studies of moral psychology show that people are more apt to kill someone (albeit for the benefit of saving others) when they are separated by some kind of technology, such as pressing a button.[13]

People's natural sense of wrongdoing is more pronounced when the act involves physically putting your hands on someone. That is, pulling a switch to kill somebody feels morally better than pushing that person in front of a moving train.[14] This is probably because we spent most of our evolutionary history without technology that allowed us to affect people at a distance, so we didn't evolve to have moral reactions to using technology. To know that pulling the switch might violate the rights of an innocent individual, you have to think through the consequences, because most people don't have a gut reaction to it.

A Dalek is an organic creature controlling a robotic body. Daleks can be seen as halfway between a creature with a metal body and a creature piloting a small tank.[15] If we look at them as creatures piloting tanks, we can speculate that perhaps this creates a psychological distance between the brain and the victims, making it easier for them to commit murder. But might they see their armored casings as their body?

My Metal Arm Is Me

"You lot, you're obsessed. You'd do anything for the latest upgrade."
—Tenth Doctor (David Tennant)[16]

For fully cybernetic individuals, the case is clearer. Cybermen have their bodies—arms, legs, everything but their brains—replaced with robotic actuators,[17] and this may someday happen to our world's humans. We can speculate on what it is like to be put in a metal body by thinking of it as amputation to the extreme—amputating just about everything except the brain. A robotic body is like one giant prosthesis. We can imagine what it might be like to be a Cyberman based on what we know about the psychology of amputees and how they adapt to prosthetics.

An argument that the Daleks might identify with their metal shells comes from research on how our minds adapt to the tools we use. After repeated use of a grasping tool (like the kind people use to pick up garbage), people actually thought their arms had gotten longer.[18] When a person uses a tool so often, they forget that the tool is there, and is able to consciously focus on the task at hand, much like one does with the keyboard after learning how to type. We can call this kind of technology *transparent*.[19] The tool feels, to the extent that it feels like anything at all, like a natural extension of our body. All this is to say that objects that are used, or remain in close proximity to our bodies, over time can become extensions of our own body image,[20] and this may apply to the controls and sensory feedback received by the Dalek mutant inside the armor.

When You Really Lose Your Soul

If we want to explain the moral problems that fictional cyborg beings demonstrate, we need to look beyond the fact that they have mechanical bodies.[21] Evidence from the cyborgs we have here on Earth suggests that the mind adapts to tools of all kinds, accepting them as part of who we are. We must instead examine how their minds have been modified by technology.

The Daleks are genetically engineered to have few emotions other than hatred or rage.[22] The Cybermen, on the other hand, feel no emotions.[23] In both the classic and the new series, their brains have electronic parts that inhibit emotions.[24] Although compassion is not the only emotion that makes us moral, it plays a large role. Social psychologist Jonathan Haidt has found evidence that many of our moral stances are actually based on emotions—anger, disgust, and so on.[25]

Changes to the mind are likely necessary to make it possible to occupy the augmented body. The Tenth Doctor tells Rose that Cybermen need to have their emotions inhibited "because it hurts,"[26] and he disables the Cybermen army simply by reenabling their emotions. By comparison, although the Dalek brain was deliberately engineered by Davros to be genocidal,[27] it's possible that a large degree of alteration would be necessary in any case to permit years of living as a blobbish mutant sealed into a small metal capsule. If so, then both species show that augmenting the body requires tampering with core emotions of the brain, a species should beware.

In the end, the Doctor's objection to the metal shells of the Daleks and the Cybermen is that they encase the ruthless, the uncompassionate, and the unsensual—that is, they are stripped of everything the Doctor values in humans. Emotions are a critical component in what we consider to be true humanity. The Doctor believes in technology—after all, it is the unimaginably advanced technology of the TARDIS that makes the adventures in time and space possible—but not when upgrading means sacrificing humanity.[28] We have good reason to think that the metal bodies of cybernetic individuals would ultimately be considered real bodies by their brains. Minds adapt to new prostheses and see them as part of their body images. We have also seen that the tools we use can be part of the body image, so we can assume that Daleks would also see their metal exoskeletons as part of themselves. In neither case can we assume that their metal bodies have contributed to their evil.

 **Daniel Saunders** was a psychology researcher and postdoctoral fellow in cognitive psychology at the Center for Mind/Brain Sciences in Trentino, Italy, when writing this chapter for the first edition. Now he is a machine-learning engineer at Spotify in Boston. He built his own Dalek out of cardboard, fiberglass, and egg cartons when he was nine, and first heard about the new series during a pilgrimage to Blackpool to see the Doctor Who Museum when he was twenty-four.

The bio for Jim Davies appears in chapter 3.

V.

CHANGE OF NATURE

With physical and mental reality intertwined, how will changes in either alter our natures as people? How much freedom and power do we wield in deciding who we are and whom we will become?

"We're all capable of the most incredible change."
—Thirteenth Doctor (Jodie Whittaker)[1]

Obviously changes to the brain can alter memory and motor function, but what about identity? What about dispositions such as grumpiness or generosity, interests in music or other people, or even the accent coming out of an individual's mouth?

16

Getting to the Hearts of Time Lord Personality Change: Regeneration on the Brain

Sarita J. Robinson

"We're all different people, all through our lives, and that's okay. That's good. You've gotta keep moving, so long as you remember all the people that you used to be."

—**Eleventh Doctor (Matt Smith)**[1]

"A musician must make music, an artist must paint, a poet must write, if he is to be ultimately at peace with himself. What a man can be, he must be."

——**psychologist Abraham Maslow**[2]

Neuropsychology is a rapidly developing field of psychology which has started to reveal how the human brain works. Advances in techniques such as neuroimaging have given us windows to the brain that scientists from previous generations did not have. By comparing our understanding of human neuropsychology to the alien we know as the Doctor, we may be able to explore how the Doctor's brain works and even speculate about the mechanisms involved in the process of regeneration.

Is an extraterrestrial's brain similar to a human's? Even though the Doctor looks human, there are some physical differences, most noticeably the Time Lord's binary vascular system: two hearts. The Gallifreyan body would also appear to have a respiratory bypass system, which means that they can avoid poison gases and even survive for a short time without taking a breath. In addition, the Doctor appears to be hardier than most humans, able to tolerate both hotter and colder temperatures or to withstand powerful electric shocks.

In addition to having many physical differences from humans, the Doctor also has some cognitive differences—for example, processing information from sources such as books and computer systems much quicker than is possible for a human and having a certain level of telepathic ability.[3] The Doctor can set up telepathic links with other incarnations to make decisions or to protect one Doctor from outside influence.[4] Gallifreyan physiology is different.

Brain Scans and the Doctor

Does size matter when it comes to your brain? Logically, if someone has a bigger brain, you might expect them to be more intelligent. However, this does not seem to be the case. One of the greatest scientists of the twentieth century, Albert Einstein, actually had a smaller brain than the typical adult male. After Einstein's death, his brain was examined and some structural differences were observed. For example, Einstein had a larger than average left parietal lobe.[5]

So even though the Doctor must have a human sized brain (going by skull size), it could be that the Doctor's brain is structured differently.

Or could it be that a Time Lord uses more of their brain? Because humans only use 10 percent of their brain, right?

WRONG!

Despite the popular myth that we only use 10 percent of our brain power, it is not true.[6] People who have even small amounts of brain damage can have major impairments in how they function. All parts of the brain have important roles, with each area responsible for a particular function. Take the *occipital lobes* (located at the back of the brain), for example. This area is responsible for visual processing. If a brain scan reveals damage to the occipital lobes, we would expect that person to have problems with their vision. But using our occipital lobes for processing visual information is only one of the things that we do during the day. Humans tend to multitask, and so we must use various areas of our brains for all the different activities we undertake. Even if we just go walking in the park on a summer's day, we use visual and auditory processing to enjoy the sights and sounds, and to maintain balance and other motor skills to walk. Next, the language processing areas for the brain would be activated to produce (in *Broca's area*) and understand (in *Wernicke's area*) speech if we stop for a chat.

As the Doctor appears to be quite psychologically different from us, we have to conclude that the Gallifreyan brain must be structured differently. The clearest way to confirm this would be to conduct a brain scan. However, although some have tried to steal the Doctor's head,[7] they do not manage to complete scans of the brain.

Looking into Skulls

Here on Earth, we don't have the benefits of alien techniques and until recently the only way to investigate someone's brain was to cut open the skull and have a look. Not until the early 1900s was it possible to look at the brain of a living person. The earliest technique, *pneumoencephalography,* was both dangerous and painful. First, the cerebrospinal fluid was drained and then replaced with air. Only then could clear brain X-rays be taken.[8]

After the 1940s, improvements in surgical techniques allowed brain surgeons to carry out operations that could alleviate conditions such as epilepsy. Patients were awake during surgery to check that no vital areas of the brain were damaged. One neurosurgeon, Wilder Penfield, used an electrical probe during these operations to stimulate parts of the brain and recorded which functions each part of the brain controlled. For example, an electric current in the *temporal lobes* (located behind the ears) caused patients to summon up memories.[9] If the Doctor agreed to undergo brain surgery, we could see if simulation of certain brain areas elicited the same responses as in humans. However, the Doctor is unlikely to agree to have brain surgery just so we can poke around.

Luckily, the development of a technique called *functional magnetic resonance imaging (fMRI)* allows us to see how different stimuli cause changes in blood flow and oxygenation levels in the brain and to see what areas of the brain are used for certain functions. Now we just need to get the Doctor into a scanner. Brain imaging has definitively come a long way in the last hundred years, but further advances are needed as the equipment is cumbersome and expensive.

What Happens to the Doctor's Brain During Regeneration?

During regeneration, the Doctor undergoes a rapid change in physical appearance as all body cells are renewed. The Doctor shows some changes in psychological makeup. Although the Doctor can retain previous memories, the changes in personality can be as marked as the changes in physical appearance. We also know that the process of regeneration can be difficult and painful, leading to emotional upset and physiological problems. In fact, some of the Doctor's behaviors around the time of regeneration are similar to those seen in teenagers. Any parent of a teenager can tell you that the adolescent years are a period of emotional, cognitive, and biological changes. In the Doctor's case, the transformation appears to be compressed in an acute phase lasting a few hours, followed by a longer period of recovery.[10]

Psychologists think that at around the age twelve, brains begin a process called *synaptic pruning*,[11] where the neural connections that are not used start to die off. For example, if a second language is learned early in life but not used in later years, it has been suggested that during the teenage years these language connections will be cut. It could be theorized that the Doctor, around the time of regeneration, undergoes an extreme form of synaptic pruning while retaining some control over which synaptic links to keep. However, much as the process of synaptic pruning gets a teenager ready for adulthood, the process of regeneration must make each Doctor's brain ready for the challenges they will face in the next regeneration. For example, we know that when the Eighth

Doctor regenerates into the War Doctor, he is actively regenerating into a form that will be able to face the challenges of the Time War.[12]

During adolescence, the process of pruning can go wrong and lead to psychiatric disorders such as *schizophrenia,* a long-term disorder that can impact on how a person thinks, feels, and behaves.[13] The Doctor can also face the problem of abnormal synaptic pruning following regeneration. The poisoned Fifth Doctor's regeneration into the Sixth Doctor proves especially problematic, with the new Doctor appearing unstable and difficult. In fact, the Sixth even attempts to strangle his companion, Peri, minutes after regenerating.[14] It is possible that the violent and traumatic event of regeneration can lead to errors in synaptic pruning, which take time to resolve.

Interestingly, neuroscientists now believe that the brain can continue to change and be shaped for the challenges we meet even after the teenage years. For example, brain regions involved in the recall of spatial information have been shown to change when London taxi drivers learn "The Knowledge" (the layout of all the roads in London).[15] Specifically, taxi drivers had different neural architecture in an area of the brain well-known for its importance to forming new memory: the *hippocampus.* So how does the process of regeneration affect the Doctor's brain and can we guess the possible structure and neurochemical balance of the Doctor in each regeneration?

Neophrenology

If no one has taken a picture of the Doctor's brain, can we make any predictions about what it might look like? In the nineteenth century, the study of *phrenology* suggested that the skull's external shape could be used to ascertain certain characteristics about a person. For example, if a person had a particular bump above their right eye, that would (supposedly) tell you something about their sense of humor. Phrenology has been discredited today, but recently some neuropsychologists have coined the phrase *neophrenology.*[16] Neophrenology suggests that by looking at a person's brain structure, you may be able to predict differences in people's mental abilities. Using this reasoning, we should be able to reverse-engineer what the Doctor's brain looks like by some of the behaviors the Time Lord displays. Obviously, the Doctor's brain may look quite different in each regeneration dependent on the skills and abilities specific to that Doctor.

The First Doctor (William Hartnell): Disinhibition

The First Doctor physically appears to be very old, very grumpy, and not shy about telling people how annoying they are. He is quite dismissive of Barbara and Ian when they first enter the TARDIS, telling Susan, "I know these Earth people better than you. Their minds reject things they don't understand."[17]

As we get older, areas at the front of our brains, the *frontal lobes*, appear to start to shrink,[18] and so some of the important functions that these lobes control (e.g., planning, judging, actively recalling)[19] start to fail. This may offer an in-story reason why the First Doctor has such trouble remembering Ian's surname. It could well be that the Doctor, toward the end of his first life, is starting to show problems with his inhibition control (*disinhibition*) and so becomes rude and unhelpful.

The Second Doctor (Patrick Troughton): Music

The Second Doctor, who has on occasion been described as a clown and can often come across as disorganized and bumbling, shows a love of music that sets him apart from other incarnations. In fact, he is often found playing his trusty recorder when he is trying to concentrate and in times of danger.[20] Psychologists have found that learning to play music can lead to enhancements in certain mental abilities such as *spatial reasoning* (ability to navigate mentally and visualize objects three-dimensionally from different angles).[21] Even people who do not play an instrument can benefit from listening to music. Listening to music helps people relax in times of high anxiety (such as before an operation)[22] and certain types of music, specifically Mozart's double piano sonata K. 448, can enhance mood and cognitive functioning. Research suggests as little as ten minutes, exposure to Mozart can improve people's reasoning ability.[23] This improvement in reasoning is thought to occur because the musical and spatial processing areas overlap in the brain. As a result, listening to music primes the area of the brain needed for spatial reasoning. Psychologists who have not replicated these findings suggest any increases in cognition are due to Mozart increasing arousal levels. Higher arousal levels mean that people are more likely to pay attention when completing any tests.[24] Whatever the reason, music does have a positive effect on the brain and the Doctor's mental abilities are likely to benefit from playing and listening to music during this incarnation.

(The Twelfth Doctor, too, will become a musician, jamming on electric guitar,[25] but this behavior does not appear as quickly after regeneration, as often overall, or as characteristically as the Second Doctor's love of recorder.)

The Third Doctor (Jon Pertwee): Inventiveness

Made to regenerate by the Time Lords and then exiled on Earth, this incarnation of the Doctor has a much-reduced ability to travel in time and space. Trapped on Earth in the twentieth century, this Doctor is inventive and makes the most of the rather primitive technology he has available. He does enjoy using the available resources to create new devices such as the Whomobile. Is it possible that great inventors have a different type of brain? That could be the case. Researchers have found that when we generate a new idea, there is activation in various areas of the brain such as the *left inferior frontal gyrus, anterior cingulate cortex,* and the *precentral gyrus.*[26] The inventive Third Doctor may have enhanced functioning in these areas of the brain.

The Fourth Doctor (Tom Baker): Generosity

The Fourth Doctor is outgoing and friendly, with an infectious sense of humor. He is generous, especially with his Jelly Babies. But what makes a person generous? Some researchers think that differences in hormone levels can affect how generous we are. In one study participants were asked to split a sum of money with a stranger. The researchers found that those who were given a dose of a hormone called *oxytocin* (the so-called cuddle hormone) were 80 percent more generous than those given a placebo.[27] Certain other hormones, such as testosterone, have been found to reduce generosity.[28]

The Fifth Doctor (Peter Davison): Mental Toughness

The Fifth Doctor enjoys playing cricket.[29] People who have a high degree of *mental toughness* (a resilient attitude, self-belief, and personal motivation) tend to make good cricketers.[30] We know little about the brain structure or neurochemistry of someone who has higher levels of mental toughness. However, some studies have suggested that there is a genetic component and the neurotransmitter serotonin, which is known to modify our responses to stress, may be involved.[31]

The Sixth Doctor (Colin Baker): Instability

Immediately after the Doctor's regeneration into his sixth incarnation, it is clear things have not gone well. Although physically the regeneration appears to have worked, mentally the Doctor is unstable in that he appears impulsive, irritable, bad-tempered, and aggressive. These changes may occur because the Doctor is experiencing poor inhibition control, suggesting that the areas that control our actions (disinhibition again), the *prefrontal lobes*, are in some way not working correctly.[32] As well as aggression, damage to the prefrontal lobes can lead to increases in extraversion, which may explain the Doctor's outlandish style in this regeneration with his multi-colored coat and bright yellow trousers.[33]

The Seventh Doctor (Sylvester McCoy): Eccentricity

The Doctor regenerates after the TARDIS comes under attack by the Rani.[34] The Seventh Doctor's new personality is eccentric, to say the least. Eccentric behavior can have a genetic component. People who have relatives who suffer from *schizophrenia* have often been found to have mild *schizotypal personality traits*, a condition marked by pervasive eccentricity. These eccentric behaviors could be the result of a lack of dopamine in the prefrontal lobes or because people with schizotypal personality traits have a smaller left temporal lobe.[35] Therefore, it is possible that this incarnation of the Doctor has less dopamine than previous regenerations or a smaller left temporal lobe.

The Eighth Doctor (Paul McGann): Memory Loss

The Doctor regenerates into his eighth incarnation when Dr. Grace Holloway performs some ill-advised heart surgery.[36] Unfortunately for him, the anesthetic nearly stops his regeneration and he is left suffering temporarily from a form of amnesia known as *transient global amnesia*—suddenly, though temporarily, forgetting everything about himself.[37] This form of amnesia is often not caused by extensive neurological damage to the brain but instead by migraine or seizures or maybe, in this case, the regeneration process. However, it is also possible that the doctor was suffering from *psychogenic amnesia*. Psychogenic (psychologically generated) amnesia can be caused by traumatic events, and so it is possible that the trauma of regeneration has caused the Doctor to temporarily forget his previous life events.[38]

The War Doctor (John Hurt): Combat Readiness

Little is known about the War Doctor on television (although audio dramas reveal more about his experiences in the Time War).[39] The Sisterhood of Karn gives the Eighth Doctor the ability to control his regeneration and so he can become the perfect soldier, the Doctor of War.[40] Because this Doctor needs to be tough and make some difficult decisions, his brain in this regeneration is likely to be designed to overcome the problems people face in war zones, such as mental fatigue. We know that people in combat situations can make errors when they are under strain. A lack of food, water, and sleep can seriously impair cognitive functioning. For example, when people are dehydrated the brain shrinks and so is unable to carry out complex thoughts.[41]

Although we are not able to redesign brains to make better soldiers, there are drugs available which can help with mental fatigue. For example, central nervous system stimulants such as amphetamines can be used to keep pilots awake during long missions, or Modafinil, a drug used to help with sleep disorders, can help keep parts of the brain in a more wakeful state. Another thing the Doctor could do to increase his resilience in war is to reduce his level of fear. Some researchers believe that the level of fear we experience is driven by our genes.[42] Maybe the Doctor in this regeneration has reduced the number of his genes that are associated with fear reactions. The War Doctor may have also reduced his levels of empathy to allow him to make the hard decisions needed to end the Last Great Time War. Lower levels of empathy could indicate differences in the structure of the cingulate and amygdala areas of the brain and also lower levels of oxytocin.[43]

The Ninth Doctor (Christopher Eccleston): Accent

Shortly after meeting the Doctor, Rose asks, "If you are an alien, how come you sound like you're from the North?" To which the Doctor replies, "Lots of planets have a North!"[44]

It appears that after his regeneration, the Doctor has had a marked change in his accent. (From this incarnation onward, the Doctors' accents vary more than before.) Accents can change in children if they move to a new regional area, but for most of us, by the time we hit adulthood, our accents are mostly fixed. Occasionally though, people have been known to develop a new accent overnight, normally as a result of a brain injury, such as a stroke. This condition is known as *foreign accent syndrome,* in which a brain trauma can lead to a sudden alteration in a person's speech rhythm and prosody. A young Englishman who suffered a stroke suddenly developed a Caribbean accent (specifically similar to the accent found on St. Lucia). In this case, the foreign accent disappeared after seventy-two hours.[45] It could well be that the changes in the Doctor's brain structure during regeneration affect his accent.

The Tenth Doctor (David Tennant): Neurorehabilitation

Newly regenerated, the Tenth Doctor struggles with the regeneration process but is restored with the healing properties of tea.[46] He then challenges the leader of the Sycorax to a duel, during which the Doctor's hand is chopped off. However, the Doctor is able to grow another hand while still within fifteen hours of his regeneration. Unlike humans who must learn to use new limbs, the Doctor appears not to need any form of *neurorehabilitation* and can start to use his new hand immediately. Even humans can learn to adapt to a hand that is not their own. In the *rubber hand illusion,* a researcher strokes both the participant's real hand (which is hidden) and the rubber hand, which the participant can see. Over time, the participant starts to believe that the rubber hand is their real hand.[47]

The Eleventh Doctor (Matt Smith): ADHD

When the Doctor turns into "a madman with a box"[48] in his eleventh incarnation, he becomes youthful and lively, with a good dose of impatience, getting quickly bored and bouncing from one task to the next.[49]

The impulsivity and hyperactivity he exhibits suggests that he has some traits of *attention-deficit/hyperactivity disorder* (ADHD). Indeed, this regeneration of the Doctor can seem quite childish. Children with ADHD can take a few years longer to mature into adulthood. Although the precise reason why ADHD occurs in humans is not fully known, it is thought that there are differences in the neurotransmitter *dopamine*[50] and atypical connectivity in reward circuitry of the brain.[51] This Doctor certainly benefits from the high levels of energy that his hyperactive traits give him.

The Twelfth Doctor (Peter Capaldi): Autism Spectrum

Despite regenerating with a face meant to remind himself to show compassion and help people[52] (or perhaps because of it), the Twelfth Doctor appears to have problems understanding complex emotions and has difficulty with empathy.[53] In fact, Clara writes a number of cards to help him give the right emotional response. Bill also struggles with the Twelfth Doctor's lack of empathy when a little boy, Spider, is sucked under the ice at the 1814 Frost Fair in London. Bill is upset when the Doctor appears to care more about retrieving his stolen sonic screwdriver than the death of the child.[54]

It could be that this regeneration has given the Doctor some of the traits of the neurodevelopmental condition previously called *Asperger's syndrome,* now subsumed under the umbrella of *autism spectrum* in modern diagnostic systems.[55] Although the Doctor learns some compensatory strategies, he does appear to have a less than complete understanding of the social world compared to other Doctors. Psychologists have found that scientists (including mathematicians) are more likely to be on the autism spectrum in this way than academics who are not scientists.[56]

Note, though, that even though he does not naturally demonstrate the same empathy as some versions of the Doctor, he nevertheless values kindness increasingly over his centuries and prioritizes it right up to his end.[57]

The Thirteenth Doctor (Jodie Whittaker): Social Connections

From a neuroanatomy perspective, the latest research would suggest that human men and women do have differences in regional brain anatomy (even when differences in overall brain size are taken into account). However, it is still unclear whether these small to moderate structural differences result in differences in cognition or behavior.[58] The physical transformation into the body of a woman may produce neurochemistry changes in her brain, but it is difficult to establish whether sex-based differences in neurochemistry would result in specific differences in cognition or behavior due to the complex way that biology and the environment interact.[59]

Regardless of how her brain is structured, we know that the Thirteenth Doctor places more importance on social connections and family bonding, referring to her companions as her "fam." (Previous Doctors who traveled with a group of three companions, specifically the First and Fifth Doctors, never referred to their companions as family.) The Doctor may become more prosocial in this regeneration in response to the Twelfth Doctor's losses and upon learning about the Master's assault on their homeworld of Gallifrey.[60] The stress caused by the loss of her fellow Time Lords could have led to an increase in *oxytocin*, a hormone that is mainly produced in an area of the brain known as the hypothalamus. In times of stress, oxytocin can be released and is associated with a greater motivation for social bonding.[61]

The Fugitive Doctor: Identity and Memory

We know little about the Fugitive Doctor other than that after escaping from Gat, the Division, and Gallifrey, she lives on twenty-first-century Earth disguised as a human, Ruth Clayton. Only when she is given a cue phrase, "Follow the light and break the glass," does she return to the lighthouse where her Time Lord essence and the TARDIS have been hidden.[62] The Fugitive Doctor has previously used the Chameleon Arch to remove memories of her life. In humans (and it would seem Time Lords), simply telling someone to forget long-term memories does not work.[63] However, we know from studies of people with dementia, it is possible to lose memories when the functioning of certain areas of the brain, such as the hippocampus, are compromised.[64] Although it is unclear exactly how the Chameleon Arch works, it does appear to rewrite, at a cellular level, the biology of the Time Lord who uses it. This suggests that the memories held in the hippocampus are overwritten, while a copy of the original memories are held in the bio-data module and can be restored later.

Alien Brains and Human Brains

Neuropsychology is a relatively young area of psychology, and advances in techniques such as brain imaging are likely to lead to further advancements in this field. From our current understanding of how the human brain works, it is clear the Doctor shares some similarities but on other occasions is quite alien. One of the most striking differences between the Doctor and humans is the ability to regenerate. Although, like the process of synaptic pruning in adolescence, regeneration is much more violent and traumatic, leading to exaggerated teenage-like behaviors in the Doctor. Errors in the regeneration process as well as changes in brain structure because of regeneration lead to each Doctor having a markedly different personality in each of their regenerations. Our understanding of the human brain allows us to guess at the neuropsychological underpinnings of the Doctor's behavior. However, like the human brain, until neuropsychological techniques improve, the brain and behavior of the Doctor cannot be fully explained.

Sarita Robinson's bio appears in chapter 10.

Change, good or bad, produces stress—

especially when unexpected, when it

transforms things we'd seen as stable,

when it violates expectations. Expectations,

though, can change, adapt, and grow. Life

is change. For a 1963 story to live and

thrive through today, it required change.

17

Regenerating Gender: Infinitely More Inside

Justine Mastin

"Everything changes and nothing stands still."
—philosopher Heraclitus[1]

"Are all people like this? . . . So much bigger on the inside."
—Idris, TARDIS personified (Suranne Jones)[2]

To assume that a TARDIS or a Time Lord will always look and act the same is unrealistic. They are made to evolve as living beings, and so are humans. These changes can range from subtle to dramatic. A Time Lord's regeneration will carry over key aspects of previous iterations, sometimes more than others, and at other times the regeneration will create new aesthetics and functionality. Each iteration is not only a piece of the whole, but it's the whole truth of the current experience. People go through great changes in their lives, too, though maybe not so dramatically.

The idea of changing something as entrenched in our culture as the concept of gender can be unsettling for some. The reality is that, like stepping into a TARDIS, human gender is bigger on the inside and can change over the course of a lifetime whether in terms of gender roles, gender concepts, or self-concept.

"C," head of MI6 (Stephen Fry): I've read the files. The Doctor is a man.

Thirteenth Doctor (Jodie Whittaker): I've had an upgrade.[3]

The Gender TARDIS

The concept of gender is as diverse as stars in the sky. At its simplest, gender is a person's self-concept of their own *masculinity* (to some, how butch they feel), *femininity* (how femme they feel), *androgyny* (how much they feel both masculine and feminine), none of the above, or maybe more.[4] Rhetoric around gender has changed significantly in recent years. Sweeping social change has questioned the strict gender roles of decades past and welcomed more fluid gender roles, as well as opened the conversation around gender diversity. *Gender diversity* includes the vast multiverse of gender experiences outside of the binary of man and woman—such as transgender, genderqueer, gender nonbinary, and gender nonconforming. Despite this increase of awareness, there are still those who believe that there are only two genders—male and female—and that these genders must line up with one's sex organs at birth. Current understanding is that gender *may* be in line with biological sex (*cisgender*) but it also may *not* be (*transgender*). There are indigenous peoples[5] for whom a spectrum of gender has been embraced for ages, and Time Lords seem to understand this basic principle as well. They recognize that gender identity and expression, as aspects of themselves, can change over time. They acknowledge that regeneration is inevitable, and that internal identity of how one experiences their gender and their external expression of how they choose to present their gender may vary widely with each regeneration.

If the Doctor has a masculine gender identity and expression in all previous known regenerations, one might assume that the Doctor will always be masculine. But as so often happens in the real world, the truth is much more complicated. In fact, when supposedly discovered by Tecteun in what is perhaps the Doctor's true first identity, the Timeless Child expresses a femme gender.[6] The Doctor also has a femme gender in at least one other known iteration, the incarnation known as Ruth Clayton, or the Fugitive Doctor.[7] Even as the Doctor's gender identity and expression are femme, inside she sometimes still identifies with the male aspects of herself. The Thirteenth Doctor occasionally speaks to this when she accidentally calls herself a man and then quickly corrects with "Every time!"[8] Remarking that "I was a different man back then"[9] recognizes that masculinity remains in her personal history even as she moves beyond that. *Gender fluidity* (change over time in gender identity, gender expression, or both)[10] is often misunderstood, both for the Doctor and for folks in the real world.

The Woman Who Fell to Earth's Gender Roles

On Gallifrey, gender identity and expression may not be meaningful in terms of social status or cultural norms, but they are most definitely significant on Earth across the ages. People *assigned female at birth* (AFAB) have different experiences and expectations than people *assigned male at birth* (AMAB). And these experiences have a profound impact on identity formation and sense of self. Much as the Thirteenth Doctor must acclimate to certain norms, so, too, do those who are gender fluid or trans in the real world. When identifying and expressing as male, the Doctor is readily welcomed into situations that the femme-expressing Doctor is not. King James, for instance, will barely deign to speak with this lowly woman, and then accuses her of witchcraft. The Doctor is taken aback at this behavior as this is the first time, in her recollection, that she has experienced this type of discrimination based on gender.[11]

The work of women in the US and Britain—where the Doctor travels extensively—has historically been less respected than the work of men. To this day, women make a fraction of the income of men, and when race is added into the equation this financial gap only widens.[12] Discrimination based on gender, like all discrimination, can negatively impact mental health. The Doctor is accustomed to being questioned about what *type* of doctor the Time Lord is, but with her new femme gender expression, she finds her name challenged, sometimes even by other women, because "doctor is a man's term."[13] The Doctor comes to terms with the new reality of her gender, such as when she considers that Punjab, India, in the 1940s was a "hard time for women"[14] and suddenly wishes that she could immediately get the respect that she is used to: "Honestly! If I was still a bloke, I could get on with the job and not have to waste time defending myself!"[15]

The Power of the Doctor's Pronouns

A person's gender identity and expression do not represent pathology. However, not being accepted for one's gender identity and expression absolutely can cause mental health concerns.[16] Gender-diverse people often experience *microaggressions,* "brief, everyday exchanges that send denigrating messages to certain individuals because of their group membership (e.g., people of color, women, or LGBTQIA+ persons)."[17] One of the simplest and also most frequent microaggressions is *misgendering,* calling or referring to someone by the incorrect pronoun(s).[18] These misgenderings can be accidental or deliberate. In *accidental misgendering,* a person may use the incorrect pronoun out of habit or carelessness if they are not making a concerted effort to change their language. Captain Jack uses "he" pronouns to speak about the Doctor and times they spent together in the past. This occurs out of habit on Jack's part, ignorance of the Doctor's change, and not as an intentional misgendering.

> **Jack Harkness (John Barrowman):** He needs to know the future of the universe is at stake.

> **Graham O'Brien (Bradley Walsh):** Not "he." She.

> **Jack:** Oh, this I gotta see![19]

Despite his misgendering when first speaking about the Thirteenth Doctor, he uses the correct pronouns as soon as he learns that she now identifies as femme. Jack makes this pivot without difficulty, immediately saying things such as "Why didn't it scoop her? Why can't I get her here?" and "Oh, she likes them mouthy then, huh?" He expresses glee when he finally meets this Doctor.[20]

In *intentional misgendering*, a person purposely uses incorrect pronouns as a form of verbal abuse. No matter what the intention is on the part of the person who does the misgendering, the impact can be harmful to the gender-diverse person.[21] It can be hurtful to feel not understood by others, particularly by those whom one trusts.[22]

While misgendering is an example of how gender-diverse people experience distress, they also have experiences of *gender affirmation*, being free to express their gender socially. When these affirmations feel particularly resonant, gender-diverse people describe the experience as gender euphoria. The phenomenon of *gender euphoria*, happiness with one's gender, is in direct contrast to the clinical language of gender dysphoria.[23] *Gender dysphoria* is a mental health diagnosis that was created by clinicians who pathologized the experience of gender diversity. *Gender euphoria* as a term was coined within the community itself, rather than assigned by clinicians, and refers to the feelings of joy that arise from engaging in activities that feel congruent with one's gender identity.[24] The Doctor displays gender euphoria when getting henna on her hands for Yaz's grandmother's wedding. She remarks that this is something she never got to do as a man.[25] The visible delight on her face as she experiences this gender-specific ritual displays one of the first times that the Doctor seems to feel in her own skin in this regeneration.

Companions

The queer community, of which trans, nonbinary, and genderqueer identities are part, have a history of being at the forefront of creating chosen family.[26] Creating a "fam" as the Doctor does with whom to travel and share her adventures is a protective factor for LGBTQIA+ individuals to aid in resiliency.[27] Many people in these communities have experienced discrimination in the various systems in which they inhabit, including in their families of origin. The Doctor is selective of who she decides to have join her fam, as are those in these communities. It's affirming to have a supportive system who will accept you no matter what changes you might go through. Even when one feels they've chosen wisely, they might feel the sting of someone they trusted not being able to tolerate the changes they go through. The Doctor across regenerations experiences companions who struggle with regeneration, as they feel this person is no longer "their" Doctor, such as when Rose initially rejects the Tenth: "Can you change back?"[28]

As with all identity formation, it takes time to become comfortable with who you are. When one makes a discovery about their gender and a change, it's only natural that there will be an additional time of transition—to figure out what clothes this iteration prefers, etc. Each time the Doctor regenerates, they must go through this process, because they have become a new iteration of themselves. It can be difficult for people around the gender-diverse person to make sense of these changes. Whether they are people who knew the Doctor before this change, who therefore may struggle with new pronoun usage, or people who know the Doctor after and have no awareness of the person the time traveler once was. While people from the Doctor's past, like Captain Jack, wrestle with integrating this new identity, her fam (Yaz, Graham, and Ryan) struggle with learning that the Doctor has previous iterations wherein she identified and presented differently.

"O" (Sacha Dhawan): Our paths crossed very briefly once, when she was a man.

Graham: When she was a what?

"O": Has she never mentioned that?

Graham: I thought she was joking.[29]

As for romantic love, one's gender and sexual or romantic preferences are not inherently related. In sharp contrast to the romantic binaries of heterosexual/homosexual, a new sexual and romantic universe unfolds with gender diversity wherein old rules need not apply.[30] No matter one's gender identity, they may be attracted to people of the same or other genders, and relationships that were once considered straight suddenly (or it appears) become queer. The Doctor is historically in heterosexual relationships (when any at all), even marrying women such as River Song.[31] The Doctor now feels a romantic pull to Yaz, which creates the potential for a queer relationship if she would engage in the romantic entanglement that she avoids.

This Universe of Possibilities

Expanding the definition of gender from the binary to make space for change and evolution allows for all people to discover their authentic selves. This may change numerous times throughout their lifespan and necessitates the people around them to also be willing to lean into the sometimes uncomfortable reality of regeneration. The Doctor revels in each new transformation, even as each mourns the version whose time is ending. Embracing the range of gender diversity in the world around us and within us invites all people to harness the power of the Doctor to regenerate. Exploring this range within your own gender TARDIS offers you this universe of possibilities, if only you will climb aboard. And if you have found your place in that time and space, perhaps offer a hand to companions who are only just discovering that it's bigger on the inside.

Justine Mastin, MA, LMFT, is a therapist, writer, podcaster, and educator. Justine cowrote *Starship Therapise: Using Therapeutic Fanfiction to Rewrite Your Life* and *The Grieving Therapist: Caring for Yourself and Your Clients When it Feels Like the End of the World.* She has contributed to numerous books in the Popular Culture Psychology series. Justine is a TEDx speaker, an instructor at University of Massachusetts Global, and cohost of the *Starship Therapise* and *Dark Side of the Mat* podcasts. Justine takes a holistic approach to healing: mind, body, and fandom.

Are boys expected to give up "softer" parts of themselves in order to become men? How does anyone escape the limitations and expectations of gender stereotypes and roles?

18

Boys to Cybermen:
Social Narratives and
Masculinity Metaphors
Billy San Juan

"Emotions! Love! Pride! Hate! Fear! Have you no emotions, sir, hmm?"
—First Doctor (William Hartnell, also David Bradley)[1]

"Foster a space that welcomes the warrior into therapy by explicitly calling for the strength
of the stereotypical male role in a different kind of battle, a 'battle for the mind and heart.'"
—psychologist Duncan Shields[2]

 As they grow up, boys are often expected to lose their "softer" qualities to become tough, strong men. Masculinity, in its stereotyped Western form, is often taught to young boys in an attempt to create an ideal "man" impervious to vulnerability. Many men suffer trying to conform to these impossible ideals.[3] A prime example is the instilled belief that men must deny their emotions,[4] because emotions are viewed as vulnerability and vulnerability is dangerous. These messages are not always conveyed directly, but they can be conveyed constantly. A boy crying on the sports field may be castigated in a variety of ways:

Stop crying. Don't be a baby. Stop acting like a girl. Be a man. Delete your emotions.

Upgrade.

219

Losing Humanity

The modern world is progressing toward an unpredictable time when advances in cybernetics can change what it means to be human. The Cybermen are robotic beings, each a "living brain jammed inside a cybernetic body with a heart of steel, emotions removed."[5] Cybermen pose formidable foes for the Doctor and companions. They also serve as a prime metaphor for the role that socialized masculinity norms play in everyday male experience. They are partially defined by their ability to regulate emotions through an emotional inhibitor.[6] Blocking emotions does not eliminate them, however. Emotional inhibitors can be hacked with a code,[7] overloaded through a strong feeling of parental love,[8] or overridden through a strong feeling of romantic love.[9] In similar fashion, strong emotions can overwhelm men who adhere to traditional values of masculinity. Instead of an emotional inhibitor being destroyed, this can lead to self-destructive actions. Men may turn to drugs, alcohol, violence, or other unsafe behaviors to cope with feelings they may not be able to truly understand. Emotions, especially those seen as vulnerable, are avoided or deleted. The reason lies in three words the Tenth Doctor whispers to Rose to explain why the Cybermen have removed their feelings: "Because it hurts."[10]

Emotional inhibition falls into four categories, fitting different themes of masculinity.

Themes of Masculinity

The values by which men are taught to live act as an operating system. These values serve as software by which actions are taken and emotions are interpreted. The values differ slightly based on various factors, but common themes emerge. There are four main themes in the underlying transmission of traditional masculinity norms.[11]

Normative, hegemonic masculine ideals are stereotyped to be the opposite of stereotyped female behaviors. This ideology encourages men to achieve social status by devaluing emotions that imply vulnerability and developing a "façade of toughness."[12] Colors, toys, actions, clothing, and interests are divided into dichotomous classes of "boy" and "girl." These *gender attitudes*, or the beliefs that dictate and constitute appropriate "boy" and "girl" behaviors, are internalized in childhood and adolescence.[13] Consider the fact that nearly all Cyber-conversion victims become Cybermen, not Cyberwomen, regardless of their original gender.[14]

Masculinity ideals value the acquisition of status and achievement. Two primary methods males use to acquire status are prestige and dominance.[15] *Prestige* is achieved by entities who receive accolades from others. A man builds prestige by developing a positive reputation, such as "wealthy businessman" or "decorated soldier." *Dominance* is a similar concept. However, it implies an agonistic process whereby influence is exerted by instilling fear. Dominance relies on acts showing physical superiority to attain status or achievement. The word is often used to describe individual athletes in competitive sports, such as boxing or mixed martial arts. The Doctor and the Cybermen exemplify prestige and dominance, respectively. The Doctor's companions follow voluntarily, such as when Donna actively searches to find the Tenth Doctor specifically so she can join his travels.[16] The Cybermen force victims to upgrade without choice.

Men are often habituated to exhibit emotional self-control. Men may have difficulty identifying and verbalizing vulnerability, due mainly to the belief that men are expected to conceal weakness.[17] Stoicism is seen as a sign of calm and a display of leadership in times of adversity. Every iteration of the Cybermen, from the cyborglike Mondasian Cybermen to the artificially designed Cybermen of Lumic Industries, features an unexpressive faceplate with a fixed expression. A fixed expression cannot show variety or reactions.

Masculinity norms value *aggression*, actions intended to inflict harm. Though anyone may perpetrate or be victims of violence, physical aggression is clearly a behavior associated with masculinity.[18] The adherence to a *masculine credo*, which includes a focus not only on emotional restriction but also on aggression, status, and sexual functioning, is correlated to men's feelings of competency, independence, and ambition.[19] The Cybermen aggress through violence, and their lack of emotion is shown through merciless actions, such as the slaughter that occurs during a funeral[20] or their unwillingness to surrender when fighting the Daleks.[21]

> "As long as men are supposed to be 'masculine' and women are supposed to be 'feminine,' many people will suffer in their attempts to conform."
> —psychologist Rebekah Smart[22]

The Doctor's Masculinity: Positive Psychology/Positive Masculinity

If the Cybermen represent a view of the maladaptive aspects of masculinity, then the Doctor represents positive aspects that may come as a result of properly adjusted masculinity narratives. In a shift in modern psychological research and literature, some researchers have begun to look at masculinity in a manner that emphasizes principles of positive psychology and seeks to focus on healthier and more constructive aspects of masculinity. It is important to note that the following qualities are not unique to men. However, they are qualities that men often use to define masculinity as a social construct. It is also important to note that this list merely reflects the myriad *positive masculine qualities*, but is not a complete and comprehensive catalogue:[23]

1. Intimate male relationships are often forged through action-oriented activities, rather than more passive activities such as long conversation. Describing the findings shown by much research,[24] psychologist David Myers has observed that men tend to prefer doing activities "side-by-side" more than communicating "face-to-face."[25] For example, watching and/or playing sports serve as stereotypical bonding activities for men. Fishing, camping, and hunting also serve as tropes by which men spend time together to strengthen friendships. This can be seen in adventure-oriented interactions between the Doctor and the Brigadier, such as when the Brigadier saves the Doctor from a glowing snakelike creature and quips, "I can't just let you out of my sight, can I, Doctor?" The Seventh Doctor marvels that the Brigadier recognizes him despite his regenerated form, at which point the Brigadier replies, "Who else would it be?"[26] In similar fashion, the intimacy between these two

characters can be observed in the span of seconds when the Doctor salutes him, a simple action indicating a strong bond because the Doctor rarely salutes anyone and does not like to be saluted.[27]

2. Men with healthy masculinity ideals often value their role as protector for friends and loved ones. A drive to fulfill such a role even motivates healthy behavior for those who want to be capable of protecting others.[28] The Doctor proclaims himself to be a protector many times, notably when the Eleventh asks the Atraxi, "Is this world protected?" and they find the answer in a series of images that show every version of him (all those known at the time, that is) from the First Doctor up to the Eleventh.[29]

3. Men tend to be characterized as "good fathers" when they take an active, responsive role in their child's life.[30] The "good father" shows accessibility (presence and availability), engagement (direct contact and shared interactions), and responsibility (taking care of his children).[31] Though initially uninterested in a relationship with his artificially created daughter, Jenny, the Tenth Doctor begins to model his method of nonviolence for conflict resolution and becomes her good father.[32]

4. Healthy men are positively socialized to value self-reliance. Though self-reliance includes consideration of opinions or data from other sources, a "healthy man" will help consider others' needs and come to his own conclusion. In several instances, the Doctor acts in a self-reliant manner based on personal knowledge and experience. However, the Time Lord will also listen to input from companions, such as when Amy helps the Eleventh Doctor find an alternative instead of harming a star whale.[33]

5. Healthy men undertake risks or engage in other forms of daring, but only after careful consideration of consequence and reward.[34] This allows for growth of character through testing their endurance, resilience, and other self "limits." Such a perception of risk-taking may account for why more men than women participate in dan-

gerous activities like skydiving.[35] Nearly every adventure the Doctor undertakes involves some sort of risk or feat of daring. Though some Doctors may be a bit more impulsive than others, each usually considers consequence and reward before taking action.

6. Male-oriented organizations often offer humanitarian services in the interest of social good. This is not to suggest that female-oriented organizations do not engage in similar activities. However, this has been noted by researchers as an area of positive expression of masculinity. Organizations such as the Knights of Columbus, Freemasons, and the Boy Scouts of America all serve as examples of male-oriented organizations that give men and boys opportunities for stereotypically male-appropriate socialization and service. The Doctor is not necessarily a member of a male-oriented organization and probably would never choose to affiliate with one because joining clubs runs contrary to inner nature. (As Groucho Marx said, more than once and in several different ways, "I don't want to belong to any club that will accept people like me as a member."[36])

7. Men use humor as a means of enjoyment, to forge intimacy with other men, as a strategic tool to manage conflict, and as a means of winning support. Researchers suggest that men may use humor as a surreptitious method of expressing affection.[37] The Doctor's sense of humor has varied between incarnations. However, it is a quality that endears the Time Lord to both companions and viewers alike.

8. Traditional masculinity is often embodied in male heroes.[38] These heroes may exhibit incredible strength, may be great leaders, or may have overcome life hurdles to reach their status as "hero." In mythology, Hercules shows great might and becomes more heroic through a series of trials. In the post-9/11 world, Americans elevated firefighters and other first responders to the status of "hero" when the perception of risk involved became greater.[39] The Doctor embodies many traits of a hero, including resilience in the face of personal tragedies such as the deaths of companions,[40] wives,[41] and seemingly their entire race.[42]

Silver Nightmares

The Cybermen and the Doctor represent two sides of masculinity. Taken to the extreme, social constructs of masculinity may inhibit beautiful aspects of life related to emotion and even cause biopsycho-social issues for men. On the other hand, in a healthy context, social constructs of masculinity can elevate men to become productive members of an emotionally literate society. Men must make a choice as they are bombarded by so-called masculine constructs throughout their social development. Will they succumb to the idea that emotions are a weakness, an exploitable vulnerability to be hidden at the cost of physical and social health? Will they be upgraded to be emotionally stunted Cybermen?

Or will their hearts grow to beat like the Doctor's?

"I'm not the man I used to be. Thank goodness."
—**Fifth Doctor (Peter Davison)**[43]

 **Billy San Juan** received his PsyD from Alliant International University in 2014. He is a regular contributor to the Popular Culture Psychology line of books, as well as a horror fiction writer. He has contributed flavor text and card names for the hit game *Magic: The Gathering.* He lives in San Diego with his wife, child, several fish, and a praying mantis.

TIME LORDS TO TIME LADIES

Travis Langley & Billy San Juan

An adventure begins with the Twelfth Doctor's student and friend Bill Potts declaring her humanity when a blue man points a gun at her, Nardole, and Missy and he demands to know which of them is human.

Bill Potts (Pearl Mackie): "Me! Me, I-I'm human."[44]

The story later takes a dark turn when Cybermen strip Bill of physical humanity by placing her brain inside a robotic body. As Missy puts it, Bill is now "dead, dismembered, fed through a grinder, and squeezed into a Cyberman, doomed to spend an eternal afterlife as a biomechanical psycho zombie."[45]

Cybermen can commit this particular atrocity only because the Doctor's "best enemy,"[46] the Master, helps them delete Bill's humanity and even her gender by turning her into *it* and *him—Cyber* and *man*. The Master does this while he's "very worried about my future."[47] He does not like discovering signs of humanity—as hints of compassion and benevolence—in Missy, the person this Master will next become after regenerating. The toxically masculine Master essentially vents his aversion to femininity through a rare act of maiming one of the Doctor's companions. The Master normally prefers to toy with them, even chatting with them as an indirect way of doing something with the Doctor.[48]

Bill's conversion is incomplete, though. Even in the Cyberman shell, she retains her personal memories and sense of self. After Missy refers to Cyberman Bill as "her," the Master scoffs, "'Her'? It's a Cyberman now," then adds with a note of disgust, "Becoming a woman is one thing, but have you got empathy?" His annoyance grows when the Doctor also refers to Cyber-Bill by female pronouns.

The Master (John Simm): Is the future going to be all girl?

Twelfth Doctor (Peter Capaldi): We can only hope.

Missy stabs the Master, forcing her past self to start regenerating into the woman he will become, and she tells him, "Welcome to the sisterhood." She sees so many ways in which he needs to grow as a person, and by bringing her predecessor's time to an end, by forcing him to become her, she retroactively chooses to become herself. The dying Master shoots her, though, thinking she will not be able to regenerate and survive. He would rather die than live as a woman again.

Wounded by Cybermen, the Twelfth Doctor ends the same adventure also about to regenerate. While stalling his regeneration, he comes face to face with the First Doctor, whose remarks remind the Twelfth of his own past. Seeing the Master's sexism and remembering his own early sexism reminds him of the *gender-role journey* he has taken thus far, broadening his perspective beyond traditional gender roles.[49] His remarks to the Master express his hope for others to outgrow socialized sexism, and so he pursues his own continued growth. The Master's attitudes and the First Doctor's reminder likely guide the Doctor's next transformation as he becomes she. For the first time in the Doctor's recollection, the man in the blue box becomes a woman.

The fact that she is now female keeps slipping her mind at first.

Thirteenth Doctor (Jodie Whittaker): Why are you calling me "Madam"?

Yaz (Mandip Gill): Because you're a woman.

Thirteenth Doctor: Am I? Does it suit me?[50]

Despite ready acceptance of this, the Doctor does not easily incorporate the gender difference into self-concept, repeatedly saying things like "'Ma'am.' Still can't get used to that"[51] and "Come to Daddy! I mean

Mummy."[52] For thousands of years, this character's self-concept has been male. *Gender identity*, a person's self-identification as male or female, varies from person to person in terms of how fixed it may be—constant and unwavering in one person, variable and fluid in another, uncertain in someone else.[53] Societal structures, social expectations, and interpersonal relations interact as both circumstance and biology influence gender identity.[54]

Before long, though, the Thirteenth Doctor stops saying such things. Gender-related aspects of the Time Lord's self-concept shift. The Doctor is on a *gender journey*,[55] discovering who she is now, growing progressively more familiar with who she becomes. Every Doctor shows personal growth. This is the Doctor who regenerated while ready to work on growing more *gender-aware*. People actively conscious of gender in themselves and in others tend to develop more egalitarian views of gender roles and report progress on their personal gender journeys.

Perhaps foreshadowing female Bill's conversion into Cyber*man* and the male Twelfth Doctor's regeneration into woman, Bill and the Twelfth discuss gender views. When Bill learns that the Time Lords are a "bit flexible on the whole man-woman thing" in terms of gender identity, the Doctor says, "We're the most civilized civilization in the universe. We're billions of years beyond your petty human obsession with gender and its associated stereotypes." Bill points out their vestigial sexism, though: "But you still call yourselves Time *Lords*."[56] Though a difference in translation might offer the simplest explanation, the Doctor offers nothing of the sort. There is a gender distinction among Gallifreyan titles. Several female Gallifreyans such as Romana are referred to as Time Ladies.[57] When the Fourth Doctor calls Romana a Time Lady, is he subscribing to the gendered term or is he deferring to Romana's personal preference?[58] When the Twelfth Doctor first calls Missy a Time Lord, she corrects him, "Time Lady, please. I'm old-fashioned,"[59] and consistently calls herself a Time Lady after that.[60] The female Thirteenth Doctor calls them all Time Lords as gender-neutral.

What do such distinctions mean? Are expectations different for Time Lords and Time Ladies? *Gender roles* (originally called *sex roles*, but that sounded sexual and confused people) are expectations regarding how people of different genders are expected to behave as part of their roles in life.[61] They are not beliefs about what different genders *are* like (*gender stereotypes*) but, rather, expectations about how they're *supposed* to act regardless of whether such expectations may be right or wrong, fair or unfair. Because societal expectations establish gender roles, we need to know more about any society before we can understand such roles and the context for what they mean. We know little about how gender-changing Time Lords incorporate gender expectations into their system, and yet Missy makes it clear that some distinctions have traditionally figured in.

For Missy, identifying as Time Lady declares acceptance of her female being. When she actively tries to be good, it is not only to save her neck or to keep a promise to the Doctor. After all, she is the one who offers to be good and puts forth that promise—her idea, her choice. After years confined to the Doctor's university vault, Missy sits weeping as she thinks about all the people she has killed throughout her lifetimes. She tells him, "Every day I think of more. Being bad—being bad drowned that out. I didn't know I even knew their names."[62] Her tears hold truth. It could be a mistake to assume she has softened compared to previous Masters simply because she has become a woman. It may be the other way around: The villain becomes a woman because womanhood symbolizes (to the Master) qualities that the sexist villain consciously resists, the inner self she is ready to explore. Missy's immediate predecessor is not the only misogynistic Master. When mortally wounded by his assistant Chantho and about to regenerate, the Professor Yana version expresses disgust: "Killed by an insect. A girl! How inappropriate."[63] In point of fact, the Master is repeatedly shown getting killed by women, Masters, or both.[64]

In any societal *system* (structure of concepts and elements organized to serve a function and provide a framework under which the society operates, a connection between two or more entities),[65] rules maintain the system's stability like chair legs stabilize a person's seat. Stability in this sense does not mean mentally stable and does not inherently mean good or bad, but instead refers to consistency and durability of the structure. When change occurs, one person may feel it threatens the stability where another sees how change might make it stronger overall. Where one finds comfort in stability, another sees stagnation. Rejecting change, some *Doctor Who* viewers will perceive changes like having a female or non-White Doctor as imperiling the system. Adapting to change, others perceive change as necessary to keep the story vital, energized, and alive. On planet Earth, stereotypical views that see masculinity as the opposite of femininity— indicative of the "opposite sex" and not simply "other sex" or "different sex"—promote "four basic rules of manhood":[66]

> Assertively, even aggressively, pursue goals and do whatever it takes to reach them.
> Relentlessly repudiate femininity: Reject feminine qualities in oneself and disdain them in others.
> Be the provider.
> Be reliable during crises.

Although (or perhaps because) the Master does not have the kind of interpersonal relationships that would fulfill the last two, he defines himself by the first and demonstrates the second when he repudiates signs of his future self's femininity. He does not mind the idea of the physical sex change (in fact, he finds himself sexually attracted to Missy) but sneers at the possibility of developing a "softer side." The Twelfth Doctor, on the other hand, feels they can each benefit by letting go of masculine preconceptions. After all, the Doctor and Master have always been ones to rebel against static systems.

Even though the Thirteenth Doctor immediately calls the gender change "brilliant"[67] and welcomes the female identity, she does not immediately think of herself as a woman in her self-concept. Is that why she always calls herself a Time Lord, never Time Lady, or is *Time Lord* simply a gender-neutral term in her mind? Other Gallifreyan women such as the

Fugitive Doctor's adversary Gat will also say "Time Lord."[68] The Fugitive herself, regardless of carrying herself with the confidence and authority stereotypically accepted as part of a masculine gender role, fully considers herself woman.

Perhaps the Thirteenth Doctor's transition is why the TARDIS determines that the time has come for her to find out about the Fugitive Doctor, to learn she has not always been a man. The TARDIS could transport any incarnation of the Doctor to the moment when Judoon invade the town of Gloucester, could have taken the Third, Fourth, or Fifth there long ago, but as the TARDIS itself (herself) once points out, it always takes the Doctor "where you needed to go."[69] As the Twelfth Doctor senses, the Doctor needs to venture into a not-so-masculine direction.

Psychology grew out of two parent disciplines when early researchers applied physiology's methods to some of philosophy's questions, but usually not the question of free will. As modern psychological science shows how one brain part after another determines both conscious and unconscious behavior, can a scientist leave room for the possibility of free will?

19

The Doctor's Brain and the Power of Choice: Regeneration, Determinism, and Free Will

David Kyle Johnson & Travis Langley

> "So, free will is not an illusion after all."
> —Third Doctor (Jon Pertwee)[1]

"We must believe in free will. We have no choice."
—author Isaac Bashevis Singer[2]

 An alien race known as the Monks, though deadly, lock the Twelfth Doctor away and quietly take over the Earth through mind control. After the Doctor deprograms his human guards, he recruits his student and friend Bill Potts to join their rebellion, but first has to make sure Bill is not under their control. While he pretends to be under their control to test her, he praises conquerors, to Bill's dismay.

Twelfth Doctor (Peter Capaldi): The Romans killed people and saved billions more from disease, war, famine, and barbarism.

Bill Potts (Pearl Mackie): No, wait. What about free will? You believe in free will. Your whole thing is— You made me write a
three-thousand-word essay on free will.

Doctor: Yes, well, I mean you had free will, and look what you
did with it.[3]

Despite this ruse, the Twelfth Doctor does value freedom of choice.
After they free the world from the Monks' six-month domination, he
reminds Bill of the homework assignment she never delivered: "Three
thousand words, *The Mechanics of Free Will.* Now six months overdue."
He still wants her to contemplate the *how* of free will.

Most areas of psychology shy away from the classic philosophical
debate over *free will versus determinism:* Do we have free will or are our
personality and actions determined by myriad influences? *Existential
psychologists,* who look at the reasons we ask who we are and why we ask
why, criticize other areas of psychology for being too deterministic, for
failing to consider free will.[4] The Doctor repeatedly opposes tyrants and
others who would deprive people of their ability to choose (*free will*),
but he does wonder if external forces determine which choices they'll
make (*determinism*).[5] Growing out of *existentialism* or *existential philosophy,* existential psychology is one of psychology's more philosophically
oriented areas. Before adopting methods from physiology, the broader
field of psychology itself began as a topic within philosophy, a topic
exploring the nature of the mind and questions like whether free will
even exists.[6]

Physiological psychology continues to study relationships between
physiology and mental processes, identifying many biological influences on behavior. When a drug unknowingly ingested can render
someone suggestible and impair memory[7] or a spike through the brain
can turn a calm, responsible person into one who is emotional and
uncontrollable,[8] how much choice do the people experiencing each
of these events have? When regeneration turns the Doctor erratic[9] or
even aggressive[10] and when the changes are so striking that the Doctor's in-fiction companions[11] or real-world TV viewers wonder if the
character is really the Doctor at all,[12] how much choice does the Time

Lord have? If the Doctor's actions are somehow the result of physical changes to the body, including brain, is the character really free? Does the Doctor have free will? Do we? As in many areas in psychology, physiological psychology and the related modern area of *neuroscience* (which focuses on the nervous system) whittle away at the arguments that favor free will by revealing one variable after another that might determine who we are and what we do.

The Cortical Vortex

Throughout *Doctor Who* stories, villains repeatedly manipulate brains in order to alter people's natures. Perhaps most notably, full Cyber-conversion deactivates parts of the brain that regulate empathy, emotions, and sense of personal identity to turn them into Cybermen. Some whose conversions are not completed retain enough humanity to assert themselves, such as when the converted Brigadier saves his daughter Kate from an exploding plane or another leads an army of other Cybermen to self-destruct and save the human race.[13] When a companion to the Doctor gets converted into the earliest model of Mondasian Cyberman, those parts of her brain (and tear ducts) clearly remain because she weeps for what she has lost and fights by the Doctor's side against fully-converted Cybermen.[14]

Although the idea that mentality is directly related to the brain goes back as far as the ancient Greek Pythagorean Alcmaeon of Croton,[15] it wasn't until the modern day that this fact became widely accepted. Arguably, one of the most important cases to help establish this idea was the case of Phineas Gage, a railroad foreman who suffered a traumatic accident in 1848 when an explosion gone wrong drove a tamping iron through his head. The resulting destruction of part of his forebrain changed his personality, something that would not have been possible were his psychological makeup not a product of his brain.[16] We see something similar when the Doctor changes. As another Time Lord says about the Doctor's regeneration from Third to Fourth: "It will shake up the brain cells a little."[17] In a way, each time the Doctor regenerates, it's as if tamping irons were flying through his skull.

Although Gage eventually partially recovered and the effects of his injury may have been exaggerated, his case nevertheless sent science down a path of discovery that revealed a direct dependence of the mind on the brain. Seeing how specific injuries affected people revealed much about which parts and pathways in the brain played roles in specific aspects of human mentality.

Emotional Responses

Every distinct emotional reaction depends on specific brain areas. Trying to reassure a frightened child, the Twelfth Doctor explains fear in terms of uncontrollable physiological response: "So much blood and oxygen pumping through your brain, it's like rocket fuel. Right now, you can run faster and you can fight harder, you can jump higher than ever in your life. And you are so alert, it's like you can slow down time. What's wrong with scared? Scared is a superpower."[18] When he calls fear a superpower, empirical evidence would suggest that he refers to the power of the brain's *amygdala* to help us recognize danger, the *hypothalamus* to activate relevant feelings and drives, and the *pituitary gland* to trigger the release of hormones that help us take action.[19]

A young man terrified by ventriloquist dummies laughs uncontrollably in a mysterious hotel where the Eleventh Doctor and others must face their greatest fears.[20] Laughing in the face of death can help a person manage fear, but those rare people who have literally laughed themselves to death (usually through asphyxiation or cardiac arrest[21]) have taught us that laughter is not a fully voluntary function. It results from activity of a series of brain regions that run through the cerebral cortex, now known as the "laughter circuit."[22]

Motor Control

Much as we might like to think we consciously control our own physical actions, we often do not. When we realize we've been humming or tapping fingers for a bit without awareness, we glimpse the control that nonverbal, perhaps subconscious, parts of the brain might have.

When the Eleventh Doctor struggles against the Cyber-Planner "Mr. Clever" for control of the Doctor's body,[23] some of his behavior is reminiscent of that shown by *split-brain patients*, people whose brain hemispheres have been separated through injury, surgery (sometimes done to treat grand mal seizures), or certain neural disorders.[24] The Doctor cannot keep his own hand from seizing an object and destroying it. "He's got control of the left arm," he says, referring to the Cyber-Planner in his head. Split-brain patients often suffer from something similar called *alien hand syndrome,* in which one side of the body acts on its own and is not under "their" control—that is, not consciously controlled by the verbal left hemisphere, but instead directed by the largely nonverbal right hemisphere. In one real-life case, a man had trouble getting dressed every morning because as soon as one hand would button his shirt, his other would unbutton it. Another young patient's left hemisphere responded to questions by indicating that he wanted to be a draftsman when he got older, while the right wanted to be a race-car driver. When resisting the Cyber-Planner, the Doctor's struggle while of two minds is realistic. Despite the Cyber-Planner's effort, the Doctor clings to his power of personal choice.

Memory

How the brain's neurons are wired and fire can direct how we act. So if regeneration makes the Doctor act differently, it's likely to some degree because regeneration rewires the brain. A partial reorganization of neurons could explain not only the memory loss that sometimes accompanies regeneration but also the attitude and personality adjustments that come with it. Neural death will damage memory, possibly beyond repair. Oxygen deprivation causes cells to degenerate rapidly. This may be why the Eighth Doctor suffers the most severe post-regeneration amnesia: because the Seventh Doctor lies in a hospital morgue for hours—seemingly dead, unbreathing and therefore deprived of oxygen—before regenerating into the Eighth.[25]

Starting with the Second Doctor,[26] most Doctors experience partial but temporary amnesia after regenerating. For hours, the Thirteenth cannot remember that she is the Doctor (nor recall the word *tongue*).[27] Post-regeneration amnesia is typically brief, but what makes the Doctor lose older memories here and there? When the Doctor forgets things over the years, it would be difficult know the extent to which such loss results from psychological or biological causes. Sometimes the Doctor chooses to forget, which would be psychological whether done consciously (*suppression*) or unconsciously (*repression*).[28] Some forgetting will be biological in origin, though. Regeneration may wipe a random memory like a magnet erases a computer disk, or it may rearrange synaptic connections, rendering the memory inaccessible for the time being like a computer file that has been supposedly erased yet is still recoverable. Regeneration alone is not the only biological process that may cause forgetting, though, as head injuries may occur between regenerations or the Doctor's brain simply loses some things over time like any other brain will.

The Third Doctor's case differs in that he suffers more persistent, long-term memory loss. At first, he spends most of his time immediately post-regeneration sleeping in a hospital bed. His disorientation and erratic behavior when awake make a physician, who does know the patient's alien nature, ponder, "I wonder if the brain's damaged." Once the Doctor is up and about, the Brigadier has questions. The Doctor dismisses them, though, saying, "My dear Brigadier, it's no earthly good asking me a lot of questions. I've lost my memory, you see?"[29] He cannot even recall the previous evening. His memory loss persists because the Time Lords, when forcing the previous Doctor to regenerate into this one, blocked access to much of his own knowledge. Even though real-world medical technology is not yet advanced enough to target and block selected knowledge for controlled periods of time, there are drugs, magnetic fields, and other phenomena that can interfere with our ability to access memories of various kinds—sometimes permanently, sometimes briefly, and sometimes temporarily yet slow to return.[30] Even the advanced Gallifreyans lack perfect ability to determine what the Doctor does and does not remember. Brains vary, after all, between individuals and—for them—between regenerations. His own mention of aliens who "communicate with their eyebrows" surprises the Doctor himself. "Well, that's strange. How on Earth did I remember that?"[31] Amnesia patients have been known to surprise themselves with what they do remember.

Recognition

And then there is Oliver Sacks's famous man who mistook his wife for a hat. A tumor made parts of his mentality wither away gradually, which often included the symptom of mistaking inanimate objects for animated ones—parking meters for children, his shoe for his foot, and (of course) his wife for his hat.[32] The man did not choose to make those mistakes any more than the Twelfth Doctor chooses to suffer some degree of *prosopagnosia*, difficulty or inability to recognize faces or tell two faces apart even when motivated to do so. In one instance, he asks if he is speaking to the same people he was with mere moments before, because the Twelfth Doctor cannot recognize any of them after a few minutes.[33] Prosopagnosia can result from brain injury, but about 2 percent of people are actually born with some level of the disorder. Sacks was a sufferer himself. Studies suggest that a malfunction of the *fusiform gyrus* (located in the brain's occipital and temporal lobes) is the culprit.[34] Thus, regenerating into the Twelfth Doctor (supposedly his first regeneration of a new cycle, after he should have run out of regenerations[35]) apparently damages his fusiform gyrus.

Concern

The Sixth and Twelfth Doctors may show the greatest difficulty feeling empathy toward others. In general, *antisocial personality disorder* and *psychopathy*—personality conditions involving extreme violations of others' rights, along with lack of empathy or other emotional aspects of a conscience[36]—could possibly be caused by anything from hormone and neurotransmitter imbalances to environmental and cultural influences. The fact that both the Sixth and Twelfth Doctors become some of the greatest fighters for justice would argue against true antisocial or psychopathic qualities. Individuals on the *autism spectrum* may be mistaken for psychopaths due to their differences in how they feel, express their feelings, and relate to others.[37] The Twelfth Doctor, in particular, starts off showing more autistic-seeming traits.

A rewiring of the Doctor's *prefrontal cortex*, which houses some of our ability to make moral decisions, might be to blame. If that area in any Doctor's brain is damaged or rewired during regeneration, they may have lost their ability to make moral decisions that show concern for others, much like how *traumatic brain injury* can result in difficulties processing emotions and make some head injury victims look like psychopaths in their lack of empathy.[38] *Transcranial magnetic stimulation,* using a magnetic field outside the cranium to manipulate the brain inside, can stimulate or inhibit neural activity, with effects that include either enhancing or inhibiting empathy and altering moral judgments, depending on how and where it is applied.[39]

Indeed, an inability to keep the *limbic system* (a set of brain regions responsible for motivation and emotion) in check is why babies and toddlers are so emotional and selfish. The connections running from their prefrontal cortex to their limbic system have not yet developed, letting the impulses and emotions that their limbic system generates essentially rule them. It is only through practice that such connections grow, which perhaps explains how the Sixth and Twelfth Doctors each show more concern for others as time wears on.

It's also possible that the Sixth or Twelfth Doctor's diminished regard for others stems from an inability to sympathize with them. If so, then perhaps their *mirror neurons,* nerve cells that fire in sympathy with what we observe in others,[40] are damaged during regeneration. When one person witnesses another performing a task, some of the neurons in the witness's brain will fire as if actually performing the task instead of merely observing, mirroring the same way they may be firing in the task performer's own brain.[41] By making the brain mimic what another person's brain might experience when experiencing different emotions, mirror neurons appear to mediate empathy.[42] If the Doctor's mirror neurons heal improperly during regeneration, like scar tissue that looks worse when cells poorly reconnect, his ability to empathize may be impaired as well.[43]

The Twelfth Doctor's growing concern that people need to show kindness may play a part in why he then regenerates into the kinder Thirteenth Doctor. The Time Lord chooses to be kind.[44]

Hidden Purpose

Repeating the same actions when circumstances are the same suggests that environment determines behavior. When the Twelfth Doctor spends billions of years stuck in a castle repeating the same behavior over and over (as he keeps reliving the same few days without remembering that he has done all these things many times before) rather than reveal a secret other Time Lords want from him, does he have any free will at all?[45] The aforementioned determinism to which the existential psychologists objected suggests that our actions are determined by specific causes. The same circumstances surrounding him and characteristics in him lead the Doctor to repeat the same set of actions, determining the outcome every time. If he truly has free will, shouldn't his journey through the castle vary?

Sublimely Subliminal

Subliminal stimuli, details that our brains detect on some level but without our conscious awareness, will influence emotions and actions, although not as powerfully as many people believe. For example, research participants in numerous studies have expressed preference for images shown to them too quickly for them to realize they'd seen them[46] or too scrambled for them to know consciously what they were viewing.[47] These tendencies are so weak, though, that it's generally more effective to present stimuli clearly enough that people can recognize them outright.[48]

When the Silence give people commands that they follow even after they forget they've seen the Silence, these commands are technically not subliminal because the witnesses are consciously aware during the initial experience, and yet they function in subliminal ways because people forget where these desires come from.[49] A more apt analogy might be *posthypnotic suggestion,* giving someone the idea to follow a command after a session of hypnosis. Again, though, evidence indicates that hypnosis is not as powerful in the real world as it is within fiction.[50] Whether it's the Master controlling Jo Grant through hypnosis[51] or the Tenth Doctor using hypnosis to calm the Globe Theatre's architect,[52] both Gallifreyan hypnotists demonstrate control beyond the scope of human practitioners. Note, though, that Gallifreyan psionic ability may boost those effects beyond the scope of earthly hypnosis.

The Doctor knows the limits of hypnosis, as mentioned earlier. When the Sycorax make two billion people climb to dangerous heights and threaten to make those people leap to their deaths, the Tenth Doctor calls their bluff and proves that they cannot make them jump.[53]

Quantum Choice

The brain is responsible for mentality, the brain produces actions, and the brain remains a vast mystery—in these ways, the Doctor is not unlike us. The way regeneration alters the Time Lord's brain and even DNA likely accounts for changes of personality, just as physiological changes can alter us too. The most random-seeming changes that happen to us may really depend on choices we make, whether we know it or not. Changes that occur to Time Lords via regeneration are not completely random either. The Second Doctor gets the chance to choose his next face, the Eighth Doctor decides to transform into a warrior,[54] the Eleventh Doctor unconsciously selects the Twelfth Doctor's face as a reminder to save people,[55] and the Twelfth Doctor's concerns over gender bias may determine where the next regeneration takes the Thirteenth Doctor's biological sex.[56]

It seems that free will can be neither proven nor disproven. Studies on the variables that influence or cause behavior reveal many patterns by looking at trends, while nevertheless failing to explain every exception. Empirical research cannot prove the *null hypothesis*, the idea that a possible cause exerts no influence in any way whatsoever, and likewise cannot prove absence of any causality. The Third Doctor decides that free will does exist after all, not because of abstract philosophical debate but because of the way he interprets visible evidence after seeing how different a parallel universe's inhabitants can become. Given "an infinity of universes—ergo an infinite number of choices," he decides, "the pattern can be changed." Without free will, each parallel person and event would turn out the same in every reality.[57]

The Doctor chooses to run. The Doctor chooses to help people and to help others find reasons to make better choices of their own.

"The last of the human freedoms—to choose one's attitude in any given set of circumstances, to choose one's own way."
—psychiatrist Viktor Frankl[58]

"People can save planets or wreck them.
That's the choice: Be the best of humanity, or—"
—Thirteenth Doctor (Jodie Whittaker)[59]

David Kyle Johnson, PhD, is a professor of philosophy at King's College and professor for The Great Courses. In addition to authoring *The Myths That Stole Christmas,* he blogs for *Psychology Today,* has written and edited extensively for Wiley-Blackwell's Philosophy and Popular Culture series, and has published in journals such as *Religious Studies, Sophia, Philo, Think,* and *Science, Religion, and Culture* regarding metaphysics and philosophy of religion.

Travis Langley's bio appears at the beginning of this book.

Sometimes even the Doctor finds

himself the long way around. . .

20

The Time Lord Who Returns: An Interview with the First Modern Doctor

Aaron Sagers & Travis Langley

"It won't be quiet, it won't be safe, and it won't be calm,
but I tell you what it will be: Trip of a lifetime."
—**Ninth Doctor (Christopher Eccleston)**[1]

When the *Doctor Who* program returned in 2005 under showrunner Russell T. Davies, the Ninth Doctor arrived in the form of actor Christopher Eccleston. A war-torn loner, this Doctor believes himself the last of the Time Lords. He has lost his people and his home. Even if the classic Doctors rarely visit Gallifrey, the character had always taken comfort in knowing the homeworld was still there. Perhaps it is because he has lost everyone that the Ninth Doctor seems more human than ever before—more emotional, more affectionate, more worried. Doctor number nine behaves and dresses with less eccentricity. Clad in leather jacket and dark colors, this Doctor blends into the crowd when walking a London or Cardiff street.

For years after leaving the series, Eccleston kept his distance from new *Who*. Eccleston wished the next showrunner, Steven Moffat, well and regarded Moffat's Ninth Doctor scripts highly. When planning *Doctor Who*'s fiftieth anniversary, though, Moffat had to create the War Doctor to complete the anniversary story because Eccleston simply did not yet feel comfortable stepping back into *Doctor Who* to play the

Ninth Doctor again. Meeting fans through conventions and hearing how much his portrayal moved them helped Eccleston heal, and so, in 2020, Big Finish Productions announced his return to the role for *The Ninth Doctor Adventures* audio dramas.[2] After fifteen years, Christopher Eccleston found it "exciting to revisit the Ninth Doctor's world, bringing back to life a character I love playing."[3] Even though returning had not felt right by *Doctor Who*'s fiftieth anniversary, he would be back by the sixtieth.[4]

Doctor Who returned with Chris Eccleston. In time, Eccleston returned to *Doctor Who*.

While working on this book's first edition, journalist Aaron Sagers interviewed *Doctor Who* stars both classic and modern for earlier chapters. For this edition, he asked Eccleston our questions about the enduring character.

The Character

Aaron Sagers: When you were developing your approach to the character, did you view the Doctor as an extravert or as an introvert who plays extraverted? How did you strike the balance between the light-heartedness and fun, and the depth?

Christopher Eccleston (Ninth Doctor): The Doctor is mercurial and charismatic, and you have to have the ability when playing the role to switch very quickly between the two.

My first thought when playing it was—because I was seen as such a miserable sod before I played Doctor Who—was I could play the loneliness of him. He is undoubtedly damaged. He's the one remaining Time Lord. He is never at home. He has fallen through time. I knew I could do that. That was my first way in. I guess that locates him as an introvert. I think the BBC and everyone who cast me were very concerned I'd play it as Hamlet. So they handed me these farting aliens and said to handle this as well.[5] Actually I enjoyed doing that.

Sagers: The Doctor is almost a Shakespearean character, especially your regeneration. He has lost everything. This seemed like a character who has experienced PTSD. Was that something you actively thought through?

Eccleston: I certainly located it. At some point, I remember thinking he's a Time Lord, he's never at home. There must be a loneliness to him, a tragedy to him. I think I was known as somebody who could do misery. So maybe some of my innate sadness was used by Russell T. Davies.

He was running from himself. He was running from the tragedy. I think that's true of all the Doctors, actually. He is a victim. Gallifrey has been destroyed. He doesn't have a home. You can't overplay that, but it's nice to have a home.

Sagers: Your favorite part about the Doctor's personality and emotion?

Eccleston: I was going to say his wit, but what I love about the character is his empathy. He has more empathy because he has two hearts. And he has an unfailing devotion to humans, which he calls "stupid apes,"[6] but it was his empathy and his love of us, because we need it. Because we don't always show it to each other. He's showing us how to behave. What's that quote? "In nine hundred years of time and space, I've never met anybody who wasn't important."[7] That'll do for me. That'll do for a tattoo. Every single one of us is important.

Sagers: Because he's lost everyone, is he more empathetic?

Eccleston: Yes. Failure is the best teacher. Tragedy deepens our humanity. Hopefully.

Sagers: When you play a military man or a preacher, these are characters we can relate to. As an actor, how did you get inside the head of a character so unlike us, who has not existed in our realm?

Eccleston: I have always been led by my writers. In drama school, I was trained on Shakespeare, Arthur Miller, Tennessee Williams, Chekhov, and Ibsen. Russell T. Davies, who was the showrunner and writer of the series I did, had done all that. He was a long-time fan of the show, watched it since he was a child. He gave me that. And I based it somewhat on Russell and some other people I know.

Sagers: Have you approached the Doctor differently in the Big Finish productions? Is he a different type of Doctor?

Eccleston: No. I have always been an actor who is led by the writers, and what's impressive about Big Finish is how well the writers have captured the character and the voice of the Ninth Doctor, because none of them have written for the TV series. For me, it's exactly the same, and exactly the same feeling, energy, wit, and heroism.

The problem we've had with the audio recordings is I'm a very physical actor. In audio recordings you're supposed to keep still so you don't rattle the buttons. I'm going to record in October in a straitjacket so I don't do that.

Favorite Scenes

Sagers: What was your favorite scene to play in *Doctor Who*?

Eccleston: I loved all the interactions with Billie. I didn't realize how special it was at the time. We were just doing our job, but people fastened on the connection we had. I loved taking that Dalek home. I knew when it was just me and that chained Dalek in the room, I was taking back television history.[8] I wanted to do something slightly different with it. It was a bit of a contemporary take, I was a bit like a football hooligan with the Dalek, wasn't I? And I loved "Are you my mummy?"[9] I knew we had something very special with those kids in gas masks. I knew my job for the children watching it was, yes, to be scared as the Doctor. But I knew I had to just hint that he was scared but enjoying himself. I knew if I did that, the kids would come along with me. I knew the adults would be terrified but keep the kids watching . . . The whole concept of it was rooted in something very real, the terror of the blitz, and the Second World War—something we knew was real and lodged in the British consciousness. The fact that the children were the enemy was a great twist, because I knew kids would love that. It kind of empowers them because they are terrifying the adults.

Sagers: Tell us about your reaction to the line from "The Doctor Dances" [part two of the aforementioned blitz story], "Everybody lives, Rose. Just this once."[10]

Eccleston: You saw right into the heart of the character when he said that. He's haunted by the tragedy of the destruction of his own race, by the destruction of his own planet. And it's almost like he's always trying to make amends for that. He knows whenever he's thwarted the Daleks, *before* he's thwarted the Daleks, they've already killed a couple thousand. And on that day, everybody lives. That's the very heart of him. He wants to save everybody.

The Love

Sagers: What was a lesson you learned by being the Doctor?

Eccleston: This show is enormously important to people. I've analyzed it, and the Doctor is an outsider. He's among us but he's apart from us. There's points in our lives where we feel like that. *Doctor Who* had a massive fanbase among the gay community in the UK, for instance. At the time *Doctor Who* was [originally] broadcast, they were criminalized. So there is great identification there. Minority groups attached themselves to him because he is unfailingly heroic and empathetic. And I have understood that since playing the role. I can see the significance . . . It's really nice to be associated with the depth of his humanity, even though he's an alien.

Sagers: Why might the Doctor rank as one of your favorite roles?

Eccleston: You know about the whole business around me leaving. But what I've realized is you never stop being the Doctor, even if you stop playing him. There is a huge amount of love towards me. My kids have witnessed that. We've been stopped in the street. Actually my son said to me a few years ago, "Someone came up to me and said 'Your dad is the best Doctor.'" He was about five, and said, "Does that mean you're good about making people feel better?"

> "Before you go, I just want to tell you: You were fantastic. Absolutely fantastic. And you know what? So was I!"
> —**Ninth Doctor (Christopher Eccleston)**[11]

Bio for Aaron Sagers appears in chapter 1. Travis Langley's appears at the beginning of this book.

Final Word:

Run!

Travis Langley

"Seriously, there's an outrageous amount of running involved."
—Donna Noble (Catherine Tate), while companion to the Tenth Doctor[1]

"When I started running, I started dreaming."
—author/marathon runner Bart Yasso[2]

We run through the moments in our lives. What we run to, from, or for may define us, and so might people we run with on our way through those moments—the *why* and *when* and *with whom* of what we do all play parts in defining who we are. The First Doctor runs away from Gallifrey with his granddaughter, and the Second Doctor then becomes known for telling his companions, "When I say run, run. Run!"[3] When the modern series comes along, the Ninth Doctor first appears by grabbing Rose Tyler's hand and saying, "Run!" The running never really stops. Even when we sit so still that time seemingly slows down, a clock ticks somewhere and time keeps running forward.

We've filled a book about the Doctor and companions. Some foes have come up, too, but they could fill volumes of their own. *Dalek Psychology: To Exterminate or Not to Exterminate* perhaps? We've explored a variety of topics herein—compassion, companionship, morality, mortality, and more—and they've all tied into issues of *personality*, that psychological term for who each person is over time. "Who?" It's part of the first question for the Doctor[4] and possibly the first question to distinguish *sentience* in human beings, a kind of subjectivity and self-awareness[5] distinct from thinking processes demonstrated by other living creatures. The question itself might define us more than any answer will. Who the Doctor is keeps changing—not only between regenerations but within each specific Doctor's time. To live instead of being stagnant requires change. We relate to this perhaps because we keep changing throughout our own lives. Change is story.

We run through our memories. Some get lost along the way, and all memories change. Memory is a reconstruction.[6] It's not a perfectly accurate record of what happened but instead a re-creation, omitting details that were never stored, dropping details over time, changing colors and other cues, and shifting to fit our evolving understanding of our own recollections. We don't simply retrieve them. We reweave them every time. Memory is story.

"Every story ever told really happened," the Twelfth Doctor tells Clara. "Stories are where memories go when they're forgotten."[7] In a sense, a fictional event is something that did not happen, and yet those fictions did not spring out of nowhere. Every fiction's creation is itself an event. The Doctor's memories are unreliable (like when the name of the Great Intelligence only "rings a bell,"[8] as one example among many) and so are ours.[9] At times, a reconsolidated memory or outright fiction wields more power than original fact.[10]

The story of *Doctor Who* keeps changing and the program keeps running. Even when it went off the air, the story continued as, among other things, the tale of fans who kept wishing it would come back. Fans become part of the story—as represented by the Doctor's ultimate fan, Petronella Osgood.[11] Interacting with the Doctor and relating to different regenerations over time thus changes her and changes the Time Lord a bit as well.[12] The Doctor's stories move us, but we move them too. *Doctor Who* originally ran for more than a quarter of a century because of its fans, it returned in 2005 because fans wanted it back, and it keeps going because fans remain part of its story.

We run with the Doctor. The Doctor runs with us—and for us. That's who the Doctor is.

"We're all stories, in the end. Just make it a good one, eh?
Cause it was, you know. It was the best!"
—Eleventh Doctor (Matt Smith)[13]

"We tell ourselves stories in order to live."
—author Joan Didion[14]

"I think we're going to be here quite some time."
—Jo Jones, née Grant, companion to the Third Doctor,
speaking to other companions[15]

Notes

Throughout these notes, episodes from the classic series (1963-1989) are identified by italicized serial titles. Those from the modern program (2005 onward) are identified by episode titles in quotations. Dates also distinguish classic from modern.

Acknowledgments
1. Ellison (1979).

Foreword
1. Serial 10-5, *The Green Death* (19 May–23 June, 1973).
2. Serial 8-1, *Terror of the Autons* (2–23 January, 1971).
3. Serial 8-5, *The Daemons*, pt. 5 (19 June, 1971).
4. All in serial 8-1, *Terror of the Autons* (2–23 January, 1971).
5. Serial 9-1, *Day of the Daleks* (1–22 January, 1972).
6. Serial 8-5, *The Daemons*, pt. 5 (19 June, 1971).
7. Serial 10-5, *The Green Death* (19 May–23 June, 1973).
8. Serial 10-5, *The Green Death* (19 May–23 June, 1973).
9. Serial 10-1, *The Three Doctors* (30 December, 1972–20 January, 1973).
10. *The Sarah Jane Adventures*, episodes 4-5 & 4-6, "Death of the Doctor," pts. 1–2 (25–26 October, 2010).
11. Fifth—*Excelis Dawn* (2002 audio drama). Sixth—*The Wormery* (2003 audio drama).
12. BBC centenary special, "The Power of the Doctor" (23 October, 2022).

Introduction to the First Edition
1. Episode 5-1, "The Eleventh Hour" (3 April, 2010).
2. Jamison (1993), p. 50.

3.   Serial 6-7, *The War Games*, pt. 10 (21, June, 1969); episode 9-11, "Heaven Sent" (28 November, 2015).

4.   Episode 6-4, "The Doctor's Wife" (14 May, 2011).

5.   Szasz (1960, 1973, 2007).

6.   Eshun & Gurung (2009); Sue & Sue (2016).

7.   For example, anniversary special, "The Day of the Doctor" (23 November, 2013); episode 9-12, "Hell Bent" (5 December, 2015).

8.   Ross & Anderson (1982).

9.   "Talk very fast, hope something good happens, take the credit. That's generally how it happens."—Eleventh Doctor in Christmas special, "The Time of the Doctor" (25 December, 2013).

10.   Episode 5-1, "The Eleventh Hour" (3 April, 2010).

11.   Kant (1764/2011), quoted by—and often misattributed to—Freud (1900/1965), pp. 121–22.

12.   Serial 25-13, *The Greatest Show in the Galaxy*, pt. 3 (28 December, 1988).

Introduction to the Second Edition

1.   Christmas special, "The Time of the Doctor" (25 December, 2013).

2.   Partly repeating Langley (2014) in this paragraph.

3.   Serial 4-3, *The Power of the Daleks*, pt. 1 (5 November, 1966).

4.   Serial 10-1, *The Three Doctors* (30 December, 1972–20 January, 1973).

5.   In Kistler (2013), p. 17.

6.   Serial 13-5, *The Brain of Morbius* (3–24 January, 1976).

7.   Anniversary special, *The Five Doctors* (23 November, 1983).

8.   Anniversary special, "The Day of the Doctor" (23 November, 2013).

9.   Episode 9-5, "The Girl Who Died" (17 October, 2015).

10.   Episode 12-12, "The Doctor Falls" (1 July, 2017); Christmas special, "Twice Upon a Time" (25 December, 2017).

11.   Episode 12-12, "The Doctor Falls" (1 July, 2017).

12.   Episode 11-1, "The Woman Who Fell to Earth" (7 October, 2018).

13.   Episodes 12-5, "Fugitive of the Judoon" (26 January, 2020); 13-3, *Flux*, chapter 3, "Once, Upon Time" (14 November, 2021).

14.   New Year's special, "The End of Time," pt. 2 (1 January, 2010); anniversary special, "The Day of the Doctor" (23 November, 2013).

15.   Episode 12-5, "Fugitive of the Judoon" (26 January, 2020).

Doctor Who History

1. *Splinters* (2022 audio drama).
2. Minisode, *Night of the Doctor* (November 14, 2013).

Roll Call: Who's Who

1. For ages when filming their first appearances, see McClure (2023).
2. First Doctor—serial 16-1, *The Ribos Operation*, pt. 1 (2 September, 1978). Second—5-1, *Tomb of the Cybermen*, pt. 1 (2 September, 1967). Third—7-2, *Doctor Who and the Silurians*, pt. 6 (7 March, 1970); repeated in 8-2, *The Mind of Evil*, pt. 1 (30 January, 1971). Fourth—quote from serial 13-3, *Pyramids of Mars*, pt. 1 (25 October, 1975); Romana says 759 when he says 756 in 16-1, *The Ribos Operation*, pt. 1 (2 September, 1978); Fourth himself reports ages ranging from 740 to 760 at different times. Fifth—none. Sixth—22-6, *Revelation of the Daleks*, pt. 1 (23 March, 1985); 23-1, *The Trial of a Time Lord: The Mysterious Planet*, pt. 1 (6 September, 1986). Seventh—serial 24-1, *Time and the Rani*, pt. 2 (14 September, 1987). Eighth—*Doctor Who* (1996 TV movie).
3. War Doctor—anniversary special, "The Day of the Doctor" (23 November, 2013). Ninth—episode 1-4, "Aliens of London" (26 April, 2005). Tenth—Christmas special, "Voyage of the Damned" (25 December, 2007). Eleventh—5-5, "Flesh and Stone" (1 May, 2010). Twelfth—8-1, "Deep Breath" (23 August, 2014). Thirteenth—12-5, "Fugitive of the Judoon" (26 January, 2020); repeated in BBC centenary special, "The Power of the Doctor" (23 October, 2022).
4. The fact that her TARDIS looks like a police box suggests she enters the sequence later than the First Doctor. Susan describes other shapes the TARDIS assumed before getting stuck as the blue box—serial 1-1, *An Unearthly Child*, pt. 2, "The Cave of Skulls" (30 November, 1963). Martin's age is confidential. Martin—12-5, "Fugitive of the Judoon" (26 January, 2020). Hurdnall—anniversary special, *The Five Doctors* (23 November, 1983). Bradley—episode 10-12, "The Doctor Falls" (1 July, 2017); Christmas special, "Twice Upon a Time" (25 December, 2017). Dhawan—BBC centenary special, "The Power of the Doctor" (23 October, 2022).
5. Bradley was the first actor to play the Doctor in other ways before appearing as the character in *Doctor Who*—first playing William Hartnell and recreating some *Doctor Who* scenes in *An Adventure in Time and Space* (2013 TV movie), then playing the First Doctor in audio starting with *The Destination Wars* (2018 audio drama).
6. Eight faces (photos of production team members) projected from the Fourth Doctor's mind were presented as incarnations that had preceded the so-called First

Doctor—serial 13-4, pt. 4, *The Brain of Morbius* (24 January, 1976). The Doctor as a boy—Michael Jones in episode 8-4, "Listen" (13 September, 2014). Timeless Child—seven children playing different incarnations in 12-10, "The Timeless Children" (1 March, 2020). Doctor Moon—screenwriter Steven Moffat intended Dr. Moon to be an A.I. copy of the deceased 45th Doctor, reunited with River in a virtual afterlife (Moffat & Davies, 2020). Played by Colin Salmon, Moon first appears in 4-8, "Silence in the Library" (31 May, 2008).

7.   Anniversary special, "The Day of the Doctor" (23 November, 2013).

8.   Watcher—serial 18-7, *Logopolis* (28 February–21 March, 1981). Valeyard—classic season 23, *The Trial of a Time Lord* (6 September–6 December, 1986). Dream Lord—episode 5-7, "Amy's Choice" (15 May, 2010).

9.   Christmas special, "The Husbands of River Song" (25 December, 2015).

I. The Hearts of Who We Are

1.   Serial 1-1, *An Unearthly Child*, pt. 1, "An Unearthly Child" (23 November, 1963).

1. The Who of You: Interview with Four Doctors and a River on the Core of Personality

1.   Serial 19-1, *Castrovalva*, pt. 1 (4 January, 1982).

2.   Allport (1955), p. 12.

3.   Watson (2004); Whitbourne (2001).

4.   Christmas special, "The Time of the Doctor" (25 December, 2013).

5.   Carducci (2009).

6.   Allport (1937).

7.   Allport & Odbert (1936).

8.   Allport (1937).

9.   Dominators—serial 6-1, *The Dominators* (10 August–7 September, 1968). Angel Bob—episodes 5-4, "The Time of Angels" (24 April, 2010); 5-5, "Flesh and Stone" (1 May, 2010).

10. For example, serial 12-4, *Genesis of the Daleks* (8 March–12 April, 1975).

11. American Psychiatric Association (2022).

12. *The Ultimate Time Lord* (2014 documentary).

13. Beginning in serial 6-1, *The Dominators* (10 August–7 September, 1968).

14. Beginning in serial 12-1, *Robot* (28 December, 1974–18 January, 1975).

15. Examples include Sagers (2012a, 2012b, 2014, 2015a, 2015b).

16. Sagers (2013).

17. *The Ultimate Time Lord* (2014 documentary).

18. For example, Grafman et al. (1996); Young et al. (2010).

19. Reid (1785); Roediger (1993); Salovey & Mayer (1990).

20. Allison & Goethals (2011).

21. Greitemeyer (2022).

22. Hamlen & Imbesi (2020); Mubarak & Ferguson (2022).

23. Du et al. (2022).

24. Hong & Lin-Siegler (2012).

25. SyFy (2018).

26. Chhaochharia et al. (2022); Doni (2021); Gillooly et al. (2021); Gladding & Villalba (2014); Merritt et al. (2021); Midgley et al. (2021).

27. Ainsworth (2010); Crane et al. (2022); Gates (2022).

28. Wernick et al. (2021).

29. Ahn et al. (2016); Hu et al. (2020).

2. Love on Board a Big Blue Box

1. Christmas special, "The Husbands of River Song" (25 December, 2015).

2. Winfrey (2000).

3. Eleventh Doctor to TARDIS: "Thanks, dear. Miss out the metal dog, why don't you?" Minisode, *Meanwhile in the TARDIS*, scene 2 (8 November, 2010).

4. Serial 17-2, *City of Death*, pt. 2 (6 October, 1979).

5. Episode 8-1, "Deep Breath" (23 August, 2014).

6. Christmas special, "The Husbands of River Song" (25 December, 2015).

7. Baird (2020); King (2018).

8. Episode 8-1, "Deep Breath" (23 August, 2014).

9. Episodes 8-4, "Listen" (13 September, 2014); 7-13, "The Name of the Doctor" (18, May, 2013).

10. Episode 2-4, "The Girl in the Fireplace" (6 May, 2006).

11. Burr et al. (2020); Ejlskov et al. (2020).

12. Christmas special, "Twice Upon a Time" (25 December, 2017).

13. Hadoke (2017).

14. Christmas special, "The Time of the Doctor" (25 December, 2013).

15. Episode 8-12, "Death in Heaven" (8 November, 2014).

16. Patience, one nickname for the Doctor's first wife—Parkin (1996). "Rubbish" quote—episode 3-10, "Blink" (9 January, 2007).

17. Serial 5-1, *Tomb of the Cybermen*, pt. 3 (16 September, 1967). Episodes 1-9, "The Empty Child" (21 May, 2005); 2-7, "Fear Her" (24 June, 2006).

18. Boelen et al. (2019).

19. Gilbert & Ho (2021); Ship (2023).

20. Held et al. (2011; 2015); Pugh et al. (2015)

21. Wegner (1989).

22. Episode 6-4, "The Doctor's Wife" (14 May, 2011).

23. Serial 1-1, *An Unearthly Child*, pt. 1, "An Unearthly Child" (23 November, 1963); 3-10, *The War Machines*, pt. 4 (16 July, 1966).

24. Serial 3-2, *The Edge of Destruction*, pt. 2, "The Brink of Disaster" (15 February, 1964).

25. After Barbara and Ian return home, for example, he tells Vicki, "I shall miss them."—serial 2-8, *The Chase*, pt. 6, "The Planet of Decision" (26 June, 1965). When Vicki leaves later, he again says after she's gone, "I shall miss you."—serial 3-3, *The Myth Makers*, pt. 4, "Horse of Destruction" (6 November, 1965). The First Doctor does not say those words to any companion when they go. Most Doctors have that problem.

26. For example, Doctor to Steven when Dodo joins: "Don't you think she looks rather like my grandchild Susan?" Steven points out that he has not met Susan. Serial 3-5 *The Massacre (of St. Bartholomew's Eve)*, pt. 4, "Bell of Doom" (26 February, 1966).

27. Serial 3-10, *The War Machines*, pt. 4 (16 July, 1966).

28. Serial 1-6, *The Aztecs* (23 May–13 June, 1963).

29. Shaw—serial 7-1, *Spearhead from Space* (3–24 January, 1970). Grant—8-1, *Terror of the Autons*, pt. 1 (2 January, 1971).

30. Serial 16-1, *The Ribos Operation*, pt. 1 (2 September, 1978).

31. Serial 5-10, *The Green Death*, pt. 6 (23 June, 1973).

32. Serial 13-6, *The Seeds of Doom*, pt. 3 (14 February, 1976).

33. Hatfield (1988); Hirsch (2007).

34. Serial 14-4, *The Face of Evil*, pt. 4 (22 January, 1977).

35. Adric—serial 18-3, pt. 4, *Full Circle* (15 November, 1980). Nyssa and Tegan—18-7, *Logopolis* (28 February–21 March, 1981).

36. Harry—serial 12-1, *Robot* (18 January, 1975). K9 Mark II—15-6, *The Invasion of Time*, pt. 6 (11 March, 1978).

37. WhoLife! (2018).

38. Serial 18-4, *State of Decay*, pt. 3 (6 December, 1980).

39. Bacon (2020). See also "Merry Christmas, Doctor Who," a.k.a. "Doug Who?" (1978, *The Armageddon Factor* bonus feature), in which the Fourth Doctor and first Romana (Tom Baker, Mary Tamm) kiss. Though non-canon, it is the first BBC-produced scene to show the Doctor romantic with a companion.

40. Serial 18-7, *Logopolis*, pt. 1 (28 February, 1981).

41. Serial 20-3, *Mawdryn Undead,* pt. 4 (9 February, 1983).

42. Abandoned—serial 19-7, *Time-Flight,* pt. 4 (30 March, 1982). Returns—20-1, *Arc of Infinity,* pt. 4 (12 January, 1983).

43. Kaufman et al. (2019); Kline & Peters (1991); Monahan & Hood (1976); Studer et al. (2020); Tobias-Webb et al. (2017).

44. Serial 20-6, *The King's Demons,* pt. 2 (16 March, 1983).

45. Serial 21-5, *Planet of Fire,* pt. 4 (2 March, 1984).

46. Serial 24-4, *Dragonfire,* pt. 1 (23 November, 1987).

47. BBC centenary special, "The Power of the Doctor" (23 October, 2022).

48. *Doctor Who* (1996 TV movie).

49. Rice (n.d.).

50. Christmas and New Year's specials, pt. 1 (25 December, 2009), pt. 2 (1 January, 2010), according to Davies & Cook (2010).

51. Flint Rehab (2020); Harrod et al. (1996).

52. Liebrenz et al. (2016); Silverman (2002).

53. Fugitive—episode 12-5, "Fugitive of the Judoon" (26 January, 2020). Tenth—3-9, "The Family of Blood" (2 June, 2007).

54. Minisode, *Night of the Doctor* (14 November, 2013).

55. Anniversary special, "The Day of the Doctor" (23 November, 2013).

56. Need for affiliation—McClelland (1965); Murray (1931). Rootedness—Fromm (1955).

57. Tenth Doctor—Christmas special, "The Christmas Invasion" (25 December, 2006). Eleventh—episode 5-1, "The Eleventh Hour" (3 April, 2010). Twelfth—Christmas special, "Twice Upon a Time" (25 December, 2017).

58. Episode 1-1, "Rose" (26 March, 2005).

59. The Second Doctor and Jamie hold hands once in serial 5-1, *The Tomb of the Cybermen,* pt. 1 (2 September, 1967), but only by mistake when they think they're each holding onto Victoria between them. Actors Patrick Troughton and Frazer Hines devised this unscripted gag without telling the director.

60. Episode 1-13, "The Parting of the Ways" (18 June, 2005).

61. Episode 1-10, "The Doctor Dances" (28 May, 2005).

62. Loses Rose—episode 2-13, "Doomsday" (8 July, 2006). Joan—3-9, "The Family of Blood" (2 June, 2007). Reinette—2-4, "The Girl in the Fireplace" (6 May, 2006). Astrid—Christmas special, "Voyage of the Damned" (25 December, 2007). Elizabeth—anniversary special, "The Day of the Doctor" (23 November, 2013).

63. Modern season 3 (2007).

64. Birtel (2014); Garbo (1977); Krantzler (1977).

65. Episode 2-3, "School Reunion" (29 April, 2006).

66. Hadden et al. (2018).

67. *Doctor Who: The Fan Show* (2018).

68. Episode 2-13, "Doomsday" (8 July, 2006).

69. Episode 4-13, "Journey's End" (5 July, 2008).

70. Episodes 4-4, "The Sontaran Stratagem" (26 April, 2008); 4-13, "Journey's End" (5 July, 2008).

71. Freud (1936); Vaillant (1977).

72. Episode 4-6, "The Doctor's Daughter" (10 May, 2008).

73. Such as episodes 7-2, "Dinosaurs on a Spaceship" (8 September, 2012); 6-7, "A Good Man Goes to War" (4 June, 2011).

74. Christmas special, "The Snowmen" (25 December, 2012).

75. Dancing at the wedding, mentioned in episode 6-8, "Let's Kill Hitler" (27 August, 2011). Despite marrying River in a timeline that ceases to exist, he calls her his wife—episodes 6-13, "The Wedding of River Song" (1 October, 2011); 7-13, "The Name of the Doctor" (18 May, 2013). He disputes the validity of his wedding with Marilyn Monroe—Christmas special, "A Christmas Carol" (25 December, 2010). For one review of all the kissing, see Kirkley (2017).

76. Mulkern (2017). Also Moffat: "Matt's more sexless, more amiable, more disconnected, more alien Doctor" (*Doctor Who: The Fan Show*, 2018).

77. Vastra to Eleventh: "I am trying to be delicate. I know how you can blush. When did this baby begin?" Episode 6-7, "A Good Man Goes to War" (4 June, 2011).

78. Christmas special, "The Time of the Doctor" (25 December, 2013); 8-1, "Deep Breath" (23 August, 2014). Admittedly, the Twelfth Doctor's subsequent attitude toward Danny Pink raises new questions. Is the Doctor's possessiveness regarding Clara passionate, romantic, narcissistic, autistic? (Compare Sheldon Cooper.) Keep in mind that Missy set up this toxic relationship to make mischief.

79. Freud (1936); Vaillant (1977).

80. Episode 6-7, "A Good Man Goes to War" (4 June, 2011).

81. Episode 8-1, "Deep Breath" (23 August, 2014).

82. Twelfth kisses Missy—episode 8-12, "Death in Heaven" (8 November, 2014). Eighth kisses Grace—*Doctor Who* (1996 TV movie).

83. Modern season 10 (2017).

84. "Fam" finally sounds right to her in episode 11-10, "The Battle of Ranskoor Av Kolos" (9 December, 2018). "Extended fam"—BBC centenary special, "The Power of the Doctor" (23 October, 2022).

85. Spring special, "Legend of the Sea Devils" (17 April, 2022).

86. Bogaert (2015); Johnson (2020).

87. Sternberg (1997).

88. Episode 2-3, "School Reunion" (29 April, 2006).

89. Episode 8-11, "Dark Water" (1 November, 2014).

90. Erikson & Erikson (1998).

91. Episode 6-4, "The Doctor's Wife" (14 May, 2011).

92. Serial 1-3, "The Edge of Destruction" (8–15 February, 1964).

93. Fromm (1956), p. 32.

94. Christmas special, "Twice Upon a Time" (25 December, 2017).

95. Neugarten & Weinstein (1964). Borrowing some text in this section from Langley (2018).

96. "In all the years my granddaughter and I have been traveling, we have never had an argument. And now you have caused one."—First Doctor in serial 1-7, *The Sensorites*, pt. 3 (4 July, 1965).

97. Zhao et al. (2011).

98. Hayslip & Glover (2009); Patrick & Goedereis (2009); Wooten Thomas (2010).

3. The Moral Foundations of *Doctor Who*

1. Episode 10-12, "The Doctor Falls" (1 July, 2017).

2. Haidt (2012).

3. Haidt (2012).

4. Haidt (2012).

5. Episode 2-5, "Rise of the Cybermen" (13 May, 2006).

6. Courtland (2006).

7. Haidt (2012).

8. Haidt (2012).

9. Serial 12-15, *Genesis of the Daleks*, pt. 5 (5 April, 1975).

10. Milgram (1974).

11. Serial 12-15, *Genesis of the Daleks*, pt. 5 (5 April, 1975).

12. Fromm (1941, 1973).

13. Gal (1985).

14. Buccafusco & Fagundes (2016); Haidt (2012).

15. Shelton & Hill (1969).

16. Episodes 3-1, "Smith and Jones" (31 March, 2007); 12-5, "Fugitive of the Judoon" (26 January, 2020).

17. Baumeister & Sommer (1997).

18. Boos et al. (2015); Puurtinen et al. (2015).

19. Delvauz et al. (2015); Pierro et al. (2015).

20. Gibson & Condor (2009).

21. Serial 7-2, *Doctor Who and the Silurians*, pt. 1 (31 January, 1970).

22. Episodes 5-8, "The Hungry Earth" (22 May, 2010); 5-9 "Cold Blood" (29 May, 2010).

23. Haidt (2012).

24. Hirai & Vernon (2011).

25. Helwig & Prencipe (1999); Simpson & Laham (2015).

26. Black (2012).

27. Richter (2008).

28. New Year's special, "Revolution of the Daleks" (1 January, 2021).

29. Episode 3-12, "The Sound of Drums" (23 June, 2007).

30. For example, episode 9-2, "The Witch's Familiar" (26 September, 2015).

31. Rachels (1995).

32. All of which the Master demonstrates in serial 18-7, *Logopolis* (28 February—21 March, 1981), and Missy in episode 9-2, "The Witch's Familiar" (26 September, 2015).

33. Zimbardo (2007).

34. Episode 12-10, "The Timeless Children" (1 March, 2020).

35. Serial 12-15, *Genesis of the Daleks*, pt. 5 (5 April, 1975).

36. Busch (2015).

37. American Psychiatric Association (2022).

38. Hare (1994).

39. Anniversary special, *The Five Doctors* (23 November, 1983).

4. Exterminate! The Mentality of a Master Race: Are You a Dalek?

1. Rome Statute of the International Criminal Court, Article 33.2.

2. New Year's special, "Resolution" (1 January, 2019).

3. Episode 9-2, "The Witch's Familiar" (26 September, 2015).

4. New Year's special, "Resolution" (1 January, 2019).

5. Atkinson & Tucker (2021).

6. Janis (1971, 1972).

7. Episode 1-6, "Dalek" (30 April, 2005).

8. Freud (1921); Le Bon (1896); Jung (1959).

9. Festinger et al. (1952).

10. Postmes & Spears (1998).

11. Spears (2017).

12. Myers & Lamm (1975).

13. Serial 4-9, *The Evil of the Daleks* (20 May–1 July, 1967).

14. Schwarz (1995).

15. Reicher (2001).

16. Post & Panis (2011).

17. Bandura (2015).

18. Kelman (1973).

19. Vaes et al. (2012).

20. Newman & Erber (2002).

21. Serial 11-3, *Death to the Daleks* (23 February–16 March, 1974).

22. New Year's special, "Revolution of the Daleks" (1 January, 2021).

23. Singer (2004).

24. New Year's special, "Eve of the Daleks" (1 January, 2022).

25. Episode 1-6, "Dalek" (30 April, 2005).

26. Bignell & O'Day (2004).

27. Williams et al. (2005).

28. Livingston Smith (2012).

29. Episode 8-2, "Into the Dalek" (30 August, 2014).

30. Episode 1-6, "Dalek" (30 April, 2005).

31. Episode 7-1, "Asylum of the Daleks" (1 September, 2012).

5. The Five Factors and Company: Constellations of Personality

1.   Rogers (1961/1995), p. 122).

2.   Serial 21-7, *The Twin Dilemma,* pt. 4 (30 March, 1984).

3.   Allport & Odbert (1936).

4.   Cattell (1943).

5.   *Doctor Who* (1996 TV movie).

6.   Serial 18-2, *Meglos,* pt. 1 (27 September, 1980).

7.   Episode 5-12, "The Pandorica Opens" (19 June, 2010).

8.   Jung (1921).

9.   Loo (1979).

10. Cohen Schmidt (1979).

11. Anniversary special, "The Day of the Doctor" (23 November, 2013); *Only the Monstrous* (2015 audio drama).

12. Eysenck (1947).

13. Hetterna et al. (2006); Spinhoven et al. (2014).

14. Wang et al. (2009); Tmka et al. (2012).

15. For example, Marcus et al. (2007).

16. Anniversary special, "The Day of the Doctor" (23 November, 1983); Christmas and New Year's specials, "The End of Time," pt. 1 (25 December, 2009) and pt. 2 (1 January, 2010).

17. Eysenck (1966).

18. Eysenck (1966).

19. Episode 2-10, "Love & Monsters" (17 June, 2006).

20. Eysenck (1993), p. 155.

21. Episode 5-10, "Vincent and the Doctor" (5 June, 2010).

22. Chowdhury (2008); Ter Borg & Frenité (2012); Viskuil (2013).

23. For example, anniversary special, "The Day of the Doctor" (23 November, 2013).

24. Eysenck & Eysenck (1985).

25. For example, Tupes & Christal (1961).

26. McCrae & Costa (1985).

27. Serial 24-4, *Dragonfire* (3 November–7 December, 1987); episode 4-2, "Fires of Pompeii" (12 April, 2008); serial 23-1, *The Mysterious Planet* (6–27 September, 1986); audio play *Terror Firma* (August, 2005); episode 1-13, "The Parting of the Ways" (18 June, 2005); episode 4-14, "Journey's End" (5 July, 2008); anniversary special, *The Five Doctors* (25 November, 1983); anniversary special, "The Day of the Doctor" (23 November, 2013); serial 4-2, *The Trial of a Time Lord: The Tenth Planet* (8–29 October, 1966); episode 11-2, "The Ghost Monument" (14 October, 2018).

28. Christmas special, "The Doctor, the Widow, and the Wardrobe" (25 December, 2011); episodes 5-1, "The Eleventh Hour" (3 April, 2010); 7-1, "Asylum of the Daleks" (1 September, 2012); 7-6 "The Bells of St. John" (30 March, 2013); 7-12, "Nightmare in Silver" (11 May, 2013).

29. Episode 4-8, "Silence in the Library" (31 May, 2008); Christmas special, "The Husbands of River Song" (25 December, 2015).

30. Goldberg (1982).

31. Fiske (1949); Funder (2001); Goldberg (1982); Tupes & Christal (1961).

32. McCrae & Costa (1987).

33. Eysenck (1992).

34. McCrae & Costa (1987).

35. Episode 1-13, "The Parting of the Ways" (18 June, 2005).

36. Christmas special, "The Time of the Doctor" (25 December, 2013).

37. Serial 3-9, *The Savages*, pt. 1 (28 May, 1966).

38. Serial *Shada*, unfinished due to technicians' strike (scheduled for January–February, 1980); eventually produced as Eighth Doctor audio drama (10 December, 2005) but later animated with the Fourth Doctor, for whom it had been written (2017 animated serial).

39. Serial 19-4, *The Visitation*, pt. 1 (15 February, 1982).

40. Anniversary special, "The Day of the Doctor" (23 November, 2013).

41. Minisode, *The Night of the Doctor* (14 November, 2015).

42. Anniversary special, "The Day of the Doctor" (23 November, 2013).

43. Christmas special, "The Time of the Doctor" (25 December, 2013).

44. Prominent examples include Freud (1909, 1940); Kohlberg (1981); Piaget (1932).

45. Episode 8-2, "Into the Dalek" (20 August, 2014).

46. Episode 6-7, "A Good Man Goes to War" (4 June, 2011).

47. Lee & Ashton (2012).

48. Serial 4-9, *The Evil of the Daleks*, pt. 5 (17 Junes, 1967).

49. Book et al. (2016); Lee & Ashton (2005; 2012); Mededović & Petrović (2015).

50. For example, De Raad et al. (2010).

51. For example, Ashton & Lee (2001).

52. For example, Tellegen & Waller (1994).

53. For example, Jo Grant in serial 8-1, *Terror of the Autons* (2–23 January, 1971); Clara Oswald in episode 8-11, "Dark Water" (1 November, 2014).

54. The Master kills Chang Lee in *Doctor Who* (1996 TV movie), although the TARDIS revives Lee; kills Chantho in episode 3-11, "Utopia" (16 June, 2007); kills Lucy Saxon in Christmas special, "The End of Time," pt. 1 (25 December, 2009); and decides to kill Yaz but fails in BBC centenary special, "The Power of the Doctor" (23 October, 2022).

55. Episode 12-12, "The Doctor Falls" (1 July, 2017).

56. Tellegen (1993); supported by Blumberg (2001), but Durrett & Trull (2005) found the Big Five to account for more variance in traits.

57. "Your leader will be angry if you kill me. I'm a genius."—Second Doctor in serial 6-5, *The Seeds of Death*, pt. 3 (8 February, 1969).

58. "Wise and wonderful person who wants to help."—Fourth Doctor in serial 16-5, *The Power of Kroll*, pt. 2 (30 December, 1978). "I'm so impressive."—Ninth Doctor in episode 1-2, "The End of the World" (2 April, 2005).

59. "We are incredibly clever."—Eleventh Doctor to War and Tenth Doctors in anniversary special, "The Day of the Doctor" (23 November, 1963).

60. Episode 6-7, "A Good Man Goes to War" (4 June, 2011).

61. Episode 5-7, "Amy's Choice" (15 May, 2010).

62. Episode 9-12, "Hell Bent" (5 December, 2015).

63. Anniversary special, "The Day of the Doctor" (23 November, 2013).

II. Deep Breadth

1. Serial 11-5, *Planet of the Spiders*, pt. 1 (4 May, 1974).

6. Dream Lords: Would the Doctor Run with Freud, Jung, Myers, and Briggs?

1. Serial 20-2, *Snakedance*, pt. 1 (17 January, 1983).

2. In Adler & Jaffé (1973), p. 33.

3. Freud (1900/1965), p. 608.

4. Rorschach (1921).

5. Freud (1936).

6. Myers & Myers (1980).

7. Jung (1921/1976).

8. Kramer (2006); McGowan (1994); North (2014); Popper (1963); Stromberg & Caswell (2015); Webster (1995); Woodworth (1917).

9. Eysenck (1985), p. 208.

10. *Doctor Who* (1996 TV movie).

11. Freud (1940).

12. Ellenberger (1970/1981); Janet (1889).

13. Episode 8-1, "Deep Breath" (23 August, 2014).

14. Vaillant (1977).

15. Freud (1936).

16. Freud (1915/1963).

17. American Psychological Association (1998); Hayne et al. (2006); McNally (2005).

18. Anniversary special, "The Day of the Doctor" (23 November, 2013).

19. Most notably in episode 6-8, "Let's Kill Hitler" (27 August, 2011).

20. Christmas special, "The Time of the Doctor" (25 December, 2013). For further analysis, see Langley (2013).

21. Wegner (1989).

22. Serial 5-1, *The Tomb of the Cybermen*, pt. 3 (16 September, 1967).

23. Episode 11-1, "The Woman Who Fell to Earth" (7 October, 2018).

24. Freud (1915/1963, 1917/1963).

25. Serial 3-10, *The War Machines* (25 June–16 July, 1966).

26. Serial 14-2, *The Hand of Fear* (2–23 October, 1976).

27. Serial 8-1, *Terror of the Autons* (2–23 January, 1971).

28. Serial 22-6, *Revelation of the Daleks* (23–30 March, 1985).

29. Christmas special, "The Christmas Invasion" (25 December, 2005).

30. Adler (1927/1963); Freud (1900/1965); Horney (1939); Jung (1963).

31. Serial 20-2, *Snakedance*, pt. 1 (18 January, 2013).

32. Murray (1940), p. 138.

33. Serial 1-15, *The Horror of Fang Rock*, pt. 4 (24 September, 1977).

34. Serial *Shada*, unfinished (scheduled for January–February, 1980).

35. Serial 17-2, *City of Death*, pt. 2 (6 October, 1979).

36. May (1983).

37. Elaborated upon in Langley (2015).

38. Serial 14-4, *The Face of Evil*, pt. 4 (22 January, 1977).

39. Jung (1907/1909).

40. *Doctor Who* (1996 TV movie).

41. Jung (1966)

42. Serial 23-4, *The Trial of a Time Lord: The Ultimate Foe* (29 November–6 December, 1986); Bernstein (2015).

43. Episode 5-7, "Amy's Choice" (15 May, 2010); Frankel (2016).

44. Jung (1917).

45. Cohen & Schmidt (1979).

46. Episode 8-1, "Deep Breath" (23 August, 2014).

47. Episode 9-5, "The Girl Who Died" (17 October, 2015).

48. Serial 18-4, *State of Decay*, pt. 1 (22 November, 1980).

49. Serial 4-1, *The Smugglers*, pt. 4 (1 October, 1966).

50. Myers & Briggs Foundation (n.d.).

51. Eveleth (2013).

52. Dickson & Kelly (1985); Krauss Whitbourne (2010).

53. Brooks (1982); Saxon (1989).

54. "People assume that time is a strict progression of cause to effect, but actually from a non-linear, non-subjective viewpoint, it's more like a big ball of wibbly-wobbly, timey-wimey stuff."—Tenth Doctor in episode 3-10, "Blink" (9 June, 2007).

7. The Unconscious: What, When, Where, Why, and of Course Who

1. Episode 4-3, "Planet of the Ood" (29 April, 2008).

2. Freud (1912), p. 264.

3. Freud (1901/1966).

4. Episode 7-5, "The Angels Take Manhattan" (29 September, 2012).

5. Episode 1-1, "Rose" (26 March, 2005).

6. Episode 2-10, "Love and Monsters" (8 December, 2006).

7. Serial 19-3, *Kinda*, pt. 1 (1 February, 1982).

8. Episode 4-11, "Turn Left" (12 June, 2008).

9. Episode 3-10, "Blink" (9 June, 2007).

10. Freud (1900/1965), p. 608.

11. Episode 5-1, "The Eleventh Hour" (3 April, 2010).

12. Bollas (1995), pp. 12–13.

13. Episode 5-1, "The Eleventh Hour" (3 April, 2010).

14. Freud (1920).

15. Episode 5-1, "The Eleventh Hour" (3 April, 2010).

16. Freud (1923).

17. Episode 5-10, "Vincent and the Doctor" (5 June, 2010).

18. Yalom (1970), p. 198.

19. See, for example, episode 2-3, "School Reunion" (29 April, 2006); Christmas special, "The Runaway Bride" (25 December, 2006); episode 7-5, "Angels Take Manhattan" (29 September, 2012).

20. Episode 8-1, "Deep Breath" (23 August, 2014); Christmas special, "Last Christmas" (25 December, 2014).

21. Serial 4-7, *The Macra Terror*, pt. 2 (18 March, 1967).

22. Episode 5-1, "The Eleventh Hour" (3 April, 2010).

23. Bollas (1995), p. 20.

24. Christmas special, "The Time of the Doctor" (25 December, 2013).

25. Episode 5-1, "The Eleventh Hour" (3 April, 2010).

26. Altman (2015).

27. Altman (2015).

28. Editor's note: When the Time Lords send the Doctor on missions, they do not accompany or maintain contact, as seen in serials 8-4, *Colony in Space* (10 April–15 May, 1971); 9-2, *The Curse of Peladon* (29 January–18 February, 1972); 10-1, *The Three Doctors* (30 December, 1972–20 January, 1973); 12-4, *Genesis of the Daleks* (8 March–12 April, 1975); 22-1, *Attack of the Cybermen* (5–12 January, 1985); and 22-4, *The Two Doctors* (16 February–2 March, 1985). The one Time Lord who helps the Fourth Doctor for a while, Romana, becomes less rigidly Gallifreyan in her ways after the completion of their original mission—serial 17-1, *Destiny of the Daleks* (1–22 Sep-

tember, 1979). Whether the Fugitive Doctor receives support when she works for the Time Lords remains, like most of her background, unknown.

29.   As Kanpo Rinpoche reports in the serial *Planet of the Spiders* (4 May–8 June, 1974).

30.   Episode 7-5, "The Angels Take Manhattan" (29 September, 2012).

31.   Episode 7-13, "The Name of the Doctor" (18 May, 2013).

32.   Christmas special, "The Time of the Doctor" (25 December, 2013).

8. Weeping Angels, Archetypes, and the Male Gaze

1.   Episode 3-10, "Blink" (9 June, 2007).

2.   Jung (1940/1969), p. 160

3.   Episode 3-10, "Blink" (9 June, 2007).

4.   Episode 3-10, "Blink" (9 June, 2007).

5.   Longhurst (2012), p. 33.

6.   Jung (1936/1969).

7.   McAdams (1994), p. 103.

8.   Godwin (1990), p. 155.

9.   Langlinais (2005).

10.   McAdams (1994).

11.   Engler (2009), p. 78.

12.   McAdams (1994), p. 105.

13.   Burger (2015), p. 102.

14.   Jung (1936/1969).

15.   Christmas special, "Twice Upon a Time" (25 December, 2017).

16.   Minisode *Night of the Doctor* (16 November, 2023).

17.   *The Sarah Jane Adventures,* episodes 7 & 8 (29 October–5 November, 2007).

18.   Episode 12-10, "The Timeless Child" (1 March, 2020).

19.   Serials 11-5, *Planet of the Spiders* (4 May–8 June, 1974); 21-7, *The Twin Dilemma* (22-30 March, 1984).

20.   Episode 7-5, "The Angels Take Manhattan" (29 September, 2012).

21.   Episode 3-10, "Blink" (9 June, 2007).

22.   Lacan (1981).

23.   Mulvey (1975).

24.   Episode 3-10, "Blink" (9 June, 2007).

25.   Episode 5-4, "The Time of Angels" (24 April, 2010).

26.   Kelly (1955).

27.   Kelly (1955).

28. Episode 5-4, "The Time of Angels" (24 April, 2010).

29. Episode 5-5, "Flesh and Stone" (1 May, 2010).

9. New Face, New Time Lord: A Personality Perspective

1. Episode 11-1, "The Woman Who Fell to Earth" (7 October, 2018).

2. Allport (1955), p. 19.

3. Myers (2015); Myers & Myers (1995).

4. Bishop (2014); McCrae & Costa (1991); Wacker et al. (2006).

5. Capraro & Capraro (2002); Carey et al. (1989); Saggino et al. (2001); Reynierse & Harker (2008a, 2008b).

6. Cohen & Schmidt (1979); Myers (1998).

7. Myers & Myers (1995).

8. Serial 10-1, *The Three Doctors* (30 December, 1972—20 January, 1973); Myers & Myers (1995).

9. Episode 7-5, "The Angels Take Manhattan" (29 September, 2012); Myers & Myers (1995); Wacker et al. (2006).

10. Reynierse & Harker (2008a, 2008b).

11. Serial 1-6, *The Aztecs*, pt. 1, "The Temple of Evil" (23 May, 1964).

12. Serial 10-1, *The Three Doctors* (30 December, 1972—20 January, 1973); Myers & Myers (1995).

13. Serial 4-2, *The Tenth Planet*, pt. 4 (29 October, 1966).

14. Serial 4-3, *The Power of the Daleks*, pt. 1 (5 November, 1966).

15. Myers & Myers (1995).

16. Serial, 4-3, *The Power of the Daleks*, pts. 1 (5 November, 1996), 5 (3 December, 1995); Wacker et al. (2006).

17. Serial 6-7, *The War Games*, pt. 10 (21 June, 1969).

18. Jin & Austin (2000); Myers (1995).

19. Serial 7-1, *Spearhead from Space* (3–24 January, 1971); Myers (1995); Reynierse & Harker (2008a, 2008b).

20. Beckham (2012).

21. Brown & Reilly (2009); Michael (2003).

22. Fishman & Ng (2013).

23. Serial 12-2, *The Ark in Space*, pt. 2 (8 February, 1975).

24. Season 19 (1982); OPP (n.d.).

25. Myers (1998); Myers & Myers (1995).

26. Serial 19-4, *The Visitation*, pt. 1 (15 February, 1982).

27. Myers (1998); Little (2004).

28. Serial 21-1, *The Twin Dilemma,* pt. 1 (24 March, 1984); Myers (1998); Myers & Myers (1995).

29. Reynierse & Harker (2008s, 2008b); Wacker et al. (2006).

30. Serial 25-2, *The Happiness Patrol* (2–16 November, 1988).

31. Myers (1998).

32. Episode 1-3, "The Unquiet Dead" (9 April, 2005); Myers (1998).

33. Episode 1-1, "Rose" (26 March, 2005); Myers (1998).

34. Episode 1-13, "The Parting of the Ways" (18 June, 2005).

35. Myers & Myers (1995).

36. Episode 2-4, "The Girl in the Fireplace" (6 May, 2006); Percival et al. (1992).

37. Episode 4-2, "The Fires of Pompeii" (12 April, 2008); Myers (1998).

38. Keirsey (1998); Myers & Myers (1995).

39. Episodes 5-13, "The Big Bang" (26 June, 2010), 6-7, "A Good Man Goes to War" (4 June, 2011); Reynierse & Harker (2008a, 2008b).

40. Myers & Myers (1998); Wacker et al. (2006).

41. Episode 7-4, "The Power of Three" (22 September, 2012); Christmas special, "The Time of the Doctor" (25 December, 2013).

42. Episode 12-10, "The Timeless Children" (1 March, 2020).

43. Bashtavenko (2005); Myers & Myers (1995).

44. Episode 4-2, "The Fires of Pompeii" (12 April, 2008).

45. Episode 8-2, "Into the Dalek" (30 August, 2014).

46. Episodes 8-2, "Into the Dalek" (30 August, 2014); 8-7, "Kill the Moon" (4 October, 2014); 10-3, "Thin Ice" (29 April, 2017).

47. New Year's special, "Revolution of the Daleks" (1 January, 2021).

48. Episode 11-9, "It Takes You Away" (2 December, 2018).

49. Episode 11-1, "The Woman Who Fell to Earth" (7 October, 2018).

50. Briggs Myers et al. (2009).

51. New Year's special, "Eve of the Daleks" (1 January, 2022).

52. War Doctor—anniversary special, "The Day of the Doctor" (23 November, 2013). Fugitive Doctor—episode 12-5, "Fugitive of the Judoon" (26 January, 2020). Eighth Doctor—*Doctor Who* (1996 TV movie).

53. TV: Classic season 23, *The Trial of a Time Lord* (6 September–6 December, 1986). Audio example: *The Trial of the Valeyard* (17 August, 2015).

54. BBC centenary special, "The Power of the Doctor" (23 October, 2022); 2023 specials.

55. Huang et al. (2017).

56.   Christmas special, "The Time of the Doctor" (25 December, 2013).

57.   Freud, A. (1919), letter to her father reprinted by Young-Bruehl (2008), p. 86.

III. Hands to Hold

1.   Episode 2-11, "Fear Her" (24 June, 2006).

10. Who Makes a Good Companion?

1.   Episode 1-13, "The Parting of the Ways" (18 June, 2005).

2.   Erikson (1987), p. 632.

3.   Jack—episode 1-1, "The Parting of the Ways" (18 June, 2005), explained in 3-6, "Utopia" (16 June, 2007). Ashildr—9-6, "The Woman Who Lived" (24 October, 20150.

4.   Romana I—serial 16-1, *The Ribos Operation*, pt. 1 (2 September, 1978); Dodo—serial 3-5, *The Massacre*, pt. 4 (26 February, 1966); Tegan—serial 18-7, *Logopolis*, pt. 1 (28 February, 1981); Donna—episode 4-1, "Partners in Crime" (5 April, 2008); Amy—episode 5-1, "The Eleventh Hour" (3 April, 2010); Yaz, Ryan, and Graham—episode 11-1, "The Woman Who Fell to Earth" (7 October, 2018).

5.   Smith (2007).

6.   Santy (1994).

7.   Chidester et al. (1991).

8.   *Doctor Who* (1996 TV movie).

9.   Duckworth & Seligman (2005).

10.   Serial 8-1, *Terror of the Autons*, pt. 1 (2 January, 1971).

11.   Serial 16-1, *The Ribos Operation*, pt. 1 (2 September, 1978).

12.   Gardner & Hatch (1989).

13.   Recorder first appeared in serial *The Power of the Daleks*, pt. 1 (5 November, 1966); electric guitar in episode 9-1, "The Magician's Apprentice" (19 September, 2015).

14.   Episode 11-1, "The Woman Who Fell to Earth" (7 October, 2018).

15.   Episode 13-1, *Flux*, chapter 1, "The Halloween Apocalypse" (31 October, 2021).

16.   Park et al. (2004).

17.   Anniversary special, "The Day of the Doctor" (23 November, 2013); episode 9-7, "The Zygon Invasion" (15 October, 2015).

18.   BBC centenary special, "The Power of the Doctor" (23 October, 2022).

19.   Episode 1-6, "Dalek" (30 April, 2015).

20.   Episode 4-2, "Fires of Pompeii" (12 April, 2008).

21.   Episode 11-5, "The Tsuranga Conundrum" (4 November, 2018).

22. Bar-Tal (1985-1986).

23. McCrae & Terracciano (2005).

24. Episode 7-8, "The Rings of Akhaten" (6 April, 2013).

25. Episode 1-7, "The Long Game" (7 May, 2005).

26. Beginning in the anniversary special, "The Day of the Doctor" (23 November, 2013).

27. Serial 24–4, *Dragonfire* (3 November–7 December, 1987).

28. *The Sarah Jane Adventures,* episode 4-6, "Death of the Doctor," pt. 2 (26 October, 2010); BBC centenary special, "The Power of the Doctor" (23 October, 2022).

29. Serial 4-9, *The Evil of the Daleks,* pt. 7 (1 July, 1967).

30. Episode 4-3, "Planet of the Ood" (19 April, 2008).

31. Episode 10-12, "The Doctor Falls" (1 July, 2017).

32. Serial 18-7, *Logopolis* (28 February–21 March, 1981).

33. Leach (1994).

34. Episode 3-12, "The Sound of Drums" (23 June, 2007).

35. BBC centenary special, "The Power of the Doctor" (23 October, 2022).

36. American Psychiatric Association (2022).

37. Gergen et al. (1970).

38. Cleckley (1941); Hare (1991); Hare & Neumann (2006); Harpur et al. (1989).

39. Episode 1-1, "Rose" (26 March, 2005).

40. Serial 12-4, *Genesis of the Daleks* (8 March–12 April, 1975).

41. Cacioppo & Cacioppo (2014).

42. Van der Horst & Coffé (2012).

43. Serial 23-4, *The Ultimate Foe,* pt. 2 (6 December, 1986).

44. Wing & Jeffery (1999).

45. Serial 6-2, *The Chase* (26 June, 1965).

46. Episode 3-13, "Last of the Time Lords" (30 June, 2007).

47. Christmas special, "The End of Time" (1 January, 2010).

48. Episode 4-8, "Silence in the Library" (31 May, 2008).

49. "That last time I was dying, I looked back on all of you. Every single one."—Eleventh Doctor to Jo in *The Sarah Jane Adventures,* episode 4-6, "Death of the Doctor" pt. 2 (26 October, 2010). Fifth Doctor interface and Tegan—BBC centenary special, "The Power of the Doctor" (23 October, 2022).

50. Serial 20-4, *Terminus,* pt. 4 (15 February, 1983).

51. *Doctor Who: P.S.* (2012 webcast); *Doctor Who: Lockdown | Rory's Story* (2020 webcast).

52. Calhoun et al. (2014).
53. Episode 4-4, "The Sontaran Stratagem" (26 April, 2008).
54. BBC centenary special, "The Power of the Doctor" (23 October, 2022).
55. Donovan (2022).
56. By her own admission, Clara has betrayed the Twelfth Doctor's trust by trying to destroy all TARDIS keys and therefore the TARDIS itself. Episode 8-11, "Dark Water" (1 November, 2014).
57. Vygotsky (1931/1997), p. 96.
58. Excerpt from Currie (2016) in *Doctor Who Psychology: A Madman with a Box* (1st edition).
59. McGlynn et al. (2009).
60. Tuckman & Jensen (1977).
61. Episode 5-1, "The Eleventh Hour" (3 April, 2010).
62. Episode 5-6, "Vampires of Venice" (8 May, 2010).
63. Episode 5-13, "The Big Bang" (26 June, 2010).
64. Episode 6-7, "A Good Man Goes to War" (4 June, 2011).
65. Episode 7-4, "The Power of Three" (22 September, 2012).
66. Episode 7-5, "The Angels Take Manhattan" (29 September, 2012).

11. The Compassionate Doctor: Caring for Self by Caring for Others

1. Episode 9-2, "The Witch's Familiar" (26 September, 2015).
2. Seppälä (2013).
3. For example, serial 12-4, *Genesis of the Daleks* (8 March–12 April, 1975).
4. Goetz (2010).
5. Goetz et al. (2010).
6. Episode 6-8, "Let's Kill Hitler" (27 August, 2011).
7. Fiske (2009); Meyer et al. (2013).
8. Serial 12-4, *Genesis of the Daleks* (8 March–12 April, 1975).
9. Fiske (2009); Meyer et al. (2013).
10. Christmas special, "A Christmas Carol" (25 December, 2010).
11. Seppälä (2013).
12. Cole et al. (2007); Kearney et al. (2013).
13. Depression—Ryan et al. (2008); anxiety—Fogarty et al. (1999); posttraumatic stress disorder (PTSD)—Kearney et al. (2013); chronic pain—Chapin et al. (2014).
14. Hutcherson et al. (2008).
15. Klimecki et al. (2012); Ryan et al. (2008).

16. Cole et al. (2007).

17. Asmundson et al. (2004).

18. Episode 1-2, "The End of the World" (2 April, 2005).

19. Jakupcak et al. (2007).

20. Kearney et al. (2013).

21. Kearney et al. (2013)

22. Episode 1-3, "The Parting of the Ways" (18 June, 2005).

23. Ryan et al. (2008).

24. Herbert (2015); Liao & Simmonds (2014); Quinn et al. (2021).

25. Ryff & Boylan (2016).

26. Episode 11-3, "Rosa" (21 October, 2018).

27. *The Sarah Jane Adventures*, episode 4-6, "Death of the Doctor," part 2 (26 October, 2010).

28. Cole et al. (2007); Ryan et al. (2008).

29. Figley (2002).

30. Serials 25-1, *Remembrance of the Daleks* (5–26 October, 1988); 26-2, *Ghost Light* (4–18 October, 1989); 26-3, *The Curse of Fenric* (25 October–15 November, 1989).

31. *Persuasion* (2013 audio drama).

32. *Time Works* (2006 audio drama).

33. Boscarino et al. (2004); Ringenbach (2009).

34. Jazaieri et al. (2014); Seppälä et al. (2014); Shapiro et al. (2005).

35. Klimecki & Singer (2012).

36. Jazaieri et al. (2014); Klimecki & Singer (2012).

37. Episode 1-2, "The End of the World" (2 April, 2005).

38. Anniversary special, "The Day of the Doctor" (23 November, 2013).

39. Serial 1-1, *An Unearthly Child*, pt. 1, "An Unearthly Child" (23 November, 1963).

40. Christmas special, "Twice Upon a Time" (25 December, 2017).

41. Episode 1-1, "Rose" (26 March, 2005).

42. Episode 2-6, "The Age of Steel" (20 May, 2006).

43. Respectively, Segerstrom & Miller (2004); Epel et al. (2001); Chandola et al. (2008).

44. Klimecki et al. (2012); Rockliff (2008).

45. Episode 2-1, "New Earth" (15 April, 2006).

46. BBC centenary special, "The Power of the Doctor" (23 October, 2022).

47. Rachel (n.d.).

48. Winthrop (1949).

49. Episode 13-6, *Flux,* chapter 6, "The Vanquishers" (5 December, 2021).

50. Episode 3-8, "Human Nature" (26 May, 2007), based on the Seventh Doctor novel by Cornell (1995).

51. BBC centenary special, "The Power of the Doctor" (23 October, 2022).

52. BBC centenary special, "The Power of the Doctor" (23 October, 2022).

53. Serial 19-6, *Earthshock,* pt. 4 (16 March, 1982).

54. Goetz et al. (2010).

55. Seppälä (2013).

56. Cole et al. (2007); Kearney et al. (2013).

57. Ryan et al. (2008).

58. Christmas special, "Twice Upon a Time" (25 December, 2017).

IV. Lost Things

1. Anniversary special, "The Day of the Doctor" (23 November, 2013).

12. Death and the Doctor: Interview on How Immortals Face Mortality

1. Episode 7-7, "The Rings of Akhaten" (6 April, 2013).

2. Yalom (2008), p. 49.

3. Yalom (2008).

4. Kastenbaum (2000).

5. For example, episode 2-3, "School Reunion" (26 April, 2006).

6. Yalom (2008).

7. Plumb et al. (2004); Yalom (2008).

8. Christmas special, "The End of Time," pt. 1 (25 December, 2009).

9. Episode 10-11, "World Enough and Time" (24 June, 2017).

10. Firestone (2015); Fritzsche (2020); Roe-Burning & Straker (1997).

11. Horner et al. (2022); Van Tongeren et al. (2022).

12. Episode 2-3, "School Reunion" (26 April, 2006).

13. Which comes up again when Yaz meets Tegan and Ace in BBC centenary special, "The Power of the Doctor" (23 October, 2022).

14. Center for Substance Abuse Treatment (1999).

15. Yalom (2008).

16. Examples: Doctor Who Amino (2015); Doctor Who Answers (2012).

17. For example, episode 2-3, "School Reunion" (26 April, 2006).

18. Christmas special, "The Snowmen" (25 December, 2012).

19. Shan (1973); Toblin et al. (2012).

20. Barr & Cacciatore (2008).

21. Bonanno et al. (2002).

22. Miles & Demi (1992).

23. Kübler-Ross (1969).

24. Episode 7-13, "The Name of the Doctor" (18 May, 2012).

25. Episode 9-11, "Heaven Sent" (28 November, 2015).

26. Episode 4-9, "Forest of the Dead" (7 June, 2008).

27. Episode 7-13, "The Name of the Doctor" (18 May, 2013).

28. Christmas special, "The Snowmen" (25 December, 2012).

29. Episode 7-13, "The Name of the Doctor" (18 May, 2012).

30. Keesee et al. (2008).

31. Keesee et al. (2008); Mikulincer et al. (2004).

32. Mikulincer et al. (2004).

33. Skinner et al. (2006).

34. Poulin et al. (2013).

35. Wong et al. (1994).

36. Ware (2012).

37. Episode 3-3, "Gridlock" (14 April, 2007).

38. Wong et al. (1994).

39. Anniversary special, "The Day of the Doctor" (5 June, 2010).

40. Episode 5-10, "Vincent and the Doctor" (5 June, 2010).

41. Wong et al. (1994).

42. Mikulincer et al. (2004); Poulin et al. (2013); Wong et al. (1994).

43. Bonanno et al. (2002).

44. Anniversary special, "The Day of the Doctor" (5 June, 2010).

45. Wong et al. (1994); Yalom (2008).

46. Episodes 12-10, "The Timeless Children" (1 March, 2020); 13-6, Flux, chapter 6, "The Vanquishers" (5 December, 2021)

13. Post-Time War Stress Disorder

1. Episode 3-3, "Gridlock" (14 April, 2007).

2. Kübler-Ross (1969), p. 169.

3. Hahn et al. (2015); Hoge & Warner (2014); Pigeon et al. (2013); Roemer et al. (1998); Stanley et al. (2016); Wilson (2015).

4. Episode 1-2, "The End of the World" (2 April, 2005).

5. Handley et al. (2009).

6.   Episode 7-13, "The Name of the Doctor" (18 May, 2013); anniversary special, "The Day of the Doctor" (23 November, 2013).

7.   Holtz (2015); PTSD Alliance (n.d.); Sidran Institute (n.d.); Staggs (n.d.).

8.   Santiago et al. (2013).

9.   Held et al. (2011; 2015); Pugh et al. (2015).

10.   Dekel et al. (2016).

11.   Anniversary special, "The Day of the Doctor" (23 November, 2013).

12.   American Psychiatric Association (2013, 2022).

13.   Christmas and New Year's specials, "The End of Time," pt. 1 (25 December, 2009) and pt. 2 (1 January, 2010); anniversary special, "The Day of the Doctor" (23 November, 2015).

14.   Anniversary special, "The Day of the Doctor" (23 November, 2013).

15.   American Psychiatric Association (2022).

16.   Anniversary special, "The Day of the Doctor" (23 November, 2013).

17.   Krebs et al. (2010); Litz et al. (1997); Wegner et al. (1987).

18.   Episode 1-2, "The End of the World" (2 April, 2005).

19.   Caplan et al. (1985); Eysenck et al. (2006); Fortunato & Furey (2011).

20.   Boyd-Wilson et al. (2002).

21.   Tanielian & Jaycox (2008).

22.   Allport (1937).

23.   Episode 9-12, "Hell Bent" (5 December, 2015).

24.   Episode 1-1, "Rose" (26 March, 2005).

25.   Freud (1936).

26.   Episode 3-3, "Gridlock" (14 April, 2007).

27.   Holowka et al. (2012).

28.   Minisode, *The Night of the Doctor* (13 November, 2013).

29.   Episode 5-7, "Amy's Choice" (15 May, 2010).

30.   Episode 6-7, "A Good Man Goes to War" (4 June, 2011).

31.   Anniversary special, "The Day of the Doctor" (23 November, 2013).

32.   Episode 8-2, "Into the Dalek" (30 August, 2014).

33.   Gonzalez et al. (2016).

34.   Episode 1-6, "Dalek" (30 April, 2005).

35.   Dixon-Gordon et al. (2014).

36.   Berger (1977); Cassell et al. (2014).

37.   Sender (2014).

38. Anniversary special, "The Day of the Doctor" (23 November, 2015); episode 1-13, "The Parting of the Ways" (18 June, 2005); 4-13, "Journey's End" (5 July, 2008); New Year's special, "The End of Time," pt. 2 (1 January, 2010).

39. Price (n.d.).

40. Husain et al. (2008).

41. Episode 6-4, "The Doctor's Wife" (14 May, 2011).

42. Serial 14-6, *The Talons of Weng-Chiang*, pt. 3 (12 March, 1977).

43. American Psychiatric Association (2022).

44. Episode 9-3, "Under the Lake" (3 October, 2015).

45. Caballero & Connell (2010).

46. Gros et al. (2015); Jacobsen et al. (2001).

47. First Doctor, mead—serial 2-9, *The Time Meddler*, pt. 1 (3 July, 1965). The Brigadier has apparently shared brandy with at least one Doctor, indicated in episode 6-13, "The Wedding of River Song" (1 October, 2011). Tenth, banana daiquiri—2-4, "The Girl in the Fireplace" (6 May, 2006). Eleventh, wine—6-1, "The Impossible Astronaut" (23 April, 2011). The first four Doctors all drink wine occasionally on screen, especially the Third and Fourth. Twelfth, whisky—9-1, "Deep Breath" (23 August, 2014); brandy—Christmas special, "Twice Upon a Time" (25 December, 2017).

48. First Doctor says three times that he never touches alcohol in serial 3-8, *The Gunfighters*, pts. 1–2 (30 April–7 May, 1966). Tenth declines champagne in episode 2-1, "New Earth" (15 April, 2006).

49. Specifically, Prime Minister David Lloyd George—1-4, "Aliens in London" (16 April, 2005).

50. American Psychiatric Association (2013, 2022).

51. Based on the seminal work of Herman (1992). See reviews by Heim et al. (2022); Ide & Paez (2000).

52. Schwartz (2016).

53. Introduced in serial 3-3, *The Myth Makers* (16 October–6 November, 1965); dies in 3-4, *The Daleks' Master Plan* (12 November, 1965–29 January, 1966).

54. Serial 3-4, *The Daleks' Master Plan* (12 November, 1965–29 January, 1966).

55. BBC centenary special, "The Power of the Doctor" (23 October, 2022).

56. Serial 18-3, *Full Circle* (25 October–15 November, 1980).

57. Serial 19-6, *Earthshock*, pt. 4 (16 March, 1982). The next silent credits would not run until the end of episode 11-3, "Rosa" (21 October, 2018).

58. Serial 21-4, *Resurrection of the Daleks* (15 February, 1984). Whether "I'll miss you" is part of what she wishes he'd said or the reply she wishes she could have given to

his unsaid "Brave heart" is unclear, but perhaps it doesn't matter either way. Decades later, they both say it.

59. BBC centenary special, "The Power of the Doctor" (23 October, 2022).

60. Examples: Jack Harness, killed, then made immortal—episode 1-13, "The Parting of the Ways" (18 June, 2005). Amy and Rory, lost in time, then deaths confirmed on gravestone—7-5, "The Angels Take Manhattan" (29 September, 2012). All of the Twelfth Doctor's companions—see subsequent note.

61. Examples: The Ninth Doctor invites Linda Moss, but a Dalek kills her in the vacuum of space—episode 1-13, "The Parting of the Ways" (18 June, 2005). Tenth, Astrid Peth, who falls to her death—Christmas special, "The Voyage of the Damned" (25 December, 2007); and as far as he knows, his daughter Jenny dies and stays dead right after they meet in 4-6, "The Doctor's Daughter" (10 May, 2008). Eleventh Doctor invites Rita to travel with him, Amy, and Rory, but she does not survive their adventure in a mysterious hotel—6-11, "The God Complex" (17 September, 2011); also Clara Oswin Oswald in one of many Clara deaths—Christmas special, "The Snowmen" (25 December, 2012). Twelfth, his ultimate fan Petronella Osgood before Missy seemingly vaporizes her—8-12, "Death in Heaven" (8 November, 2014).

62. Clara's boyfriend Danny Pink—episode 8-11, "Dark Water" (1 November, 2014). Clara—9-10, "Face the Raven (21 November, 2015). Both Bill (last of her human form) and Missy—10-12, "The Doctor Falls" (1 July, 2017). Nardole (death confirmed)—Christmas special, "Twice Upon a Time" (25 December, 2017). Plus, even though River Song dies in 4-9, "Silence in the Library," right after the Tenth Doctor first meets her, it is the Eleventh who says farewell to her A.I. vestige in 7-13, "The Name of the Doctor" (18 May, 2013) and the Twelfth who goes on their final date in Christmas special, "The Husbands of River Song" (25 December, 2015), knowing she will soon die.

63. Ryan and Graham—New Year's special, "Revolution of the Daleks" (1 January, 2021); Dan and Yaz—BBC centenary special, "The Power of the Doctor" (23 October, 2022).

64. Serial 2-2, "The Dalek Invasion of Earth," pt. 6 (26 December, 1964).

65. Serial 14-2, "The Hand of Fear," pt. 4 (23 October, 1976).

66. Episode 10-12, "The Doctor Falls" (1 July, 2017); Christmas special, "Twice Upon a Time" (25 December, 2017).

67. Episode 12-2, "Spyfall," pt. 2 (5 January, 2020); 12-10, "The Timeless Children" (1 March, 2020).

68. American Psychiatric Association (2013, 2022).

69. World Health Organization (2022).

70. World Health Organization (n.d.). Their manual says *post traumatic* as opposed to the DSM's unbroken *posttraumatic*. Neither hyphenates the term.

71. Christmas specials, "The Runaway Bride" (25 December, 2006); "The Next Doctor" (25 December, 2008); "The Doctor, the Widow, and the Wardrobe" (25 December, 2011).

72. New Year's special, "Revolution of the Daleks" (1 January, 2021).

73. New Year's special, "The End of Time," pt. 2 (1 January, 2010).

74. Zeigarnik (1927/1938).

75. Ovsiankina (1928).

76. Kahneman & Miller (1986); McGraw et al. (2005); Medvec et al. (1995).

14. Behind Two Hearts: Grief and Vulnerability

1. Christmas special, "The Snowmen" (25 December, 2012).

2. Brown (2012), p. 37.

3. Bonanno (2004).

4. Shear et al. (2007).

5. Bonanno (2004).

6. Shear (2010).

7. Bonanno & Kaltman (2001).

8. Episode 9-11, "Heaven Sent" (28 November, 2015).

9. Prigerson et al. (1997).

10. Episodes 6-13, "The Wedding of River Song" (1 October, 2011); 7-5, "The Angels Take Manhattan (29 September, 2012); 7-1, "Asylum of the Daleks" (1 September, 2012); Christmas special, "The Snowmen" (25 December, 2012).

11. Christmas special, "Twice Upon a Time" (25 December, 2017).

12. Shear et al. (2007).

13. Boelen et al. (2010).

14. Orcutt et al. (2005).

15. Episode 4-13, "Journey's End" (5 July, 2008).

16. Cole et al. (2007).

17. Burley et al. (2021); Ternes et al. (2019); Zhou et al. (2022).

18. Miller et al. (2008).

19. Minisode, *The Great Detective* (16 November, 2012).

20. Barr (2004).

21. Boelen et al. (2006).

22. Episode1-2, "The End of the World" (2 April, 2005).

23. Anniversary special, "The Day of the Doctor" (23 November, 2013).

24. Brown (2012).

25. Episode 6-4, "The Doctor's Wife" (14 May, 2011).

26. Episode 3-10, "Blink" (9 June, 2007).

27. Episode 9-3, "Before the Flood" (1 October, 2015).

28. Episode 2-2, "Tooth and Claw" (22 April, 2006).

29. Episode 4-9, "Forest of the Dead" (7 June, 2008); Christmas special, "The Husbands of River Song" (25 December, 2015).

30. Episode 9-2, "The Witch's Familiar" (26 September, 2015).

31. Brown (2012).

32. Episode 9-1, "The Magician's Apprentice" (19 September, 2015).

33. Brown (2012).

34. Episode 4-9, "Forest of the Dead" (7 June, 2008).

35. Kanter et al. (2006).

36. J. McGonigal (2015); K. McGonigal (2015).

37. Fredrickson (2001); K. McGonigal (2015); Tugade & Fredrickson (2004).

15. From Human to Machine: At What Point Do You Lose Your Soul?

1.   Serial 25-1, *Remembrance of the Daleks,* pt. 1 (5 October, 1988).

2.   Moravec (1999), p. 111

3.   Giritli (2012); Kirk & Kirk (1997).

4.   Castelnuovo-Tedesco (1989); Walters (2001).

5.   Episode 2-6, "The Age of Steel" (20 May, 2006).

6.   Serial 12-4, *The Genesis of the Daleks* (12 March–12 April, 1975).

7.   Serial 12-5, *Revenge of the Cybermen* (19 April–10 May, 1975).

8.   For example, Barlett (2015).

9.   Zhong et al. (2010).

10. Miller & Rowold (1979).

11. Van Swearingen et al. (1999).

12. Franco et al. (1995).

13. Greene (2013).

14. Greene et al. (2001).

15. Serial 1-2, *The Daleks* (21 December, 1963–1 February, 1964).

16. Episode 2-5, "Rise of the Cybermen" (13 May, 2006).

17.   Serial 4-2, *The Tenth Planet* (8–29 October, 1966).

18.   Cardinali et al. (2009).

19.   Clark (2003), p. 37.

20.   Desmond & MacLachlan (2002).

21.   Kelly & Davies (this volume).

22.   Serial 1-2, *The Daleks* (21 December, 1963–1 February, 1964).

23.   Serial 4-2, *The Tenth Planet* (8–29 October, 1966).

24.   Episodes 8-2, "Into the Dalek" (30 August, 2014); 6–12, "Closing Time" (24 September, 2011).

25.   Haidt (2012). See also Kelly & Davies (this volume).

26.   Episode 2-6, "The Age of Steel" (20 May, 2006).

27.   Serial 12-4, *Genesis of the Daleks* (12 March–12 April, 1975).

28.   Episode 2-5, "Rise of the Cybermen" (13 May, 2006).

V. Change of Nature

1.   Episode 11-1, "The Woman Who Fell to Earth" (7 October, 2018).

16. Getting to the Hearts of Time Lord Personality Change: Regeneration on the Brain

1.   Christmas special, "The Time of the Doctor" (25 December, 2013).

2.   Maslow (1943), p. 382.

3.   Episode 1-11, "Boom Town" (4 June, 2005).

4.   Serial 10-1, *The Three Doctors* (30 December, 1972–20 January, 1973); anniversary special, *The Five Doctors* (25 November, 1983).

5.   Witelson et al. (1999).

6.   Bernstein (1999).

7.   Serial 13-5, *The Brain of Morbius* (3–24 January, 1976).

8.   Lyons et al. (2014).

9.   Penfield (1968).

10.   Serials: 4-3, *The Power of the Daleks* (November 5–December 10, 1966); 7-1, *Spearhead from Space* (3–24 January, 1970); 12-1, *Robot* (28 December, 1974–18 January, 1975); 19-1, *Castrovalva* (4–13 January, 1982); 21-7, *The Twin Dilemma* (22–30 March, 1984); 24-1, *Time and the Rani* (7–28 September, 1987). *Doctor Who* (1996 television movie). Episodes: Christmas special, "The Christmas Invasion" (25 December, 2006); 5-1, "The Eleventh Hour" (3 April, 2010); 8-1, "Deep Breath" (23 August, 2014); 11-1, "The Woman Who Fell to Earth" (7 October, 2018).

11.   Blakemore & Choudhury (2006).

12. Anniversary special, "The Day of the Doctor" (23 November, 2013).

13. McGlashan & Hoffman (2000).

14. Serial 21-7, *The Twin Dilemma* (22–30 March 1984).

15. Maguire et al. (2006).

16. Friston (2002).

17. Serial 1-1, *An Unearthly Child*, pt. 1 (23 November, 1963).

18. Von Hippel et al. (2008).

19. Goldberg (2002).

20. Classic Serial 10-1, *The Three Doctors* (30 December, 1972–20 January, 1973).

21. Gardner (2006); Rauscher et al. (1993).

22. Steelman (1990).

23. Rauscher et al. (1993

24. Thompson et al. (2001).

25. For example, episode 9-1, "The Magician's Apprentice" (19 September, 2015).

26. Beaty et al. (2014).

27. Zak et al. (2007).

28. Zak et al. (2009).

29. Serials 19-1 *Castrovalva* (4–12 January, 1982) and 19-5, *Black Orchid* (1–2 March, 1982).

30. Weissensteiner et al. (2012).

31. Sheard (2012).

32. Brower & Price (2001).

33. Grafman et al. (1996).

34. Serial 24-1, *Time and the Rani*, pt. 2 (14 September, 1987).

35. Rosell et al. (2014).

36. *Doctor Who* (1996 TV movie).

37. Romero et al (2013).

38. Carelli (2015).

39. Starting with *The War Doctor: Only the Monstrous* (2015 audio drama).

40. Minisode, *The Night of the Doctor* (14 November, 2005).

41. Lieberman et al. (2005).

42. Moreno (2006).

43. Paradiso et al. (2021).

44. Episode 1-1, "Rose" (26 March, 2005).

45. Roque et al. (2012).

46. Christmas special, "The Christmas Invasion" (25 December, 2005).

47. Botvinick & Cohen (1998).

48. Episode 5-1, "The Eleventh Hour" (3 April, 2010).

49. Episode 5-10, "Vincent and the Doctor" (5 June, 2010).

50. Barkley (2014).

51. Núñez-Jaramillo et al. (2021).

52. Episode 9-5, "The Girl Who Died" (17 October, 2015)

53. Frith (2004).

54. Episode 10-3, "Thin Ice" (29 April, 2017)

55. American Psychiatric Association (2013, 2022); World Health Organization (2022).

56. Baron-Cohen et al. (2001).

57. Christmas special, "Twice Upon a Time" (25 December, 2017).

58. DeCasien et al. (2022).

59. Marrocco & McEwen (2022).

60. Episode 12-2, "Skyfall" pt. 2 (5 January, 2020)

61. Dief et al. (2018).

62. Episode 12-5, "Fugitive of the Judoon" (26 January, 2020)

63. Oberauer & Greve (2022).

64. Jahn (2013).

17. Regenerating Gender: Infinitely More Inside

1. Heraclitus, quoted in 4th century BC by Plato (1999 trans.)

2. Episode 6-4, "The Doctor's Wife" (14 May, 2011).

3. Episode 12-1, "Spyfall," pt. 1 (1 January, 2020).

4. Lindqvist et al. (2020).

5. Elm et al. (2016).

6. Episode 12-10, "The Timeless Children" (1 March, 2020).

7. Episode 12-5, "Fugitive of the Judoon" (26 January, 2020).

8. Episode 12-2, "Spyfall," pt. 2 (5 January, 2020).

9. Episode 13-8, "Legend of the Sea Devils" (17 April, 2022).

10. Fontanella et al. (2014); Gabbard & Wilkinson (1996).

11. Episode 11-8, "The Witchfinders" (25 November, 2018).

12. Hazel & Kleyman (2019).

13. Episode 12-8, "The Haunting of Villa Diodati" (16 February, 2020).

14. Episode 11-6, "Demons of the Punjab" (11 November, 2018).

15. Episode 11-8, "The Witchfinders" (25 November, 2018).

16. Kattari et al. (2020).

17. Sue & Spanierman (2020), p. 36.

18. Ross et al. (2022).

19. Episode 12-5, "Fugitive of the Judoon" (26 January, 2020).

20. New Year's special, "Revolution of the Daleks" (1 January, 2021).

21. McLemore (2018).

22. Earnshaw et al. (2020); Galupo et al. (2020); Truszczynski et al. (2022).

23. Beischel et al. (2021).

24. Austin et al. (2022).

25. Episode 11-6 "Demons of the Punjab" (11 November, 2018).

26. Jackson et al. (2020).

27. Episode 11-1 "The Woman Who Fell to Earth" (7 October, 2018).

28. Minisode, *Children in Need Special*, "Born Again" (18 November, 2005).

29. Episode 12-1, "Spyfall," pt. 1 (1 January, 2020).

30. Hammack et al. (2018).

31. Episode 6-13, "The Wedding of River Song" (1 October, 2011).

18. Boys to Cybermen: Social Narratives and Masculinity Metaphors

1. Hartnell—serial 4-2, *The Tenth Planet* (8–29 October, 1966). Partly repeated by Bradley—Christmas special, "Twice Upon a Time" (25 December, 2017).

2. Shields (2015).

3. Smart (2006).

4. Kilmartin (2010).

5. Episode 2-5, "Rise of the Cybermen" (13 May, 2006).

6. Episode 2-6, "The Age of Steel" (20 May, 2006).

7. Episode 2-6, "The Age of Steel" (20 May, 2006).

8. Episode 6-12, "Closing Time" (24 September, 2011).

9. Episode 8-12, "Death in Heaven" (8 November, 2014).

10. Episode 2-5, "Rise of the Cybermen" (13 May, 2006).

11. Brannon (1985).

12. Smith et al. (2015), p. 162.

13. Farkas & Leaper (2016).

14. Even the Cyberwoman in episode 2-13, "Doomsday" (July 1, 2006), looks like a Cyberman.

15. Geary et al. (2016).

16. Episode 4-2, "Partners in Crime" (5 April, 2008).

17. Levant (2006).
18. Kilmartin & McDermott (2015).
19. Meyers et al. (2015).
20. Christmas special, "The Next Doctor" (25 December, 2008).
21. Episode 2-13, "Doomsday" (8 July, 2006).
22. Smart (2006), p. 320.
23. Kiselica & Englar-Carlson (2010).
24. For example, Wright (1989).
25. Myers (2004), p. 165.
26. Serial 26-1, *Battlefield* (6–27 September, 1989).
27. Episode 8-12, "Death in Heaven" (8 November, 2014).
28. Snipes et al. (2015).
29. Episode 5-1, "The Eleventh Hour" (3 April, 2010).
30. Morman & Floyd (2006).
31. Lamb et al. (1987).
32. Episode 4-6, "The Doctor's Daughter" (10 May, 2008).
33. Episode 5-2, "The Beast Below" (10 April, 2010).
34. Kiselica & Englar-Carlson (2010).
35. Stuessy (2007).
36. Marx (1959), p. 321.
37. Kiselica & Englar-Carlson (2010).
38. Boon (2005).
39. Boon (2005); Farthing (2005).
40. Examples: Adric in serial 19-6, *Earthshock*, pt. 4 (16 March, 1982); Clara in episode 9-10, "Face the Raven" (21 November, 2015); and, as far as the Doctor is concerned, Bill in episode 12-12, "The Doctor Falls" (1 July, 2017).
41. "Four wives, all dead."—Clara in episode 8-12, "Death in Heaven" (8 November, 2014).
42. Episodes 1-2, "The End of the World" (2 April, 2005); 12-2, "Spyfall," pt. 2 (5 January, 2020).
43. Anniversary special, *The Five Doctors* (23 November, 1983).
44. Episode 10-11, "World Enough and Time" (24 June, 2017).
45. Episode 12-12, "The Doctor Falls" (1 July, 2017).
46. Anniversary special, *The Five Doctors* (23 November, 1983).
47. Episode 10-11, "World Enough and Time" (24 June, 2017).
48. The Master kills Dr. Grace Holloway in *Doctor Who* (1996 TV movie), but he also kills his own companion Chang Lee in that story and the TARDIS revives both victims.

49. O'Neil & Egan (1992).

50. Episode 11-1, "The Woman Who Fell to Earth" (7 October, 2018).

51. Episode 11-3, "Rosa" (21 October, 2018).

52. Episode 11-2, "The Ghost Monument" (14 October, 2018).

53. Diamond (2021); Fontanella et al. (2014); Gabbard & Wilkinson (1996).

54. De Vries et al. (2014); Roselli (2018); Steensma et al. (2013).

55. Philpot et al. (1997).

56. Episode 10-11, "World Enough and Time" (24 June, 2017).

57. Serial 4-18, "State of Decay," pt. 4 (13 December, 1980).

58. Serial, 17-2, *City of Death*, pt. 1 (29 September, 19).

59. Episode 8-11, "Dark Water" (1 November, 2014).

60. For example, episodes 9-1, "The Magician's Apprentice," and 9-2, "The Witch's Familiar" (19 & 26 September, 2015).

61. Bem (1974, 1976).

62. Episode 8-10, "The Lie of the Land" (3 June, 2017).

63. Episode 3-11, "Utopia" (16 June, 2007).

64. Executed by Daleks and, after getting a new body, the Master refuses to let the Doctor save him from falling into the Eye of Harmony—*Doctor Who* (1996 TV movie). Chantho wounds Yana—see previous note. Wife kills Master as Harold Saxon and he refuses to regenerate—3-13, "Last of the Time Lords" (30 June, 2007). Resurrected Saxon Master and Missy kill each other—10-12, "The Doctor Falls" (1 July, 2017). When the Master impersonating Rasputin appears to be dying, the Thirteenth Doctor points out, "Your body's failing because of what you put it through," and he acknowledges, "Maybe."—BBC centenary special, "The Power of the Doctor" (23 October, 2022).

65. American Psychological Association (n.d.).

66. Mendoza (2013). See also O'Neil (2008).

67. Christmas special, "Twice Upon a Time" (25 December, 2017).

68. Episode 12-5, "Fugitive of the Judoon" (26 January, 2020).

69. Episode 6-4, "The Doctor's Wife" (14 May, 2011).

19. The Doctor's Brain and the Power of Choice: Regeneration, Determinism, and Free Will

1. Serial 7-4, *Inferno,* pt. 4 (30 May, 1970).

2. Kanfer (1997).

3. Episode 10-8, "The Lie of the Land" (3 June, 2017).

4. Hanly (1979).

5.   Serial 7-4, *Inferno,* pt. 4 (30 May, 1970).

6.   Wertheimer (1987).

7.   Bramness et al. (2006).

8.   Harlow (1848).

9.   As K'anpo Rinpoche predicts in serial 11-5, *Planet of the Spiders* (4 May–8 June, 1974).

10.   Serial 21-7, *The Twin Dilemma,* pt. 1 (22 March, 1984).

11.   Serial 4-3, *The Power of the Daleks,* pt. 1 (5 November, 1966).

12.   Johnson (2010).

13.   Episode 8-12, "Death in Heaven" (8 November, 2014).

14.   Episode 12-12, "The Doctor Falls" (1 July, 2017).

15.   Geschwind (1965); Goldberg & Bloom (1990); Goldstein (1908); Gross (1987).

16.   Carter (2010), p. 64.

17.   Serial 11-5, *Planet of the Spiders,* pt. 6 (8 June, 1974).

18.   Episode 8-4, "Listen" (13 September, 2014).

19.   McCullough (2015).

20.   Episode 6-11, "The God Complex" (17 September, 2011).

21.   Lo & Cohen (2007); Mikkelson (2012).

22.   Ramachandran & Blakeslee (1999).

23.   Episode 7-12, "Nightmare in Silver" (13 May, 2013).

24.   Caixeta et al. (2007).

25.   *Doctor Who* (1996 TV movie).

26.   Serial 4-3, *The Power of the Daleks,* pt. 1 (5 November, 1966).

27.   Episode 11-1, "The Woman Who Fell to Earth" (7 October, 2018)

28.   Such as when the Eleventh Doctor says he has forgotten how many children died on Gallifrey in anniversary special, "The Day of the Doctor" (23 November, 2013).

29.   Serial 7-1, "Spearhead from Space," pts. 1–2, (3–10 January, 1970).

30.   Cogan et al. (2019); Imbernón et al. (2022).

31.   Serial 7-1, "Spearhead from Space," pt. 2, (10 January, 1970).

32.   Sacks (1985).

33.   Christmas special, "Last Christmas" (25 December, 2014).

34.   Lewis (2013).

35.   Christmas special, "The Time of the Doctor" (25 December, 2013).

36.   American Psychiatric Association (2013, 2022); Hare (1996).

37.   Rogers et al. (2006); Schramme (2018).

38.   Shamay-Tsoory (2010). Discussed previously in Langley (2014).

39. Carr et al. (2003); Geddes (2011); Hetu et al. (2012); Young et al. (2010).

40. Bonini et al. (2022).

41. Carter (2010).

42. Carter (2010).

43. Baird et al. (2011); Kaplan & Iacoboni (2006); Milston et al. (2013).

44. Christmas special, "Twice Upon a Time" (25 December, 2017).

45. Episode 9-11, "Heaven Sent" (28 November, 2015).

46. For example, Ferguson & Zayas (2009).

47. For example, Jiang et al. (2006).

48. Blankenburg et al. (2003); Dehaene (2009); Haynes & Rees (2006).

49. Episodes 6-1, "The Impossible Astronaut" (23 April, 2011); 6-2, "Day of the Moon" (30 April, 2011).

50. For example, Spanos (1996).

51. Serial 8-1, *Terror of the Autons* (2–23 January, 1971).

52. Episode 3-2, "The Shakespeare Code" (7 April, 2007).

53. Christmas special, "The Christmas Invasion" (25 December, 2006).

54. Serial 6-7, *The War Games*, pt. 10 (21 June, 1969); Minisode, *The Night of the Doctor* (14 November, 2015).

55. Realized in episode 9-5, "The Girl Who Died" (17 October, 2015).

56. Episode 12-12, "The Doctor Falls" (1 July, 2017); Christmas special, "Twice Upon a Time" (25 December, 2017).

57. Serial 7-4 *Inferno*, pt. 7 (20 June, 1970).

58. Frankl (1956/2006).

59. Episode 12-3, "Orphan 55" (12 January, 2020).

20. The Time Lord Who Returns: An Interview with the First Modern Doctor

1. Modern season 1 teaser trailer, "The Trip of a Lifetime" (8 March, 2005).

2. Staring with *The Ravagers* 1-1, *Sphere of Freedom* (13 May, 2021).

3. Big Finish (2020).

4. Tharries (2022).

5. Episodes 1-4, "Aliens in London," and 1-5, "World War Three" (16 & 23 April, 2005).

6. Episodes 1-1, "Rose" (26 March, 2005); 1-8, "Father's Day" (14 May, 2005).

7. The Tenth Doctor (Matt Smith) in Christmas special, "A Christmas Carol" (25 December, 2010).

8. Episode 1-6, "Dalek" (30 April, 2005).

9.   Episode 1-9, "The Empty Child" (21 May, 2005).

10. Episode 1-10, "The Doctor Dances" (28 May, 2005).

11. Episode 1-13, "The Parting of the Ways" (18 June, 2005).

Final Word: Run!

1.   Episode 4-6, "The Doctor's Daughter" (10 May, 2008).

2.   Spencer (2010).

3.   For example, serial 4-9, *The Evil of the Daleks*, pt. 6 (24 June, 1967).

4.   Episode 6-13, "The Wedding of River Song" (1 October, 2011).

5.   Clark (2000).

6.   Mori (2008).

7.   Episode 9-12, "Hell Bent" (5 December, 2015).

8.   In the Christmas special, "The Snowmen" (25 December, 2012), the Eleventh Doctor does not seem to recall that the Second Doctor fought this foe before, first in the serial 5-2, *The Abominable Snowmen* (30 September–4 November, 1967).

9.   Bernstein & Loftus (2009).

10. Loftus (2001); Roediger et al. (1993).

11. First seen cosplaying as the Doctor in the anniversary special "The Day of the Doctor" (23 November, 2013).

12. Episode 9-8, "The Zygon Inversion" (7 November, 2015).

13. Episode 5-13, "The Big Bang" (26 June, 2010).

14. Didion (1979), p. 1.

15. BBC centenary special, "The Power of the Doctor" (23 October, 2022).

References

Adler, A. (1927/1963). *Understanding human nature*. Premier.

Adler, G., & Jaffé, A. (Eds.) (1973). *C. G. Jung letters, vol. 1: 1906–1950*. Princeton University Press.

Ahn, J. N., Luna-Lucero, M., Lamnina, M., Nightingale, M., Novak, D., & Lin-Siegler, X. (2016). Motivating students' STEM learning using biographical information. *International Journal of Designs for Learning, 7*(1), 71–85.

Ainsworth, J. W. (2010). Does the race of neighborhood role models matter? Collective socialization effects on educational achievement. *Urban Education, 45*(4), 401–23.

Alleyne, E., & Fernandes, I., & Pritchard, E. (2014). Denying humanness to victims: How gang members justify violent behavior. *Group Processes & Intergroup Relations, 17*(6), 750–62.

Allison, S. T., & Goethals, G. R. (2011). *Heroes: What they do & why we need them*. Oxford University Press.

Allport, G. W. (1937). *Personality: A psychological interpretation*. Holt.

Allport, G. W. (1955). *Becoming: Basic considerations for a psychology of personality*. Yale University Press.

Allport, G. W., & Odbert, H. S. (1936). Trait-names: A psycho-lexical study. *Psychological Monographs, 47*(1), i–171.

Altman, N. (2015). *Psychoanalysis in an age of accelerated cultural change: Spiritual globalization*. Routledge.

American Psychiatric Association (2013). *Diagnostic and statistical manual of mental disorders* (5th ed.) [DSM-5]. American Psychiatric Association.

American Psychiatric Association. (2022). *Diagnostic and statistical manual of mental disorders* (5th ed., text rev.) [DSM-5-TR]. American Psychiatric Association.

American Psychological Association (1998). Final conclusions of the American Psychological Association Working Group on the Investigation of Child Abuse. *Psychology, Public Policy, & Law, 4*(4), 933–40.

American Psychological Association (n.d.). *System*. APA Dictionary of Psychology. https://dictionary.apa.org/system

Archiniegas, D. B., Lauterbach, E. C., Anderson, K. E., Chow, T. W., Flashman, L. A., Hurley, R. A., Kaufer, D., McAllister, T. W., Reeve, A., Schiffer, R. B., & Silver, J. M. (2005). The differential diagnosis of pseudobulbar affect (PBA): Distinguishing PBA among disorders of mood and affect. *CNS Spectrums, 10*(5), 1–14.

Ashton, M. C., & Lee, K. (2001). A theoretical basis for the major dimensions of personality. *European Journal of Personality, 15*(5), 327–53.

Asmundson, G. J., Stapleton, J. A., & Taylor, S. (2004). Are avoidance and numbing distinct PTSD symptom clusters? *Journal of Traumatic Stress, 17*(6), 467–75.

Atkinson, R., & Rymill, G., & Tucker, M. (2021). *Doctor Who: Dalek Mark III travel machine combat training manual*. BBC Books.

Austin, A., Papciak, R., & Lovins, L. (2022). Gender euphoria: A grounded theory exploration of experiencing gender affirmation. *Psychology & Sexuality, 13*(5), 1406–26.

Bacon, T. (2020, June 14). *Doctor Who Tom Baker era's flirty ads suggest Romana relationship*. Screen Rant. https://screenrant.com/doctor-who-tom-baker-romana-ads-romance

Bains, S. (2007, April 1). *Mixed feelings*. Wired. http://www.wired.com/2007/04/esp

Baird, A. (2020). *Sex in the brain: How seizures, strokes, dementia, tumors, and trauma can change your sex life*. Columbia University Press.

Baird, A. D., Scheffer, I. E., & Wilson, S. J. (2011). Mirror neuron system involvement in empathy: A critical look at the evidence. *Social Neuroscience, 6*(4), 327–35.

Bandura, A. (2015). *Moral disengagement: How people do harm and live with themselves*. Worth.

Barkley, R. A. (Ed.). (2014). *Attention-deficit hyperactivity disorder: A handbook for diagnosis and treatment*. Guilford.

Barlett, C. P. (2015). Anonymously hurting others online: The effect of anonymity on cyberbullying frequency. *Psychology of Popular Media Culture, 4*(2), 70–79.

Baron-Cohen, S., Wheelwright, S., Skinner, R., Martin, J., & Clubley, E. (2001). The autism-spectrum quotient (AQ): Evidence from Asperger syndrome/high-functioning autism, males and females, scientists and mathematicians. *Journal of Autism & Developmental Disorders, 31*(1), 5–17.

Bar-Tal, D. (1985-1986). Altruistic motivation to help: Definition, utility and operationalization. *Humboldt Journal of Social Relations, 13*(1-2), 3–14.

Barr, P. (2004). Guilt- and shame-proneness and the grief of perinatal bereavement. *Psychology & Psychotherapy: Theory, Research, & Practice, 77*(4), 493–510.

Barr, P., & Cacciatore, J. (2008). Personal fear of death and grief in bereaved mothers. *Death Studies, 32*(5), 445–60.

Bashtavenko, A. (2008). *Principles of typology.* AuthorHouse.

Baum, S. K. (2008). *The psychology of genocide: Perpetrators, bystanders, and rescuers.* Cambridge University Press.

Baumeister, R. F., & Sommer, K. L. (1997). What do men want? Gender differences and two spheres of belongingness: Comment on Cross and Madson (1997). *Psychological Bulletin, 122*(1), 38–44.

Beaty, R. E., Benedek, M., Wilkins, R. W., Jauk, E., Fink, A., Silvia, P. J., & Neubauer, A. C. (2014). Creativity and the default network: A functional connectivity analysis of the creative brain at rest. *Neuropsychologia, 64,* 92–98.

Beckham, M. H. (2012). Building momentum: The unconventional strengths of perceiving college students. *Journal of Psychological Type, 72*(2), 27–40.

Beischel, W.J., Gauvin, S.E.M, van Anders, S.M. (2021). "A little shiny gender breakthrough": Community understandings of gender euphoria. *International Journal of Transgender Health, 23*(3), 274–94.

Bem, S. L. (1981). Gender schema theory: A cognitive account of sex typing. *Psychological Review, 88*(4), 354–64.

Bem, S. L. (1974). The measurement of psychological androgyny. *Journal of Consulting & Clinical Psychology, 42*(2), 155–62.

Bem, S. L. (1976). Sex typing and androgyny: Further explorations of the expressive domain. *Journal of Personality & Social Psychology, 34*(5), 1016–23.

Berger, D. M. (1977). The survivor syndrome: A problem of nosology and treatment. *American Journal of Psychotherapy, 31(*2), 238–51.

Bernstein, D. M., & Loftus, E. F. (2009). How to tell if a particular memory is true or false. *Perspectives in Psychological Science, 4*(4), 370–74.

Bernstein, Z. (2015, September 3). *The Valeyard and the stolen Earth. Doctor Who TV.* Doctor Who TV. http://www.doctorwhotv.co.uk/the-valeyard-and-the-stolen -earth-75606.htm

Beyerstein, B. L. (1999). Whence cometh the myth that we only use 10% of our brains? In S. Della Sala (Ed.), *Mind-myths: Exploring popular assumptions about the mind and brain* (pp. 3–24). Wiley.

Big Finish (2020, August 9). *Christopher Eccleston returns to Doctor Who.* Big Finish. https://www.bigfinish.com/news/v/christopher-eccleston-returns-to-doctor-who

Bignell, J., & O'Day, A. (2004). *Terry Nation.* Manchester University Press.

Birtel, M. (2014). 'You may say I'm a dreamer...' *The Psychologist, 27*(5), 340–43.

Bishop, P. (2014). *Carl Jung*. Reaktion.

Black, E. (2012). *War against the weak: Eugenics and America's campaign to create a master race* (expanded ed.). Dialog.

Blakemore, S. J., & Choudhury, S. (2006). Development of the adolescent brain: Implications for executive function and social cognition. *Journal of Child Psychology & Psychiatry, 47*(3–4), 296–312.

Blankenburg, F., Taskin, B., Ruben, J., Moosmann, M., Ritter, P., Curio, G., & Villringer, A. (2003). Imperceptive stimuli and sensory processing impediment. *Science, 299*(2514), 1864.

Blumberg, H. H. (2001). The common ground of natural language and social interaction in personality description. *Journal of Research in Personality, 35*(3), 289–312.

Boelen, P. A., Olff, M., & Smid, G. E. (2019). Traumatic loss: Mental health consequences and implications for treatment and prevention. *European Journal of Psychotraumatology, 10*(1), Artl 1591331.

Bogaert, A. F. (2015). *Understanding asexuality*. Rowman & Littlefield.

Bohns, V. K., Lucas, G. M., Molden, D. C., Finkel, E. J., Coolsen, M. K., Kumashiro, M., Rusbult, C. E., & Higgins, E. T. (2013). Opposites fit: Regulatory focus complementarity and relationship well-being. *Social Cognition, 31*(1), 1–14.

Bollas, C. (1995). *Cracking up: The work of unconscious experience*. Psychology Press.

Bonanno, G. A., Wortman, C. B., Lehman, D. R., Tweed, R. G., Haring, M., Sonnega, J., Carr, D., & Nesse, R. M. (2002). Resilience to loss and chronic grief: A prospective study from preloss to 18-months postloss. *Journal of Personality & Social Psychology, 83*(5), 1150.

Bond, M. H., Kwan, V. S. Y., & Li, C. (2000). Decomposing a sense of superiority: The differential social impact of self-regard and regard for others. *Journal of Research in Personality, 34*(4), 537–53.

Bonini, L., Rotunno, C., Arcuri, E., & Gallese, V. (2022). Mirror neurons 30 years later: Implications and applications. *Trends in Cognitive Sciences, 26*(9), 767–81.

Book, A. S., Visser, B., Blais, J., & D'Agata, M. T. (2016). Unpacking more "evil": What is at the core of the dark tetrad? *Personality & Individual Differences, 90*, 269–72.

Boon, K. A. (2005). Heroes, metanarratives, and the paradox of masculinity in contemporary Western culture. *Journal of Men's Studies, 13*(3), 301–12.

Boos, M., Franiel, X., & Belz, M. (2015). Competition in human groups—impact on group cohesion, perceived stress and outcome satisfaction. *Behavioural Processes, 120*(1), 65–68.

Boscarino, J. A., Figley, C. R., & Adams, R. E. (2004). Compassion fatigue following the September 11 terrorist attacks: A study of secondary trauma among New York City social workers. *International Journal of Emergency Mental Health*, *6*(2), 57–66.

Botvinick, M., & Cohen, J. (1998). Rubber hands "feels" touch that eyes see. *Nature*, *391*, 756.

Boyd-Wilson, B. M., Walkey, F. H., & McClure, J. (2002). Present and correct: We kid ourselves unless we live in the moment. *Personality & Individual Differences*, *33*(5), 691–702.

Bramness, J. G., Skurtveit, S., & Mørland, J. (2006). Flunitrazepam: Psychomotor impairment, agitation, and paradoxical reactions. *Forensic Science International*, *159*(2–3), 83–91.

Brannon, R. (1985). Dimensions of the male sex role in America. In A. G. Sargent (Ed.), *Beyond sex roles* (pp. 296–316). West.

Briggs Myers, I., McCauley, M. H., Quenk, N. L., & Hammer, A. L. (2009). *MBTI manual: A guide to the development and use of the Myers Briggs Type Indicator* (3rd ed.). Consulting Psychologists Press.

Brooks, A. (1982, October 3). Debunking the myth of P. T. Barnum. *The New York Times*, Section 11(1).

Brower, M. C., & Price, B. H. (2001). Neuropsychiatry of frontal lobe dysfunction in violent and criminal behaviour: A critical review. *Journal of Neurology, Neurosurgery & Psychiatry*, *71*(6), 720–26.

Brown, B. (2012). *Daring greatly: How the courage to be vulnerable transforms the way we live, love, parent, and lead*. Gotham.

Brown, F. W., & Reilly, M. D. (2009). The Myers-Briggs Type Indicators and transformational leadership. *Journal of Management Development*, *28*(10), 916–32.

Buccafusco, C., & Fagundes, D. (2016). The moral psychology of copyright infringement. *Minnesota Law Review*, *100*(6), 2433–2507.

Burger, J. M. (2015). *Personality* (9th ed.). Cengage.

Burley, D. T., Genc, S., & Silk, T. J. (2021). Childhood conduct problems are associated with reduced white matter fibre density and morphology. *Journal of Affective Disorders*, *281*, 638–45.

Burr, J. A., Han, S. H., & Peng, C. (2020). Childhood friendship experiences and cognitive functioning in later life: The mediating roles of adult social disconnectedness and adult loneliness. *The Gerontologist*, *60*(8), 1456–65.

Busch, J. (2015, July 9). *Doctor Who: 13 things to know about season 9*. Collider. http://collider.com/doctor-who-13-things-to-know-about-season-9

Caballero, A., & Connell, J. E. (2010). Evaluation of the social cue cards for preschool age children with autism spectrum disorders. *Journal of Behavior Assessment & Intervention in Children, 1*(1), 25–42.

Cacioppo, J. T., & Cacioppo, S. (2014). Social relationships and health: The toxic effects of perceived social isolation. *Social & Personality Psychology Compass 8*(2), 58–72.

Caixeta, L., Maciel, P., Nunes, J., Nazareno, L., Araújo, L., & Borges, R. R. (2007). Alien hand syndrome in AIDS: Neuropsychological features and physiopathological considerations based on a case report. *Dementia & Neuropsychologia, 1*(4), 418–21.

Calhoun, L. G., Tedeschi, R. G., & Tedeschi, R. G. (Eds.). (2014). *Handbook of posttraumatic growth: Research and practice.* Routledge.

Caplan, R. D., Tripathi, R. C., & Naidu, R. K. (1985). Subjective past, present, and future fit: Effects on anxiety, depression, and other indicators of well-being. *Journal of Personality & Social Psychology, 48*(1), 180–97.

Capraro, R. M., & Capraro, M. M. (2002). Myers-Briggs Type Indicator score reliability across studies: A meta-analytic reliability generalization study. *Educational & Psychological Measurement, 62*(4), 590–602.

Cardinali, L., Frassinetti, F., Brozzoli, C., Roy, A. C., Urquizar, C., & Farnè A. (2009). Tool-use induces morphological updating of the body schema. *Current Biology, 19*(12), R478–79.

Carducci, B. J. (2009). *The psychology of personality: Viewpoints, research, and applications* (2nd ed.). Wiley.

Carelli, F. (2015). Dissociative amnesia or psychogenic amnesia as results of war's shocking events. *London Journal of Primary Care, 7*(4), 78–79.

Carey, J. C., Fleming, S. D., & Roberts, D. Y. (1989). The Myers-Briggs Type Indicator as a measure of aspects of cognitive style. *Measurement & Evaluation in Counseling & Development, 22*(2), 94–99.

Carr, L., Iacoboni, M., Dubeau, M., Mazziotta, J. C., & Lenzi, G. L. (2003). Neural mechanisms of empathy in humans: A relay from neural systems for imitation to limbic areas. *Proceedings of the National Academy of Sciences 100*(9), 5497–5502.

Carter, R. (2010). Mapping the mind (2nd ed.). University of California Press.

Carruthers, S. L., Lawrence, S., & Stich, S. (Eds.) (2007). *The innate mind* (Vol. 3, pp. 367–391). Oxford University Press.

Cassell, W. A., Charles, T., Dubey, B. L., & Janssen, H. (2014). SIS incites long term PTSD combat memories and survivor guilt. *Journal of Projective Psychology & Mental Health, 21*(2), 68–80.

Castelnuovo-Tedesco, P. (1989). The fear of change and its consequences in analysis and psychotherapy. *Psychoanalytic Inquiry, 9,* 101–18.

Cattell, R. B. (1943). The description of personality: Basic traits resolved into clusters. *Journal of Abnormal & Social Psychology, 38*(4), 476–506.

Cattell, R. B. (1944). Interpretation of the twelve primary personality factors. *Character & Personality: A Quarterly for Psychodiagnostic & Allied Studies, 13,* 55–91.

Cattell, R. B. (1956). Validation and intensification of the Sixteen Personality Factor Questionnaire. *Journal of Clinical Psychology, 12*(3), 205–14.

Celesia, G. (2010). Visual perception and awareness: A modular system. *Journal of Psychophysiology, 24*(2), 62–67.

Center for Substance Abuse Treatment. (1999). Brief interventions and brief therapies for substance abuse. In *Treatment improvement protocol series* (no. 34, pp. 105–119). Substance Abuse and Mental Health Services Administration.

Chandola, T., Britton, A., Brunner, E., Hemingway, H., Malik, M., Kumari, M., Badrick, E., Kivimaki, M., & Marmot, M. (2008). Work stress and coronary heart disease: What are the mechanisms? *European Heart Journal, 29*(5), 640–48.

Chapin, H. L., Darnall, B. D., Seppälä, E. M., Doty, J. R., Hah, J. M., & Mackey, S. C. (2014). Pilot study of a compassion meditation intervention in chronic pain. *Journal of Compassionate Health Care, 1*(1), 1–12.

Charlop-Christy, M. H., & Kelso, S. (2003). Teaching children with autism conversational speech using a cue card written script program. *Education & Treatment of Children, 26*(2), 108–27.

Chhaochharia, V., Du, M., & Niessen-Ruenzi, A. (2022). Counter-stereotypical female role models and women's occupational choices. *Journal of Economic Behavior & Organization, 196,* 501–23.

Chidester, T. R., Helmreich, R. L., Gregorich, S. E., & Geis, C. E. (1991). Pilot personality and crew coordination: Implications for training and selection. *International Journal of Aviation Psychology, 1*(1), 25–44.

Chowdhury, A. N. (2008). Vincent van Gogh and mental illness. *British Journal of Psychiatry, 193*(2), 167–68.

Clark, A. (2000*). A theory of sentience.* Clarendon.

Clark, A. (2003). *Natural born cyborgs: Minds, technologies, and the future of human intelligence.* Oxford University Press.

Cleckley, H. M. (1941/1976). *The mask of sanity: An attempt to clarify some issues about the so-called psychopathic personality.* Mosby.

Cogan, E. S., Shapses, M. A., Robinson, T. E., & Tronson, N. C. (2019). Disrupting reconsolidation: Memory erasure or blunting of emotional/motivational value? *Neuropsychopharmacology, 44*(2), 399–407.

Cohen, D., & Schmidt, J. P. (1979). Ambiversion: Characteristics of midrange responders on the introversion-extraversion continuum. *Journal of Personality Assessment, 43*(5), 513–16.

Cole, S. W., Hawkley, L. C., Arevalo, J. M., Sung, C. Y., Rose, R. M., & Cacioppo, J. T. (2007). Social regulation of gene expression in human leukocytes. *Genome Biology, 8*(9), R189.

Connolly, P. (2006). *Greece and Rome at war.* Greenhill.

Cornell, P. (1995). *Human nature.* Virgin.

Costa, P. T., & McCrae, R. R., Jr. (1992). Four ways five factors are basic. *Personality & Individual Differences, 13*(6), 667–73.

Courtland, L. (2011) Cybermen evil? I don't think so. In C. Lewis & P. Smithka (Eds.), *Doctor Who and philosophy: Bigger on the inside* (pp. 199–210). Carus.

Cramer, T. (2013, April 18). *PTSD Study: Men versus women.* Inside Veterans' Health. http://www.va.gov/health/NewsFeatures/2013/April/PTSD-Study-Men-Versus-Women.asp

Crane, P. R., Talley, A. E., & Piña-Watson, B. (2022). This is what a scientist looks like: Increasing Hispanic/Latina women's identification with STEM using relatable role models. *Journal of Latinx Psychology, 10*(2), 112–27.

Currie, E. (2016). A companion's choice: Do opposites attract? In T. Langley (Ed.), *Doctor Who psychology: A madman with a box* (1st ed., pp. 154-166). Sterling.

Daniels, T. (2011, May 1). *Why the BBC tried to . . . Exterminate Nazi Daleks! As Doctor Who's most notorious enemies return to our screens, we reveal what inspired their creator.* Mail Online. http://www.dailymail.co.uk/tvshowbiz/article-1382252/Daleks-Doctor-Whos-notorious-enemies-return-screens.html

Davies, R. T., & Cook, B. (2010). *Doctor Who: The writer's tale—the final chapter.* Random House UK.

DeCasien, A.R., Guma, E., Liu, S, & Raznahan, A. (2022). Sex differences in the human brain: A roadmap for more careful analysis and interpretation of a biological reality. *Biology of Sex Differences, 13*(1), 1–21.

Dehaene, S. (2009, November 24). *Signatures of consciousness.* Edge. https://www.edge.org/conversation/stanislas_dehaene-signatures-of-consciousness

De Mijolla-Mellor, S. (2009). *Au risque des Affinités électives* [The risks of falling in love again]. *Topique: Revue Freudienne, 107,* 165–82.

De Raad, B., Barelds, D. P. H., Mlac̆ic̆, B., Church, A. T., Katigbak, M. S., Ostendorf, F., Hřebíčková, M., Di Blas, L., & Szirmák, Z. (2010). Only three personality factors are fully replicable across languages: Reply to Ashton and Lee. *Journal of Research in Personality, 44*(4), 442–45.

Dekel, S., Mamon, D., Solomon, Z., Lanman, O., & Dishy, G. (2016). Can guilt lead to psychological growth following trauma exposure? *Psychiatry Research, 236,* 196–98.

Delvaux, E., Meeussen, L., & Mesquita, B. (2015). Feel like you belong: On the bidirectional link between emotional fit and group identification in task groups. *Frontiers in Psychology, 6,* 1106.

Desmond, D., & MacLachlan, M. (2002). Psychosocial issues in the field of prosthetics and orthotics. *Journal of Prosthetics & Orthotics, 14*(1), 19–22.

Diamond, L. M. (2021). The new genetic evidence on same-gender sexuality: Implications for sexual fluidity and multiple forms of sexual diversity. *Journal of Sex Research, 58*(7), 818–37.

Dickson, D. H., & Kelly, I. W. (1985). The 'Barnum effect' in personality assessment: A review of the literature. *Psychological Reports, 57*(1), 367–82.

Didion, J. (1979). *The white album.* Simon & Schuster.

Dief, A. E., Sivukhina, E. V., & Jirikowski, G. F., 2018. Oxytocin and stress response. *Open Journal of Endocrine & Metabolic Diseases, 8*(03), 93.

Diener, E. (1979). Deindividuation, self-awareness, and disinhibition. *Journal of Personality & Social Psychology, 37*(7), 1160–71.

Dixon-Gordon, K. L., Tull, M. T., & Gratz, K. L. (2014). Self-injurious behaviors in posttraumatic stress disorder: An examination of potential moderators. *Journal of Affective Disorders, 166,* 359–67.

Doctor Who (2022, October 23). *Doctor Who returns 2023. . .* [Video]. YouTube. https://www.youtube.com/watch?v=i5CAsSzUxzU

Doctor Who Amino (2015, June 20). *Regeneration.* Doctor Who Amino. http://www.aminoapps.com/page/doctor-who/4815354/regeneration

Doctor Who Answers (2012). *Saddest regeneration.* Doctor Who Answers. http://doctorwho.answers.wikia.com/wiki/Forum:Saddest_Regeneration

Doctor Who: The Fan Show (2018, August 3). *The Steven Moffat interview: Part 3* [Video]. YouTube. https://www.youtube.com/watch?v=styqnGNTffM

Doni, E. (2021). Exposing preschool children to counterstereotypical professional role models using audiovisual means: A small study in preschool Greece. *Early Childhood Education Journal, 49*(2), 295–302.

Donovan, N. (2022). Peer support facilitates post-traumatic growth in first responders: A literature review. *Trauma, 24*(4), 277-85.

Droselle Vries, A. L. C., Kreukels, B. P. C., Steensma, T. D., & McGuire, J. K. (2014). Gender identity development: A biopsychosocial perspective. In B. P. C. Kreukels, T. D. Steensma, & A. L. C. de Vries (Eds.), *Gender dysphoria and disorders of sex development: Progress in care and knowledge* (pp. 53–80). Springer Science + Business Media.

Du, X., Bai, X., Liu, Y., & Yuan, S. (2022). Reading struggle stories of role models can improve the perseverance of undergraduates with low perseverance. *Current Psychology: A Journal for Diverse Perspectives on Diverse Psychological Issues.* Advance online publication. https://link.springer.com/article/10.1007/s12144-022-04168-7

Duckworth, A. L., & Seligman, M. E. (2005). Self-discipline outdoes IQ in predicting academic performance of adolescents. *Psychological Science, 16*(12), 939–44.

Durrett, C., & Trull, T. J. (2005). An evaluation of evaluative personality terms: A comparison of the Big Seven and five-factor model in predicting psychopathology. *Psychological Assessment, 17*(3), 359–68.

Dutton, D. G. (2007). *The psychology of genocide, massacres, and extreme violence: Why normal people commit atrocities.* Praeger Security International.

Dvorsky, G. (2013). *Scientific evidence that you probably don't have free will.* io9. http://io9.com/5975778/scientific-evidence-that-you-probably-dont-have-free-will

Earnshaw, V. A., Menino, D. D., Sava, L. M., Perrotti, J., Barnes, T. N., Humphrey, D. L., & Reisner, S. L. (2020). LGBTQ bullying: A qualitative investigation of student and school health professional perspectives. *Journal of LGBT Youth, 17*(3), 280–97.

Ejlskov, L., Bøggild, H., Kuh, D., & Stafford, M. (2020). Social relationship adversities throughout the lifecourse and risk of loneliness in later life. *Ageing & Society, 40*(8), 1718–34.

Ellenberger, H. F. (1970/1981). *The discovery of the unconscious.* Basic.

Ellison, H. (1979). Introducing Doctor Who. In T. Dicks (Author), *Doctor Who and the day of the Daleks.* Pinnacle.

Elm, J. H., Lewis, J. P., Walters, K. L., Self, J. M. (2016). "I'm in this world for a reason": Resilience and recovery among American Indian and Alaska Native two-spirit women. *Journal of Lesbian Studies, 20*(3–4), 352–71.

Engler, B. (2009). *Personality theories* (8th ed.). Wadsworth.

Epel, E., Lapidus, R., McEwen, B., & Brownell, K. (2001). Stress may add bite to appetite in women: A laboratory study of stress-induced cortisol and eating behavior. *Psychoneuroendocrinology, 26*(1), 37–49.

Erikson, E. H. (1987). Late adolescence (1959). In S. Schlein (Ed.), *A way of looking at things: Selected papers from 1930 to 1980—Erik Erikson.* Norton.

Erikson, E. H., & Erikson, J. M. (1998). *The life cycle completed* (extended version). Norton.

Eshun, S., & Gurung, R. A. R. (2009). *Culture and mental health: Sociocultural influences, theory, and practice.* Wiley-Blackwell.

Eveleth, R. (2013, March 26). *The Myers-Briggs personality test is pretty much meaning-less.* Smithsonian. http://www.smithsonianmag.com/smart-news/the-myers-briggs -personality-test-is-pretty-much-meaningless-9359770/

Eysenck, H. J. (1947). *Dimensions of personality.* Trubner.

Eysenck, H. J. (1966). Personality and experimental psychology. *Bulletin of the British Psychological Society, 19*(1), 1–28.

Eysenck, H. J. (1985). *Decline and fall of the Freudian empire.* Viking.

Eysenck, H. J. (1992). Four ways five factors are *not* basic. *Personality & Individual Dif-ferences, 13*(6), 653–65.

Eysenck, H. J. (1993). Creativity and personality: Suggestions for a theory. *Psychological Inquiry, 4*(3), 147–78.

Eysenck, H. J., & Eysenck, M. W. (1985). *Personality and individual differences: A natural science approach.* Plenum.

Eysenck, M. W., Payne S., & Santos, R. (2006). Anxiety and depression: Past, present, and future events. *Cognition & Emotion, 20*(2), 274–94.

Farkas, T., & Leaper, C. (2016). The psychology of boys. In W. J. Wong & S. R. Wester (Eds.), *APA handbook of men and masculinities* (pp. 357–87). American Psycholog-ical Association.

Farthing, G. W. (2005). Attitudes toward heroic and nonheroic physical risk takers as mates and as friends. *Evolution & Human Behavior, 26*(2), 171–85.

Ferguson, M., & Zayas, V. (2009). Automatic evaluation. Current Directions in Psycho-logical *Science, 18*(6), 362–66.

Festinger, L., Pepitone, A., & Newcomb, T. (1952). Some consequences of deindividua-tion in a group. *Journal of Abnormal & Social Psychology, 47*(2 Suppl.), 382–89.

Figley, C. R. (2002). Compassion fatigue: Psychotherapists' chronic lack of self care. *Journal of Clinical Psychology, 58*(11), 1433–41.

Firestone, R. W. (2015). The ultimate resistance. *Journal of Humanistic Psychology, 55*(1), 77–101.

Fishman, I., & Ng, R. (2013). Error-related brain activity in extraverts: Evidence for altered response monitoring in social context. *Biological Psychology, 93*(1), 225–30.

Fiske, S. T. (2009). From dehumanization and objectification to rehumanization. *Annals of the New York Academy of Sciences, 1167*(1), 31–34.

Flint Rehab (2020, March 27). *Disinhibition after brain injury: Causes, treatment, and management.* Flint Rehab. https://www.flintrehab.com/disinhibition-after-brain-injury

Fogarty, L. A., Curbow, B. A., Wingard, J. R., McDonnell, K., & Somerfield, M. R. (1999). Can 40 seconds of compassion reduce patient anxiety? *Journal of Clinical Oncology, 17*(1), 371–79.

Fontanella, L., Maretti, M., & Sarra, A. (2014). Gender fluidity across the world: A multilevel item response theory approach. *Quality & Quantity: International Journal of Methodology, 48*(5), 2553–68.

Fortunato, V. J., & Furey, J. T. (2011). The theory of MindTime: The relationships between future, past, and present thinking and psychological well-being and distress. *Personality & Individual Differences, 50*(1), 20–24.

Franco, V., Hu, H-Y., Lewenstein, B., Piirto, R., Underwood, R., & Vidal, N. K. (1995). Anatomy of a flame: Conflict and community building on the internet. *IEEE Technology & Society Magazine, 14*(2), 12–21.

Frankel, V. E. (2016). *Doctor Who and the Hero's Journey: The Doctor and companions as chosen ones.* CreateSpace.

Frankl, V. E. (1956/2006). *Man's search for meaning* (I. Lasch, Trans.). Pocket.

Fredrickson, B. L. (2001). The role of positive emotions in positive psychology: The broaden-and-build theory of positive emotions. *American Psychologist, 56*(3), 218–26.

Freud, A. (1936). *The ego and defense mechanisms.* Imago.

Freud, S. (1900/1965). *The interpretation of dreams.* Avon.

Freud, S. (1901/1966). The psychopathology of everyday life. In *The standard edition of the complete psychological works of Sigmund Freud* (Vol. VI, pp. 8–12). Hogarth.

Freud, S. (1909). Analysis of a phobia in a 5-year-old boy. In *Jahrbuch für psychoanalytische under psychopathologische Forshugen,* Bd. 1. Reprinted with translation in *The sexual enlightenment of children* (1963). Collier.

Freud, S. (1912). A note on the unconscious in psycho-analysis. In A. Strachey & A. Tyson (Eds.) *The standard edition of the complete psychological works of Sigmund Freud* (Vol. XII, pp. 255–66). Hogarth.

Freud, S. (1915/1963). Repression. In P. Rieff (Ed.), *General psychological theory* (pp. 104–15). Collier.

Freud, S. (1917/1963). Introductory lectures on psycho-analysis: Part III. General theory of the neurosis. In J. Strachey (Ed. & Trans.), *The standard edition of the complete works of Sigmund Freud* (Vol. 16, pp. 241–477). Hogarth.

Freud, S. (1920). *Beyond the pleasure principle.* Norton.

Freud, S. (1923). *The ego and the id.* Hogarth.

Freud, S. (1921). *Group psychology and the analysis of the ego.* International Psychoanalytic Publishing House.

Freud, S. (1933). *New introductory lectures on psychoanalysis. The standard edition of the complete psychological works of Sigmund Freud,* Volume XXII (1932–36): *New introductory lectures on psycho-analysis and other works* 1–182. Hogarth.

Freud, S. (1937). Analysis terminable and interminable. *International Journal of Psychoanalysis, 18*(4), 373–405.

Freud, S. (1940). An outline of psychoanalysis. In *Standard edition of the complete works of Sigmund Freud* (vol. 23, pp. 141–207). Hogarth.

Friston, K. (2002). Beyond phrenology: What can neuroimaging tell us about distributed circuitry? *Annual Review of Neuroscience, 25*(1), 221–50.

Fritzsche, K. (2020). The terminally ill and dying patient. In K. Fritzsche, S. H. McDaniel, & M. Wirsching (Eds.), *Psychosomatic medicine: An international guide for the primary care setting* (pp. 267–74). Springer Nature Switzerland AG.

Fromm, E. (1941). *Escape from freedom.* Holt, Rinehart & Winston.

Fromm, E. (1973). *The anatomy of human destructiveness.* Holt, Rinehart & Winston.

Fromm, E. (1955). *The sane society.* Rinehart.

Fromm, E. (1956). *The art of loving.* Harper & Row.

Funder, D. (2001). Personality. *Annual Review of Psychology, 52,* 197–221.

Gabbard, G. O., & Wilkinson, S. M. (1996). Nominal gender and gender fluidity in the psychoanalytic situation. *Gender & Psychoanalysis, 1*(4), 463–81.

Gal, R. (1985). Commitment and obedience in the military: An Israeli case study. *Armed Forces & Society, 11*(4), 553–64.

Galupo, M. P., Pulice-Farrow, L., & Lindley, L. (2020). "Every time I get gendered male, I feel a pain in my chest": Understanding the social context for gender dysphoria. *Stigma & Health, 5*(2), 199–208.

Ganguly, K., & Carmena, J. M. (2009). Emergence of a stable cortical map for neuroprosthetic control. *PLoS Biology, 7*(7), e1000153.

Garbo, N. (1977). *To love again: A psychiatrist's search for love.* McGraw-Hill.

Gardner, H. (2006). *Multiple intelligences: New horizons.* Basic.

Gardner, H., & Hatch, T. (1989). Educational implications of the theory of multiple intelligences. *Educational Researcher, 18*(8), 4–10.

Gates, Z. Y. (2022). What if LeBron James was a scientist? The influence of role models on Black male youth in STEM programs. In A. G. Robins, L. Knibbs, T. N.

Ingram, M. N. Weaver, Jr., & A. A. Hilton (Eds.), *Young, gifted and missing: The underrepresentation of African American males in science, technology, engineering and mathematics disciplines* (pp. 115–28). Emerald.

Geary, D. C., Winegard, B., & Winegard, B. (2016). Evolutionary influences on men's lives. In W. J. Wong & S. R. Wester (Eds.), *APA handbook of men and masculinities* (pp. 211–29). American Psychological Association.

Geddes, L. (2011, August 24). *Empathy enhanced by magnetic stimulation of the brain.* New Scientist. https://www.newscientist.com/article/mg21128274.300-empathy-enhanced -by-magnetic-stimulation-of-the-brain

Gergen, K. J., Christie, R., & Geis, F. (Sep 3 - Sep 8, 1970). *Machiavellianism* [Conference session]. APA 78th Annual Convention, Miami Beach, FL.

Geschwind, N. (1965). Disconnexion syndromes in animals and man. I. *Brain 88*(2), 237–94.

Gibson, S., & Condor, S. (2009). State institutions and social identity: National representation in soldiers' and civilians' interview talk concerning military service. *British Journal of Social Psychology, 48*(2), 313–36.

Gilbert, K. R., & Ho, A. H. Y. (2021). Katana: Spousal bereavement and continuing bonds. In J. A. Harrington & R. A. Neimeyer (Eds.), *Superhero grief: The transformative power of loss* (pp. 117–22). Routledge/Taylor & Francis Group.

Gillooly, S. N., Hardt, H., & Smith, A. E. (2021). Having female role models correlates with PhD students' attitudes toward their own academic success. *PLOS One, 16*(8), Article e0255095.

Giritli Nygren, K. (2012). Narratives of ICT and organizational change in public administration. *Gender, Work, & Organization, 19*(6), 615–30.

Gladding, S. T., & Villalba, J. (2014). Imitation, impersonation, and transformation: Using male role models in films to promote maturity. *Journal of Counseling & Development, 92*(1), 114–21.

Godwin, M. (1990). *Angels: An endangered species.* Simon & Schuster.

Goetz, J. L., Keltner, D., & Simon-Thomas, E. (2010). Compassion: An evolutionary analysis and empirical review. *Psychological Bulletin, 136*(3), 351–74.

Goldberg, E. (2002). *The executive brain: Frontal lobes and the civilized mind.* Oxford University Press.

Goldberg, G., & Bloom, K. K. (1990). The alien hand sign. *American Journal of Physical Medicine & Rehabilitation, 69*(5), 228–38.

Goldberg, L. R. (1982). From Ace to Zombie: Some explorations in the language of personality. In C. D. Spielberger & J. N. Butcher (Eds.), *Advances in personality assessment* (Vol. 1, pp. 203–234). Erlbaum.

Goldstein, K. (1908). *Zur Lehre von der motorischen Apraxie* [On the doctrine of the motor apraxia]. *Journal für Psychologie und Neurologie, 11*(4–5), 169–87, 270–83.

Gonzalez, O. I., Novaco, R. W., Eger, M. A., & Gahm, G. A. (2016). Anger intensification with combat-related PTSD and depression comorbidity. *Psychological Trauma: Theory, Research, Practice, & Policy, 8*(1), 9–16.

Grafman, J., Schwab, K., Warden, D., et al. (1996). Frontal lobe injuries, violence and aggression: A report of the Vietnam head injury study. *Neurology, 46*(5), 1231–38.

Grafman, J., Schwab, K., Warden, D., Pridgen, A., Brown, H. R., & Salazar, A. M. (1996). Frontal lobe injuries, violence and aggression: A report of the Vietnam head injury study. *Neurology, 46*(5), 1231–38.

Greene, J. (2009). The cognitive neuroscience of moral judgment. In M. Gazzaniga (Ed.) *The cognitive neurosciences* (4th ed., pp. 987–1002). MIT Press.

Greene, J. (2013). *Moral tribes: Emotion, reason, and the gap between us and them.* Penguin.

Greene, J. D., Somerville, R. B., Nystrom, L. E., Darley, J. M., & Cohen, J. D. (2001). An fMRI investigation of emotional engagement in moral judgment. *Science, 293*(14), 2105–08.

Greitemeyer, T. (2022). Prosocial modeling: Person role models and the media. *Current Opinion in Psychology, 44*, 135–39.

Gros, D., Szafranski, D. D., Brady, K. T., & Back, S. E. (2015). Relations between pain, PTSD symptoms, and substance use in veterans. *Psychiatry: Interpersonal & Biological Processes, 78*(3), 277–87.

Gross, C. (1987). Neuroscience, the early history of. In G. E. Adelman (Ed.), *Encyclopedia of neuroscience* (pp. 843–47). Elsevier.

Hadden, B. W., Agnew, C. R., & Tan, K. (2018). Commitment readiness and relationship formation. *Personality & Social Psychology Bulletin, 44*(8), 1242–57.

Hadoke, T. (2017). *Toby Hadoke's Who Round: 232: Steven Moffat (2017).* Big Finish. https://www.bigfinish.com/releases/v/toby-hadoke-s-who-s-round-232-steven-moffat-2017-1808

Hahn, A. M., Tirabassi, C. K., Simons, R. M., & Simons, J. S. (2015). Military sexual trauma, combat exposure, and negative urgency as independent predictors of PTSD and subsequent alcohol problems among OEF/OIF veterans. *Psychological Services, 12*(4), 378–83.

Haidt, J. (2001). The emotional dog and its rational tail: A social intuitionist approach to moral judgment. *Psychological Review, 108*(4), 814–34.

Haidt, J. (2012). *The righteous mind: Why good people are divided by politics and religion.* Pantheon.

Haidt, J., & Joseph, C. (2004) Intuitive ethics: How innately prepared intuitions generate culturally variable virtues. *Daedalus, 133*(4) 55–66.

Haidt, J., & Joseph, C. (2007). The moral mind: How five sets of innate moral intuitions guide the development of many culture-specific virtues, and perhaps even modules. In P. Carruthers, S. Lawrence, & S. Stich (Eds.) *The innate mind* (Vol. 3, pp. 367–92). Oxford University Press.

Haidt, J., Koller, S., & Dias, M. (1993). Affect, culture and morality, or is it wrong to eat your dog? *Journal of Personality & Social Psychology, 65*(4), 613–28.

Hamlen, K. R., & Imbesi, K. J. (2020). Role models in the media: A content analysis of preschool television programs in the U.S. *Journal of Children & Media, 14*(3), 302–23.

Hammack, P. L., Frost, D. M., & Hughes, S. D. (2018). Queer Intimacies: A new paradigm for the study of relationship diversity. *Journal of Sex Research, 56*(4–5), 556–92.

Hamner, C. H. (2011). *Enduring battle: American soldiers in three wars, 1776–1945.* University Press of Kansas.

Handley, R. V., Salkovskis, P. M., Scragg, P., & Ehlers, A. (2009). Clinically significant avoidance of public transport following the London bombings: Travel phobia or subthreshold posttraumatic stress disorder? *Journal of Anxiety Disorders, 23*(8), 1170–76.

Hanly, C. M. T. (1979). *Existentialism and psychoanalysis.* International Universities Press.

Hare, R. D. (1996). Psychopathy: A clinical construct whose time has come. *Criminal Justice & Behavior, 23*(1), 25–54.

Harlow, J. M. (1848). Passage of an iron rod through the head. *Boston Medical & Surgical Journal, 39*(20), 389–93.

Harris, M. (1983). *The Doctor Who technical manual.* Random House.

Harrod, S. B., Metzger, M. M., & Riccio, D. C. (1996). Does induced recovery from amnesia represent a disinhibition effect? *Physiology & Behavior 60*(5), 1375–78.

Harvey, R. J., Murry, W. D., & Stamoulis, D. T. (1995). Unresolved issues in the dimensionality of the Myers-Briggs Type Indicator. *Education & Psychological Measurement, 55*(4), 535–44.

Hatfield, E. (1988). Passionate and companionate love. In R. J. Sternberg & M. L. Barnes (Eds.), *The psychology of love* (pp. 191–217). Yale University Press.

Hayne, H., Garry, M., & Loftus, E. F. (2006). On the continuing lack of evidence for repression. *Behavioral & Brain Sciences, 29*(5), 521–22.

Haynes, J., & Rees, G. (2006). Decoding mental states from brain activity in humans. *Nature Reviews Neuroscience, 7*(7), 523–34.

Hayslip, B., Jr., & Glover, R. J. (2009). Custodial grandparenting: Perceptions of loss by non-custodial grandparent peers. *Omega: Journal of Death & Dying, 58*(3), 163–75.

Hazel, K. L., & Kleyman, K. S. (2019). Gender and sex inequalities: Implications and resistance. *Journal of Prevention & Intervention in the Community, 48*(4), 281–92.

Heim, E., Karatzias, T., & Maercker, A. (2022). Cultural concepts of distress and complex PTSD: Future directions for research and treatment. *Clinical Psychology Review, 93*, 1–14.

Held, P., Owens, G. P., & Anderson, S. E. (2015). The interrelationships among trauma-related guilt and shame, disengagement coping, and PTSD in a sample of treatment-seeking substance users. *Traumatology, 21*(4), 285–92.

Held, P., Owens, G. P., Schumm, J. A., Chard, K. M., & Hansel, J. E. (2011). Disengagement coping as a mediator between trauma-related guilt and PTSD severity. *Journal of Traumatic Stress, 24*(6), 708–15.

Helwig, C. C., & Prencipe, A. (1999). Children's judgments of flags and flag-burning. *Child Development, 70*(1), 132–43.

Herbert, C. P. (2015). Perspectives in primary care: Values-driven leadership is essential in health care [Editorial]. *Annals of Family Medicine, 13*(6), 512–13.

Herman, J. L. (1992). Complex PTSD: A syndrome in survivors of prolonged and repeated trauma. *Journal of Traumatic Stress, 5*(1), 377–91.

Hettema, J. M., Neale, M. C., Myers, J. M., Prescott, C. A., & Kendler, K. S. (2006). A population-based twin study of the relationship between neuroticism and internalizing. *American Journal of Psychiatry, 163*(5), 857–64.

Hetu, S., Taschereau-Dumouchel, V., & Jackson, P. L. (2012). Stimulating the brain to study social actions and empathy. *Brain Stimulation, 5*(2), 95–102.

Hijazi, A. M., Keith, J. A., & O'Brien, C. (2015). Predictors of posttraumatic growth in a multiwar sample of U. S. combat veterans. *Journal of Peace Psychology, 21*(3), 395–408.

Hirai, M., & Vernon, L. (2011). The role of disgust propensity in blood-injection-injury phobia: Comparisons between Asian Americans and Caucasian members. *Cognition & Emotion, 25*(8), 1500–9.

Hirsch, J. S. (2007). "Love makes a family": Globalization, companionate marriage, and the modernization of gender inequality. In M. B. Padilla, J. S. Hirsch, M. Muñoz-Laboy, R. Sember, & R. G. Parker (Eds.), *Love and globalization: Transformations of intimacy in the contemporary world* (pp. 93–106). Vanderbilt University Press.

Hofmann, S. G., Grossman, P., & Hinton, D. E. (2011). Loving-kindness and compassion meditation: Potential for psychological interventions. *Clinical Psychology Review, 31*(7), 1126–32.

Hoge, C. W, & Warner, C. H. (2014). Estimating PTSD prevalence in US veterans: Considering combat exposure, PTSD checklist cutpoints, and PTSD. *Journal of Clinical Psychiatry, 75*(12), e1439–41.

Holmes, J. M., Repka, M. X., Kraker, R. T., & Clarke, M. P. (2006). The treatment of amblyopia. *Strabismus, 15*(1), 37–42.

Holowka, D. W., Marx, B. P., Kaloupek, D. G., & Keane, T. M. (2012). PTSD symptoms among male Vietnam veterans: Prevalence and associations with diagnostic status. *Psychological Trauma: Theory, Research, Practice, & Policy, 4*(2), 285–92.

Holtz, P. (2015, February 3). *8 common myths about PTSD debunked.* Task and Purpose. http://taskandpurpose.com/8-common-myths-ptsd-debunked

Hong, H., & Lin-Siegler, X. (2012). How learning about scientists' struggles influences students' interest and learning in physics. *Journal of Educational Psychology, 104*(2), 469–84.

Horner, D. E., Sielaff, A., & Greenberg, J. (2022). Self-determined immortality: Testing the role of autonomy in promoting perceptions of symbolic immortality and well-being. *Motivation & Emotion.* Advance online publication. https://doi.org/10.1007/s11031-022-09944-3

Horney, K. (1939). *New ways in psychoanalysis.* Norton.

Hu, D., Ahn, J. N., Vega, M., & Siegler, X. L. (2020). Not all scientists are equal: Role aspirants influence role modeling outcomes in stem. *Basic & Applied Social Psychology, 42*(3), 192–208.

Huang, N., Zuo, S., Wang, F., Cai, P., & Wang, F. (2017). The dark side of malleability: Incremental theory promotes immoral behaviors. *Frontiers in Psychology, 8.* https://doi.org/10.3389/fpsyg.2017.01341

Husain, S. A., Allwood, M. A., & Bell, D. J. (2008). The relationship between PTSD symptoms and attention problems in children exposed to Bosnian war. *Journal of Emotional & Behavioral Disorders, 16*(1), 52–62.

Hutcherson, C. A., Seppälä, E. M., & Gross, J. J. (2008). Loving-kindness meditation increases social connectedness. *Emotion, 8*(5), 720–24.

Ide, N., & Paez, A. (2000). Complex PTSD: A review of current issues. *International Journal of Emergency Mental Health, 2*(1), 43–51.

Imbernón, J. J., Aguirre, C., & Gómez-Ariza, C. J. (2022). Selective directed forgetting is mediated by the lateral prefrontal cortex: Preliminary evidence with transcranial direct current stimulation. *Cognitive Neuroscience, 13*(2), 77–86.

International Criminal Court (1998). *Rome Statute of the International Criminal Court.* International Criminal Court.

Jackson Levin, N., Kattari, S. K., Piellusch, E. K., & Watson, E. (2020). "We just take care of each other": Navigating 'chosen family' in the context of health, illness, and the mutual provision of care amongst queer and Transgender Young Adults. *International Journal of Environmental Research & Public Health*, *17*(19), 7346.

Jacobsen, L. K., Southwick, S. M., & Kosten, T. R. (2001). Substance use disorders in patients with posttraumatic stress disorder: A review of the literature. *American Journal of Psychiatry*, *158*(8), 1184–90.

Jahn, H. (2013). Memory loss in Alzheimer's disease. *Dialogues in Clinical Neuroscience*, *15*, 445–54.

Jakupcak, M., Conybeare, D., Phelps, L., Hunt, S., Holmes, H. A., Felker, B., Klevens, M., & McFall, M. E. (2007). Anger, hostility, and aggression among Iraq and Afghanistan war veterans reporting PTSD and subthreshold PTSD. *Journal of Traumatic Stress*, *20*(6), 945–54.

Jamison, K. R. (1993). *Touched with fire: Manic-depressive illness and the artistic temperament*. Free Press.

Janet, P. (1889). *L'automatisme psychologique* [Psychological automatism]. *Revue Philosophique de la France Et de l'Etranger*, *29*, 186-200.

Janis, I. L. (1971). Groupthink. *Psychology Today*, *5*(6), 43–46, 74–76.

Janis, I. L. (1972). *Victims of groupthink: A psychological study of foreign-policy decisions and fiascoes*. Houghton Mifflin.

Jazaieri, H., McGonigal, K., Jinpa, T., Doty, J. R., Gross, J. J., & Goldin, P. R. (2014). A randomized controlled trial of compassion cultivation training: Effects on mindfulness, affect, and emotion regulation. *Motivation & Emotion*, *38*(1), 23–35.

Jiang, Y., Costello, P., Fang, F., Huang, M., & He, S. (2006). A gender- and sexual orientation-dependent spatial attentional effect of invisible images. *Proceedings of the National Academy of Science*, *103*(45), 17048–52.

Jin, B., & Austin, D. R. (2000). Personality types of therapeutic recreation students based on the MBTI. *Therapeutic Recreation Journal*, *34*(1), 33–41.

Johnson, D. K. (2013). Do souls exist? *Think: Philosophy for Everyone*, *12*(35), 61–76.

Johnson, D. K. (2006). Does free will exist? *Think: Philosophy for Everyone*, *15*(42), 53–70.

Johnson, D. K. (2010). Is the Doctor still the Doctor? Am I still me? In C. Lewis & S. Smithka (Eds.), *Doctor Who and philosophy: Bigger on the inside* (pp. 41–52). Open Court.

Johnson, S. L. (2020). *Love without sex*. Audible.

Jung, C. G. (1959). *The archetypes and the collective unconscious*. Routledge & Kegan Paul.

Jung, C. G. (1966). *Two essays on analytical psychology* (3rd ed.). Princeton University Press.

Jung, C. G. (1907/1909). *The psychology of dementia praecox*. Journal of Nervous and Mental Disease Publishing.

Jung, C. G. (1917). On the psychology of the unconscious. In R. F. C. Hull (Trans.), *Collected works* (vol. 7). Routledge & Kegan Paul.

Jung, C. G. (1921/1976). *Psychological types*. Princeton University Press.

Jung, C. G. (1936/1969). The archetypes and the collective unconscious. In R. F. C. Hull (Ed.), *The collected words of C. G. Jung* (Vol. 9, pp. 87–110). Princeton University Press.

Jung, C. G. (1963). *Memories, dreams, reflections*. Pantheon.

Kahneman, D., & Tversky, A. (1972). Subjective probability: A judgment of representativeness. *Cognitive Psychology*, *3*(3), 430–54.

Kanfer, S. (1997, summer). *Isaac Singer's promised city*. City Journal. http://www.city -journal.org/html/isaac-singer%E2%80%99s-promised-city-11935.html

Kant, I. (1764/2011). Essay on the maladies of the head. In P. Frierson & P. Guyer (Eds.), *Observations on the feeling of the beautiful and sublime and other writings*. Cambridge University Press.

Kanter, J. W., Baruch, D. E., & Gaynor, S. T. (2006). Acceptance and commitment therapy and behavioral activation for the treatment of depression: Description and comparison. *The Behavior Analyst*, *29*(2), 161.

Kaplan, J. T., & Iacoboni, M. (2006). Getting a grip on other minds: Mirror neurons, intention understanding, and cognitive empathy. *Social Neuroscience*, *1*(3–4), 175–83.

Karekla, M., & Constantinou, M. (2010). Religious coping and cancer: Proposing an acceptance and commitment therapy approach. *Cognitive & Behavioral Practice*, *17*(4), 371–81.

Kastenbaum, R. (Ed.). (2000). *The psychology of death*. Springer.

Kattari, S. K., Kattari, L., Johnson, I., Lacombe-Duncan, A., Misiolek, B. A. (2020). Differential experiences of mental health among trans/gender diverse adults in Michigan. *International Journal of Environmental Research & Public Health 17*(18), 6805.

Kaufmann, M., Goetz, T., Lipnevich, A. A., & Pekrun, R. (2019). Do positive illusions of control foster happiness? *Emotion*, *19*(6), 1014–22.

Kearney, D. J., Malte, C. A., McManus, C., Martinez, M. E., Felleman, B., & Simpson, T. L. (2013). Loving-kindness meditation for posttraumatic stress disorder: A pilot study. *Journal of Traumatic Stress*, *26*(4), 426–34.

Keesee, N. J., Currier, J. M., & Neimeyer, R. A. (2008). Predictors of grief following the death of one's child: The contribution of finding meaning. *Journal of Clinical Psychology*, *64*(10), 1145–63.

Keirsey, D. (1998). *Please understand me II: Temperament, character, intelligence.* Prometheus Nemesis.

Kelly, G. A. (1955). *The psychology of personal constructs.* Norton.

Kelman, H. G. (1973). Violence without moral restraint: Reflections on the dehumanization of victims and victimizers. *Journal of Social Studies, 29*(4), 25–61.

Kilmartin, C. (2010). *The masculine self* (4th ed.). Sloan.

Kilmartin, C., & McDermott, R. C. (2015). Violence and masculinities. In W. J. Wong & S. R. Wester (Eds.), *APA handbook of men and masculinities* (pp. 615–36). American Psychological Association.

King, B. M. (2018). *Human sexuality today* (9th ed.). Prentice Hall.

Kirk, J., & Kirk, L. (1997). Computer pains. *Journal of Workplace Learning, 9*(2), 678–72.

Kirkley, P. (2017, February 14). *The 24 best kisses on Doctor Who.* RadioTimes. https://www.radiotimes.com/tv/sci-fi/the-24-best-kisses-in-doctor-who

Kiselica, M. S., & Englar-Carlson, M. (2010). Identifying, affirming, and building upon male strengths: The positive psychology/positive masculinity model of psychotherapy with boys and men. *Psychotherapy Theory, Research, Practice, Training, 47*(3), 276–87.

Kistler, A. (2013). *Doctor Who: A history.* Lyons.

Klimecki, O. M., Leiberg, S., Lamm, C., & Singer, T. (2012). Functional neural plasticity and associated changes in positive affect after compassion training. *Cerebral Cortex, 23*(7), 1552–61.

Klimecki, O. M., & Singer, T. (2012). Empathic distress fatigue rather than compassion fatigue? Integrating findings from empathy research in psychology and social neuroscience. In B. Oakley. A. Knafo, G. Madhavan, & D. S. Wilson (Eds.), *Pathological altruism* (pp. 368–383). Oxford University Press.

Kline, C. J., & Peters, L. H. (1991). Behavioral commitment and tenure of new employees: A replication and extension. *Academy of Management Journal, 34*(1), 194–204.

Kohlberg, L. (1981). *Essays on moral development.* Harper & Row.

Kramer, P. D. (2006). *Freud: Inventor of the modern mind.* Harper Perennial.

Krantzler, M. (1977). *Learning to love again.* Crowell.

Krauss Whitbourne, S. (2010, August 10). *When it comes to personality tests, a dose of skepticism is a good thing.* Psychology Today. https://www.psychologytoday.com/blog/fulfillment-any-age/201008/when-it-comes-personality-tests-dose-skepticism-is-good-thing

Krebs, G., Hirsch, C. R., & Mathews, A. (2010). The effect of attention modification with explicit vs. minimal instructions on worry *Behavioural Research & Therapy, 48*(3), 251–56.

Kübler-Ross, E. (1969). *On death and dying*. Routledge.

Lacan, J. (1981). *The four fundamental concepts of psychoanalysis*. Norton.

Lamb, M. E., Pleck, J. H., Charnov, E., & Levine, J. A. (1987). A biosocial perspective on paternal behavior and involvement. In J. B. Lancaster, J. Altman, A. S. Rossi, & L. R. Sherrod (Eds.), *Parenting across the lifespan: Biosocial dimensions* (pp. 111–42). De Gruyter.

Langley, T. (2013, December 27). *Doctor Who: The man who regrets and the man who forgets*. Psychology Today. https://www.psychologytoday.com/blog/beyond-heroes-and-villains/201312/doctor-who-the-man-who-regrets-and-the-man-who-forgets

Langley, T. (2014, August 20). *Doctor Who: Regeneration and a dilemma of Doctor identities*. Psychology Today. https://www.psychologytoday.com/us/blog/beyond-heroes-and-villains/201408/doctor-who-regeneration-and-dilemma-doctor-identities

Langley, T. (2014, August 31). *Doctor Who and the neuroscience of morality malfunctions*. Psychology Today. https://www.psychologytoday.com/blog/beyond-heroes-and-villains/201408/doctor-who-and-the-neuroscience-morality-malfunctions

Langley, T. (2015, March 7). *Would "Doctor Who" call Freud, Jung, Myers & Briggs stupid?* Psychology Today. https://www.psychologytoday.com/blog/beyond-heroes-and-villains/201603/would-doctor-who-call-freud-jung-myers-briggs-stupid

Langley, T. (2018, March 13). *What kind of grandparent will I be?* Psychology Today. https://www.psychologytoday.com/us/blog/beyond-heroes-and-villains/201803/which-kind-grandparent-will-i-be

Langlinais, C. (2005). Framing the Victorian heroine: Representations of the ideal woman in art and fiction. *Interdisciplinary Humanities Journal, 22*(2), 73–87.

Leach, J. (1994). *Survival psychology*. Macmillan.

Le Bon, G. (1896). *The crowd: A study of the popular mind*. T Fisher Unwin.

Lee, E. J. (2007). Deindividuation effects on group polarization in computer-mediated communication: The role of group identification, public-self-awareness, and perceived argument quality. *Journal of Communication, 57*(2), 385–403.

Lee, K., & Ashton, M. C. (2005). Psychopathy, Machiavellianism, and narcissism in the five-factor model and the HEXACO model of personality structure. *Personality & Individual Differences, 38*(7), 1571–82.

Lee, K., & Ashton, M. C. (2012). *The H factor of personality: Why some people are manipulative, self-entitled, materialistic, and exploitative—and why it matters for everyone*. Wilfred Laurier University Press.

Levant, R. (2006). Foreword. In M. Englar-Carlson & M. Stevens (Eds.), *In the room with men: A casebook of therapeutic change* (pp. xv–xx). American Psychological Association.

Lewis, J. G. (2013, September 23). *Prosopagnosia: Why some are blind to faces.* Psychology Today. https://www.psychologytoday.com/blog/brain-babble/201309/prosopagnosia-why -some-are-blind-faces

Lewis, J. W. (2006). Cortical networks related to human use of tools. *Neuroscientist,* *12*(3), 211–31.

Liao, L.-M., & Simmonds, M. (2014). A values-driven and evidence-based health care psychology for diverse sex development. *Psychology & Sexuality, 5*(1), 83–101.

Lieberman, H. R., Bathalon, G. P., Falco, C. M., Kramer, F. M., Morgan, C. A., & Niro, P. (2005). Severe decrements in cognition function and mood induced by sleep loss, heat, dehydration, and undernutrition during simulated combat. *Biological Psychiatry, 57*(4), 422–29.

Liebrenz, M., Schneider, M., Buadze, A., Gehring, M.-T., Dube, A., & Caflisch, C. (2016). High-dose benzodiazepine users' perceptions and experiences of anterograde amnesia. *Journal of the American Academy of Psychiatry & the Law, 44*(3), 328–37.

Lindqvist, A., Sendén, M. G., & Renström, E. A. (2020). What is gender, anyway: A review of the options for operationalising gender. *Psychology & Sexuality, 12*(4), 332–44.

Little, B. R. (2014). *Me, myself, and us: The science of personality and the art of well-being.* Public Affairs.

Litz, B. T., Weathers, F. W., Monaco, V., Herman, D. S., Wulfsohn, M., Marx, B., & Krane, T. M. (1996). Attention, arousal, and memory in posttraumatic stress disorder. *Journal of Traumatic Stress, 9*(3), 497–518.

Livingston Smith, D. (2012). *Less than human: Why we demean, enslave, and exterminate others.* St. Martin's.

Lo, R., & Cohen, T. J. (2007). Laughter-induced syncope: No laughing matter. *American Journal of Medicine, 120*(11), e5.

Loftus, E. F. (2001). Imagining the past. *The Psychologist, 14*(11), 584–87.

Longhurst, C. E. (2012, September/October). The science of angelology in the modern world: The revival of angels in contemporary culture. *The Catholic Response* 32–36.

Loo, R. (1979). A psychometric investigation of the Eysenck Personality Questionnaire. *Journal of Personality Assessment, 43*(1), 54–58.

Lovell, C. (1945). A study of the factor structure of thirteen personality variables. *Educational & Psychological Measurement, 5*(4), 335–50.

Lyons, M., Harrison, N., Brewer, G., Robinson, S., & Sanders, R. (2014). *Biological psychology.* Learning Matters.

Maguire, E. A., Woollett, K., & Spiers, H. J. (2006). London taxi drivers and bus drivers: A structural MRI and neuropsychological analysis. *Hippocampus, 16*(12), 1091–1101.

Marcus, B., Lee, K., & Ashton, M. C. (2007). Personality dimensions explaining relationships between integrity tests and counterproductive behavior: Big five, or one in addition? *Personnel Psychology, 60*(1), 1–34.

Marrocco, J., & McEwen, B. S., (2016). Sex in the brain: hormones and sex differences. *Dialogues in clinical neuroscience, 18*(4), 373–383. McGlashan, T. H., & Hoffman, R. E. (2000). Schizophrenia as a disorder of developmentally reduced synaptic connectivity. *Archives of General Psychiatry, 57*(7), 637–48.

Martin, E. D. (1920). *The behavior of crowds: A psychological study.* Harper & Brothers.

Marx, G. (1959). *Groucho and me: The autobiography of Groucho Marx.* Gollancz.

Maslow, A. (1943). A theory of human motivation. *Psychological Review, 50*(4), 370–396

May, R. (1983). *The discovery of being: Writings in existential psychology.* Norton.

McAdams, D. P. (1994). *The person: An introduction to personality psychology* (2nd ed.). Harcourt Brace.

McClelland, D. (1965). Toward a theory of motive acquisition. *American Psychologist, 20*(5), 321–33.

McClure, B. (2021, July 15). *Doctor Who: How old was each actor to play the Doctor?* Blue Towel Productions. https://bluetowel.wordpress.com/2021/07/15/doctor-who-how-old-was-each-actor-to-play-the-doctor

McCormack, L., & McKellar, L. (2015). Adaptive growth following terrorism: Vigilance and anger as facilitators of posttraumatic growth in the aftermath of the Bali bombings. *Traumatology, 21*(2), 71–81.

McCrae, R. R., & Costa, P. T., Jr. (1991). The NEO Personality Inventory: Using the five-factor model in counseling. *Journal of Counseling & Development, 69*(4), 367–72.

McCrae, R. R., & Costa, P. T., Jr. (1985). Openness to experience. In R. Hogan & W. H. Jones (Eds.), *Perspectives in personality* (Vol. 1, pp. 145–172).

McCrae, R. R., & Costa, P. T., Jr. (1987). Validation of the five-factor model of personality across instruments and observers. *Journal of Personality & Social Psychology, 52*(1), 81–90.

McCrae, R. R., & Costa, P. T., Jr. (1995). Positive and negative valence within the five-factor model. *Journal of Research in Personality, 29*(4), 443–60.

McCrae, R. R., & Terracciano, A. (2005). Universal features of personality traits from the observer's perspective: Data from 50 cultures. *Journal of Personality & Social Psychology, 88*(3), 547.

McCullagh, S., Moore, M., Gawel, M., & Feinstein, A. (1999). Pathological laughing and crying in amytrophic lateral sclerosis: An association with prefrontal cognitive dysfunction. *Journal of the Neurological Sciences, 169*(1), 43–48.

McCullough, M. (2015, January 26). *Sciency wiency: Listen.* Doctor Who TV. http://www.doctorwhotv.co.uk/sciencey-wiencey-listen-71329.htm

McGlashan, T. H., & Hoffman, R. E. (2000). Schizophrenia as a disorder of developmentally reduced synaptic connectivity. *Archives of General Psychiatry, 57*(7), 637–48.

McGlynn, R. P., Harding, D. J., & Cottle, J. L. (2009). Individual-group discontinuity in group-individual interactions: Does size matter? *Group Processes & Intergroup Relations, 12*(1), 129–43.

McGonigal, J. (2015). *Superbetter: A revolutionary approach to getting stronger, happier, braver, and more resilient.* Penguin.

McGonigal, K. (2015). *The upside of stress: Why stress is good for you, and how to get good at it.* Penguin.

McGowan, D. (1994). *What is wrong with Jung?* Prometheus.

McGraw, A. P., Mellers, B. A., & Tetlock, P. E. (2005). Expectancies and emotions of Olympic athletes. *Journal of Experimental Social Psychology, 41*(4), 438–46.

McLemore, K. A. (2018). A minority stress perspective on transgender individuals' experiences with misgendering. *Stigma & Health, 3*(1), 53–64.

McNally, R. J. (2005). Debunking myths about trauma and memory. *Canadian Journal of Psychiatry, 50*(13), 817–22.

Mededović, J., & Petrović, B. (2015). The Dark Tetrad: Structural properties and location in the personality space. *Journal of Individual Differences, 36*(4), 228–36.

Medvec, V. H., Madey, S. F., & Gillovich, T. (1995). When less is more: Counterfactual thinking and satisfaction among Olympic medalists. *Journal of Personality & Social Psychology, 69*(4), 603–10.

Mendoza, G. (2013, August 4). *Reviewing masculinity.* Dartmouth Review. https://dartreview.com/reviewing-masculinity

Merritt, S. K., Hitti, A., Van Camp, A. R., Shaffer, E., Sanchez, M. H., & O'Brien, L. T. (2021). Maximizing the impact of exposure to scientific role models: Testing an intervention to increase science identity among adolescent girls. *Journal of Applied Social Psychology, 51*(7), 667–82.

Meyer, M. L., Masten, C. L., Ma, Y., Wang, C., Shi, Z., Eisenberger, N. I., & Han, S. (2013). Empathy for the social suffering of friends and strangers recruits distinct patterns of brain activation. *Social Cognitive & Affective Neuroscience, 4*(8), 446–54.

Meyers, N. M., Chapman, J. C., Gunthert, K. C., & Weissbrod, C. S. (2015). The effect of masculinity on community reintegration following TBI in Military Veterans. *Military Psychology, 28*(1), 14–24.

Michael, J. (2003). Using the Myers-Briggs Type Indicator as a tool for leadership development? Apply with caution. *Journal of Leadership & Organizational Studies, 10*(1), 68–81.

Midgley, C., DeBues-Stafford, G., Lockwood, P., & Thai, S. (2021). She needs to see it to be it: The importance of same-gender athletic role models. *Sex Roles, 85*(3-4), 142–60.

Mikkelson, D. (2012, June 12). *The last laugh's on him: Have people died laughing?* Snopes. http://www.snopes.com/horrors/freakish/laughing.asp

Mikulincer, M., Florian, V., & Hirschberger, G. (2004). The terror of death and the quest for love: An existential perspective on close relationships. In J. Greenberg, S. L. Koole, T. Pyszczynski, J. Greenberg, S. L. Koole, & T. Pyszczynski (Eds.), *Handbook of experimental existential psychology* (pp. 287–304). Guilford.

Miles, M. S., & Demi, A. S. (1992). A comparison of guilt in bereaved parents whose children died by suicide, accident, or chronic disease. *Omega: Journal of Death & Dying, 24*(3), 203–15.

Miller, D. H., Weinshenker, B. G., Filippi, M., . . . & Polman, C. H. (2008). Differential diagnosis of suspected multiple sclerosis: A consensus approach. *Multiple Sclerosis, 14*(9), 1157–74.

Miller, F., & Rowold, K. (1979). Halloween masks and deindividuation. *Psychological Reports, 44*(2), 422–22.

Millis, W. (1981). *Arms and men: A study in American military history.* Rutgers University Press.

Milston, S. I., Vanman, E. J., & Cunnington, R. (2013). Cognitive empathy and motor activity during observed actions. *Neuropsychologia, 51*(6), 1103–8.

Moffat, S., & Davies, R. T. (2020, June). Showrunner showdown. *Doctor Who Magazine, 1*(555).

Monahan, J., & Hood, G. L. (1976). Psychologically disordered and criminal offenders: Perceptions of their volition and responsibility. *Correctional Psychologist, 3*(2), 123–34.

Moravec, H. (1999). *Robot: Mere machine to transcendent mind.* Oxford University Press.

Moreno, J. D. (2006). Juicing the brain. *Scientific American Mind, 17*(6), 66–73.

Mori, N. (2008). Styles of remembering and types of experience: An experimental investigation of reconstructive memory. *Integrative Psychological & Behavioral Science, 42*(3), 291–314.

Morman, M. T., & Floyd, K. (2006). Good fathering: Father and son perceptions of what it means to be a good father. *Fathering: A Journal of Research, Theory, & Practice about Men as Fathers, 4*(2), 113–36.

Mubarak, N., & Ferguson, C. J. (2022). Pride and prejudice and zombies . . . and statistics: Effects of powerful female role-models in media on attitudes towards women, and female viewer anxiety. *Current Psychology, 41*(2), 691–96.

Mulkern, P. (2017, December 8). *Jodie Whittaker "will be brilliant," Chris Chibnall "is going to be bold"—and there could be more Sherlock says Steven Moffat.* Radio Times. https://www. radiotimes.com/tv/sci-fi/doctor-who-steven-moffat-interview-jodie-whittaker -chris-chibnall-sherlock

Mulvey, L. (1975). Visual pleasure and narrative cinema. *Screen, 16*(3), 6–18.

Murray, A. (1938). *Explorations in personality.* Oxford University Press.

Murray, D. (2020). *The madness of crowds: Gender, race and identity.* Bloomsbury Continuum.

Murray, H. A. (1940). Sigmund Freud: 1856–1939. *American Journal of Psychology, 53*(1), 134–38.

Myers & Briggs Foundation (n.d.). *MBTI basics.* Myers & Briggs Foundation. http:// www.myersbriggs.org/my-mbti-personality-type/mbti-basics

Myers, D. G., & Lamm, H. (1975). The polarizing effect of group discussion. *American Scientist, 63*(3), 297–303.

Myers, D. G. (2004). *Psychology in modules.* Worth.

Myers, I. B. (1998). *Introduction to type* (6th ed.). CPP.

Myers, I. B., & Myers, P. B. (1995). *Gifts differing: Understanding personality type.* Consulting Psychologists Press.

Neal, D. T., & Chartrand, T. L. (2011). Embodied emotion perception amplifying and dampening facial feedback modulates emotion perception accuracy. *Social Psychological & Personality Science, 2*(6), 673–78.

Neugarten, B. L., & Weinstein, K. K. (1964). The changing American grandparent. *Journal of Marriage & the Family, 26*(2), 199–204.

Newman, L. S., & Erber, R. (Eds.) (2002). *Understanding genocide: The social psychology of the Holocaust.* Oxford University Press.

North, A. (2014, July 18). *Why Myers-Briggs is totally useless—but wildly popular.* New York Times. http://op-talk.blogs.nytimes.com/2014/07/18/why-myers-briggs-is-totally-useless -but-wildly-popular

Núñez-Jaramillo, L., Herrera-Solís, A., & Herrera-Morales, W. V. (2021). ADHD: Reviewing the causes and evaluating solutions. *Journal of Personalized Medicine, 11*(3), 166.

Oberauer, K., & Greve, W. (2022). Intentional remembering and intentional forgetting in working and long-term memory. *Journal of Experimental Psychology: General*, *151*(3), 513.

O'Neil, J. M. (2008). Summarizing 25 years of research on men's gender role conflict using the Gender Role Conflict Scale: New research paradigms and clinical implications. *Counseling Psychologist*, *36*(3), 358–445.

O'Neil, J. M., & Egan, J. (1992). Men's and women's gender role journeys: A metaphor for healing, transition, and transformation. In B. R. Wainrib (Ed.), *Gender issues across the life cycle* (pp. 107–123). Springer.

OPP (n.d.). *INTP: MBTI personality profile*. OPP. https://www.opp.com/tools/mbti/mbti-personality-types/intp

Orcutt, H. K., Pickett, S. M., & Pope, E. B. (2005). Experiential avoidance and forgiveness as mediators in the relation between traumatic interpersonal events and posttraumatic stress disorder symptoms. *Journal of Social & Clinical Psychology*, *24*(7), 1003–29.

Ovsiankina, Maria (1928). *Die Wiederaufnahme unterbrochener Handlungen* [The resumption of interrupted actions]. *Psychologische Forschung*, *11*, 302–79.

Paradiso, E., Gazzola, V., & Keysers, C. (2021). Neural mechanisms necessary for empathy-related phenomena across species. *Current Opinion in Neurobiology 68*, 107–15.

Park, N., Peterson, C., & Seligman, M. E. P. (2004). Strengths of character and well-being. *Journal of Social & Clinical Psychology*, *23*(5), 603–19.

Parkin, L. (1996). *Cold fusion* (*Doctor Who: The missing adventures* #29). Virgin.

Patrick, J. H., & Goedereis, E. A. (2009). The importance of context and the gain-loss dynamic for understanding grandparent caregivers. In K. Shifren (Ed.), *How caregiving affects development: Psychological implications for child, adolescent, and adult caregivers* (pp. 169–90). American Psychological Association.

Penfield, W. (1968). Engrams in the human brain: Mechanisms of memory. *Proceedings of the Royal Society of Medicine*, *61*(8), 831.

Philaretou, A. G., & Allen, K. R. (2001). Reconstructing masculinity and sexuality. *Journal of Men's Studies*, *9*(3), 301–24.

Philpot, C. L., Brooks, G. R., Lusterman, D.-D., & Nutt, R. L. (1997). Gender coevolution. In C. L. Philpot, G. R. Brooks, D.-D. Lusterman, & R. L. Nutt, *Bridging separate gender worlds: Why men and women clash and how therapists can bring them together* (pp. 253–96). American Psychological Association.

Piaget, J. (1932). *The moral judgment of the child*. Harcourt Brace Jovanovich.

Pierro, A., Sheveland, A., Livi, S., & Kruglanski, A. W. (2015). Person-group fit on the need for cognitive closure as predictor of job performance, and the mediating role of group identification. *Group Dynamics: Theory, Research, & Practice, 19*(2), 77–90.

Pigeon, W. R., Campbell, C. E., Possemato, K., & Ouimette, P. (2013). Longitudinal relationships of insomnia, nightmares, and PTSD severity in recent combat veterans. *Journal of Psychosomatic Research, 75*(6), 546–50.

Plato (1999, orig. 4th century BC). *Cratylus* (B. Jowett, Trans.) Project Gutenberg. https://www.gutenberg.org/files/1616/1616-h/1616-h.htm

Plumb, J. C., Orsillo, S. M., & Luterek, J. A. (2004). A preliminary test of the role of experiential avoidance in post-event functioning. *Journal of Behavior Therapy & Experimental Psychiatry, 35*(3), 245–57.

Popper, K. R. (1963). *Conjectures and refutations: The growth of scientific knowledge.* Routledge & Kegan Paul.

Post, J. M., & Panis, L. K. (2011). Crimes of obedience: "Groupthink" at Abu Ghraib. *International Journal of Group Psychotherapy, 61*(1), 48–66.

Postmes, T., & Spears, R. (1998). Deindividuation and antinormative behavior: A meta-analysis. *Psychological Bulletin, 123*(3), 238–59.

Potts, A. (2005). Cyborg masculinity in the Viagra era. *Sexualities, Evolution, & Gender, 7*(1), 3–16.

Poulin, M. J., Brown, S. L., Dillard, A. J., & Smith, D. M. (2013). Giving to others and the association between stress and mortality. *American Journal of Public Health, 103*(9), 1649–55.

Pretz, J. E., & Totz, K. S (2007). Measuring individual differences in affective, heuristic, and holistic intuition. *Personality & Individual Differences, 43*(5), 1247–57.

Price, J. L. (n.d.). *Findings from the National Vietnam Veterans' Readjustment Study.* U.S. Department of Veterans Affairs. http://www.ptsd.va.gov/professional/research-bio /research/vietnam-vets-study.asp

Prigerson, H. G., Bierhals, A. J., Kasl, S. V., Reynolds, C. F. III, Shear, M. K., Day, N., Beery, L. C., Newsom, J. T., & Jacobs, S. (1997). Traumatic grief as a risk factor for mental and physical morbidity. *American Journal of Psychiatry, 154,* 616–23.

Psytech (2002). *The 15FQ+ technical manual* (2nd ed.). Psytech. http://www.psytech.com /Content/TechnicalManuals/EN/15FQplusman.pdf

PTSD Alliance (n.d.). *Posttraumatic stress disorder myths.* PTSD Alliance. http://www. ptsdalliance.org/common-myths

Pugh, L. R., Taylor, P. J., & Berry, K. (2015). The role of guilt in the development of posttraumatic stress disorder: A systematic review. *Journal of Affective Disorders, 182,* 138–50.

Puurtinen, M., Heap, S., & Mappes, T. (2015). The joint emergence of group competition and within-group cooperation. *Evolution & Human Behavior, 36*(3), 211–17.

Quinn, K., Mollet, N., & Dawson, F. (2021). The Compassionate Schools Framework: Exploring a values-driven, hope-filled, relational approach with school leaders. *Educational & Child Psychology, 38*(1), 24–36.

Rachel, N. (n.d.). *Trauma and fragmentation.* Natalia Rachel. https://www.nataliarachel.com/trauma/trauma-and-fragmentation

Rachels, J. (1995). *Elements of moral philosophy.* McGraw Hill.

Ramachandran, V. S., & Blakeslee, S. (1999). *Phantoms in the brain: Probing the mysteries of the human mind.* HarperCollins.

Rauscher, F. H., Shaw, G. L., & Ky, K. N. (1993). Music and spatial task performance. *Nature, 365,* 611.

Rees, V. (2015). *From Gabriel to Lucifer: A cultural history of angels.* I. B. Tauris.

Reicher, S. (2001). The psychology of crowd dynamics. In Hogg, M. A., & Tindale, S. (Eds.), *Blackwell handbook of social psychology: Group processes.* Blackwell.

Reicher, S. D., & Spears, R., & Postmes, T. (1995). A social identity model of deindividuation phenomena. *European Review of Social Psychology, 6*(1), 161–98

Reid, T. (1785). *Essays on the intellectual powers of man.* John Bell, G. G. J. & J. Robinson.

Renier, L. A., Anurova, I., De Volder, A. G., Carlson, S., VanMeter, J., & Rauschecker, J. P. (2010). Preserved functional specialization for spatial processing in the middle occipital gyrus of the early blind. *Neuron, 68*(1), 138–48.

Reynierse, J. H., & Harker, J. B. (2008a). Preference multidimensionality and the fallacy of type dynamics: Part 1 (Studies 1–3). *Journal of Psychological Type, 68*(10), 90–112.

Reynierse, J. H., & Harker, J. B. (2008b). Preference multidimensionality and the fallacy of type dynamics: Part 2 (Studies 4–6). *Journal of Psychological Type, 68*(11), 113–38.

Rice, B. (n.d.). 'Doctor Who'—*everything we know about the Doctor's mother.* Fansided. https://winteriscoming.net/2015/05/10/doctor-who-everything-we-know-about -the-doctors-mother

Richter, E. D. (2008). Genocide: Can we predict, prevent, and protect? *Journal of Public Health Policy, 29*(3), 265–74.

Ringenbach, R. T. (2009). *A comparison between counselors who practice meditation and those who do not on compassion fatigue, compassion satisfaction, burnout, and self-compassion* [Doctoral dissertation]. OhioLINK. https://etd.ohiolink.edu/pg_10?0::NO:10:P10 _ACCESSION_NUM:akron1239650446

Rockliff, H., Gilbert, P., McEwan, K., Lightman, S., & Glover, D. (2008). A pilot exploration of heart rate variability and salivary cortisol responses to compassion-focused imagery. *Journal of Clinical Neuropsychiatry, 5*(3), 132–39.

Roe-Burning, S., & Straker, G. (1997). The association between illusions of invulnerability and exposure to trauma. *Journal of Traumatic Stress, 10*(2), 319–27.

Roediger, H. L., III, Wheeler, M. A., & Rajaram, S. (1993). Remembering, knowing, and reconstructing the past. In D. L. Medin (Ed.), *The psychology of learning and motivation: Advances in research and theory* (Vol. 30, pp. 97–134). Academic Press.

Roemer, L., Litz, B. T., Orsillo, S. M., Ehlich, P. J., & Friedman, M. J. (1998). Increases in retrospective accounts of war-zone exposure over time: The role of PTSD symptom severity. *Journal of Traumatic Stress, 11*(3), 597–605.

Rogers, C. R. (1961/1995). *On becoming a person: A therapist's view of psychotherapy.* Houghton Mifflin.

Rogers, J., Viding, E., Blair, R. J., Frith, U., & Happe, F. (2006). Autism spectrum disorder and psychopathy: Shared cognitive underpinnings or double hit? *Psychological Medicine, 36*(12), 1789–98.

Romero, J. R., Mercado, M., Beiser, A. S., Pikula, A., Seshadri, S., Kelly-Hayes, M., & Kase, C. S. (2013). Transient global amnesia and neurological events: The Framingham heart study. *Frontiers in Neurology, 4*(article 47). http://journal.frontiersin.org /article/10.3389/fneur.2013.00047/full

Roque, D., Kottapally, M., & Nahab, F. (2012). A transient loss of British charm: A case of foreign accent syndrome and proposed neuroanatomical pathway (P02. 050). *Neurology, 78*(Meeting Abstracts 1), P02–050.

Rorschach, H. (1921). *Psychodiagnostics.* Grune & Stratton.

Rosell, D. R., Futterman, S. E., McMaster, A., & Siever, L. J. (2014). Schizotypal personality disorder: A current review. *Current Psychiatry Reports 16*(7), 1–12.

Roselli, C. E. (2018). Neurobiology of gender identity and sexual orientation. *Journal of Neuroendocrinology, 30*(7), 1–8.

Ross, L., & Anderson, C. A. (1982). Shortcomings in the attribution process: On the origins and maintenance of erroneous social assessments. In D. Kahneman, P. Slovic, & A. Tversky (Eds.), *Judgment under uncertainty: Heuristics and biases* (pp. 268–83). Cambridge University Press.

Rossman, K. M. (1995). Gender-awareness and the psychosocial process of counseling: A study of the pastoral counseling of women. *Dissertation Abstracts International Section A: Humanities & Social Sciences, 55*(10-A), 3144.

Ryan, R. M., Huta, V., & Deci, E. L. (2008). Living well: A self-determination theory perspective on eudaimonia. *Journal of Happiness Studies, 9*(1), 139–70.

Ryff, C. D., & Boylan, J. M. (2016). Linking happiness to health: Comparisons between hedonic and eudaimonic well-being. In L. Bruni & P. L. Porta (Eds.), *Handbook of research methods and applications in happiness and quality of life* (pp. 53–70).

Sacks, O. (2012). *Hallucinations.* Vintage.

Sacks, O. (1985). *The man who mistook his wife for a hat.* Touchstone.

Sadalla, E. K., Kenrick, D. T., & Vershure, B. (1987). Dominance and heterosexual attraction. *Journal of Personality & Social Psychology, 52*(4), 730–38.

Safran, J. D. (2012). *Psychoanalysis and psychoanalytic therapies.* American Psychological Association.

Sagers, A. (2012a, October 4). 'He doesn't like endings,' but ultimately Whovians don't mind. CNN. http://geekout.blogs.cnn.com/2012/10/04/he-doesnt-like-endings-but-ultimately -whovians-dont-mind

Sagers, A. (2012b, December 24). *Matt Smith on a very Time Lord 'Doctor Who' Christmas.* Paranormal Pop Culture. http://www.paranormalpopculture.com/2012/12 /matt-smith-on-very-time-lord-doctor-who.html

Sagers, A. (2013, November 19). *Exclusive: Tom Baker to appear in 'Doctor Who' 50th anniversary special.* Huffington Post. http://www.huffingtonpost.com/aaron-sagers /exclusive-tom-baker-to-ap_b_4295773.html

Sagers, A. (2014, August 14). *Doctor Who in NYC: Peter Capaldi, Jenna Coleman, Steven Moffat talking Time Lord.* Blastr. http://www.blastr.com/2014-8-14/doctor-who -nyc-peter-capaldi-jenna-coleman-steven-moffat-talking-time-lord

Sagers, A. (2015a, October 9). Exclusive: *Doctor Who writer Toby Whithouse on sonic sunglasses and the bootstrap paradox.* Blastr. http://www.blastr.com/2015-10-9/exclusive -doctor-who-writer-toby-whithouse-sonic-sunglasses-and-bootstrap-paradox

Sagers, A. (2015b, November 12). *Doctor Who's Mark Gatis teases 'Sleep No More,' his most terrifying episode yet.* Blastr. http://www.blastr.com/2015-11-12/doctor-whos-mark -gatiss-teases-sleep-no-more-his-most-terrifying-episode-yet

Saggino, A., Cooper, C., & Kline, P. (2001). A confirmatory factor analysis of the Myers-Briggs Type Indicator. *Personality & Individual Differences, 30*(1), 3–9.

Salomonson, R. G. (2018). Synthesizing theories of traumatic grief: using applied theory to create a new theory of grief shame. *Dissertation Abstracts International: Section B: The Sciences & Engineering 79*(10-B(E)).

Salovey, P., & Mayer, J. D. (1990). Emotional intelligence. *Imagination, Cognition & Personality, 9*(3), 185–211.

Sanna, L. J., Chang, E. C., Miceli, P. M., & Lundberg, K. B. (2011). Rising up to higher virtues: Experiencing elevated physical height uplifts prosocial actions. *Journal of Experimental Social Psychology, 47*(2), 472–76.

Santiago, P. N., Ursano, R. J., Gray, C. L., Rynoos, R. S., Spiegel, D., Lewis-Fernandez, R., Friedman, M. J., & Fullerton, C. S. (2013, April 11). *A system review of PTSD prevalence and trajectories in DSM-5 defined trauma exposed populations: Intentional and non-intentional traumatic events.* PLOS One. http://journals.plos.org/plosone/article?id=10.1371/journal.pone.0059236

Santy, P. A. (1994). *Choosing the right stuff: The psychological selection of astronauts and cosmonauts.* Praeger.

Saxon, A. H. (1989). *P. T. Barnum: The legend and the man.* Columbia University Press.

Schramme, T. (2018). The role of empathy in an agential account of morality: Lessons from autism and psychopathy. In N. Roughley & T. Schramme (Eds.), *Forms of fellow feeling: Empathy, sympathy, concern and moral agency* (pp. 307–26). Cambridge University Press.

Schwartz, A. (2016). *The complex PTSD workbook.* Sheldon.

Schwartz, J. (1999). *Cassandra's daughter: A history of psychoanalysis.* Viking.

Schwarz, H. (1995). *Evil: A historical and theological perspective.* Fortress Press.

Segerstrom, S. C., & Miller, G. E. (2004). Psychological stress and the human immune system: A meta-analytic study of 30 years of inquiry. *Psychological Bulletin 130*(4), 601–30.

Selby, D. (2014). *Into the (mind of the) Dalek.* Doctor Who TV. https://www.doctorwhotv.co.uk/into-the-mind-of-the-dalek-66074.htm

Sell, A., Hone, L. S., & Pound, N. (2012). The importance of physical strength to human males. *Human Nature, 23*(1), 30–44.

Sender, H. (2014, August 22). *Doctor Who season 8: How old is the Doctor? Recap of the Doctor's real age leading up to Peter Capaldi (timeline).* International Business Times. http://www.ibtimes.com/doctor-who-season-8-how-old-doctor-recap-doctors-real-age-leading-peter-capaldi-timeline-1667064

Seppälä, E. (2013). The compassionate mind: Science shows why it's healthy and how it spreads. *APS Observer, 26*(5). Psychological Science. http://www.psychologicalscience.org/index.php/publications/observer/2013/may-june-13/the-compassionate-mind.html

Seppälä, E. M., Hutcherson, C. A., Nguyen, D. T., Doty, J. R., & Gross, J. J. (2014). Loving-kindness meditation: A tool to improve healthcare provider compassion, resilience, and patient care. *Journal of Compassionate Health Care, 1*(1), 1–5.

Shakespeare-Finch, J., & Lurie-Beck, J. (2014). A meta-analytic clarification of the relationship between posttraumatic growth and symptoms of posttraumatic stress disorder. *Journal of Anxiety Disorders, 28*(2), 223–29.

Shamay-Tsoory, S. G. (2010). The neural bases for empathy. *The Neuroscientist 17*(1), 18–24.

Shapiro, S. L., Astin, J. A., Bishop, S. R., & Cordova, M. (2005). Mindfulness-based stress reduction for health care professionals: Results from a randomized trial. *International Journal of Stress Management, 12*(2), 164–76.

Shatan, C. F. (1973). The grief of soldiers: Vietnam combat veterans' self-help movement. *American Journal of Orthopsychiatry, 43*(4), 640–53.

Shear, K., Monk, T., Houck, P., Melhem, N., Frank, E., Reynolds, C., & Sillowash, R. (2007). An attachment-based model of complicated grief including the role of avoidance. *European Archives of Psychiatry & Clinical Neuroscience, 257*(8), 453–61.

Sheard, M. (2012). *Mental toughness: The mindset behind sporting achievement.* Routledge.

Shelton, J., & Hill, J. P. (1969). Effects of cheating on achievement anxiety and knowledge of peer performance. *Developmental Psychology, 1*(5), 449–55.

Shields, D. (2015, November 10). *Culturally competent care for male veterans.* Society for the Psychological Study of Men and Women. http://division51.net/homepage-slider/culturally-competent-care-for-male-veterans

Ship, A. N. (2023). Losing them. In M. Loscalzo, M. Forstein, & L. A. Klein (Eds.), *Loss and grief: Personal stories of doctors and other healthcare professionals* (pp. 46–78). Oxford University Press.

Sidran Institute (n.d.). *Myths and facts about PTSD.* Sidran Institute. http://www.sidran.org/resources/for-survivors-and-loved-ones/myths-and-facts-about-ptsd

Silverman, A. F. (2002). Disinhibition, memory, and attention deficit hyperactivity disorder. *Dissertation Abstracts International: Section B: The Sciences & Engineering, 63*(5-B), 2604.

Simpson, A., & Laham, S. M. (2015). Different relational models underlie prototypical left and right positions on social issues. *European Journal of Social Psychology, 45*(2), 204–17.

Singer, M. G. (2004). The concept of evil. *Philosophy, 79*(308), 185–214.

Skinner, M. D., Goodfriend, W., Christiansen, A. K., Davis, R. L., & Pearson, C. L. (2006, April). *Terror management theory and commitment to friendship* [Conference presentation]. Rocky Mountain Psychological Association.

Smart, R. (2006). A man with a "woman's problem": Male gender and eating disorders. In M. Englar-Carlson & M. Stevens (Eds.), *In the room with men: A casebook of therapeutic change* (pp. 319–38). American Psychological Association.

Smith, M. (2007). *Polar crusader: A life of Sir James Wordie.* Birlinn.

Smith, R. M., Parrot, D. J., Swartout, K. M., & Tharp, A. T. (2015). Deconstructing hegemonic masculinity: The roles of antifemininity, subordination to women, and sexual dominance in men's perpetration of sexual aggression. *Psychology of Men & Masculinity, 16*(2), 160–69.

Snipes, S. A., Hayes Constant, T. K., Trumble, B. C., Goodreau, S. M., Morrison, D. M., Shell-Duncan, B. K., Pelman, R. S., & O'Connor, K. A. (2015). Masculine perspectives about work and family concurrently promote and inhibit men's healthy behaviors. *International Journal of Men's Health, 14*(1), 1–20.

Spanos, N. P. (1996). *Multiple identities and false memories: A sociocognitive perspective.* American Psychological Association.

Spears, R. (2017). Deindividuation. In Harkins, S. G., & Williams, K. D., & Burger, J. M. (Eds.), *The Oxford handbook of social influence.* Oxford University Press.

Spencer, A. (2010, August 13). *Interview with Bart Yasso.* Marathon Training Academy. http://marathontrainingacademy.com/interview-with-bart-yasso

Spinhoven, P., Penelo, E., de Rooij, M., Penninx, B. W., & Ormel, J. (2014). Reciprocal effects of stable and temporary components of neuroticism and affective disorders: Results of a longitudinal cohort study. *Psychological Medicine 44*(2), 337–48.

Spotila, J. R. (2004). *Sea turtles: A complete guide to their biology, behavior, and conservation.* Baltimore, MD: John Hopkins University Press.

Staggs, S. (n.d.). *Myths & facts about PTSD.* Psych Central. http://psychcentral.com/lib /myths-and-facts-about-ptsd

Stanley, I. H., Hom, M. A., & Joiner, T. E. (2016). A systematic review of suicidal thoughts and behaviors among police officers, firefighters, EMTs, and paramedics. *Clinical Psychology Review, 44*(1), 25–44.

Steelman, V. M. (1990). Intraoperative music therapy: Effects on anxiety, blood pressure. *AORN Journal, 52*(5), 1026–34.

Steensma, T. D., Kreukels, B. P. C., de Vries, A. L. C., & Cohen-Kettenis, P. T. (2013). Gender identity development in adolescence. *Hormones & Behavior 64*(2), 288–97.

Sternberg, R. J. (1997). Construct validation of a triangular love scale. *European Journal of Social Psychology, 27*(3), 313–35.

Sternberg, R. J. (1997). *Thinking styles.* Cambridge University Press.

Stickgold, R., & Walker, M. P. (2010, May 22). *The neuroscience of sleep.* Academic Press.

Strack, F., Martin, L. L., & Stepper, S. (1988). Inhibiting and facilitating conditions of the human smile: A nonobtrusive test of the facial feedback hypothesis. *Journal of Personality & Social Psychology, 54*(5), 768–77.

Stromberg, J., & Caswell, E. (2015, October 8). *Why the Myers-Briggs test is totally meaningless.* Vox. http://www.vox.com/2014/7/15/5881947/myers-briggs-personality-test-meaningless

Studer, B., Geniole, S. N., Becker, M. L., Eisenegger, C., & Knecht, S. (2020). Inducing illusory control ensures persistence when rewards fade and when others outperform us. *Psychonomic Bulletin & Review, 27*(4), 809–18.

Stuessy, T. (2007). *Risk perception: A quantitative analysis of skydiving participation.* Pro-Quest.

Sue, D. W., & Spanierman, L. B. (2020). *Microaggressions in everyday life* (2nd ed.). Wiley.

Sue, D. W., & Sue, D. (2016). Counseling the culturally diverse: *Theory and practice* (6th ed.). Wiley.

SyFy (2018, July 19). *Doctor Who's Jodie Whittaker and new companions preview the new season* [Video]. YouTube. https://www.youtube.com/watch?v=Xz1Rez4R7CE

Szasz, T. (1960). The myth of mental illness. *American Psychologist, 15*(2), 113–18.

Szasz, T. (1973). *Ideology and insanity: Essays on the psychiatric dehumanization of man.* Penguin.

Szasz, T. (2007). *The medicalization of everyday life.* Syracuse University Press.

Tanielian, T., & Jaycox, L. (2008). *Invisible wounds of war.* RAND.

Tellegen, A. (1993). Folk concepts and psychological concepts of personality and personality disorder. *Psychological Inquiry, 4*(2), 122–30.

Tellegen, A., & Waller, N. G. (1994). Exploring personality through test construction: Development of the Multidimensional Personality Questionnaire. In S. R. Briggs & J. M. Cheek (Eds.), *Personality measures: Development and evaluation* (Vol. 1, pp. 133–61). JAI Press.

Ter Borg, M., & Trenité, D. K. (2012). The cultural context of diagnosis: The case of Vincent van Gogh. *Epilepsy & Behavior, 25*(3), 431–39.

Ternes, A.-M., Clough, M., Foletta, P., White, O., & Fielding, J. (2019). Executive control deficits correlate with reduced frontal white matter Vol. in multiple sclerosis. *Journal of Clinical & Experimental Neuropsychology, 41*(7), 723–29.

Tharries (2022, July 16). *Christopher Eccleston reveals his involvement in the 60th anniversary!* [Video]. YouTube. https://www.youtube.com/watch?v=V5HXjlFzCBo

Thomas, B. (2012, November 6). *What's so special about mirror neurons?* Scientific American. http://blogs.scientificamerican.com/guest-blog/whats-so-special-about-mirror-neurons

Thompson, W. F., Schellenberg, E. G., & Husain, G. (2001). Arousal, mood, and the Mozart effect. *Psychological Science, 12*(3), 248–51.

Thoreau, H. D. (1854). *Walden; or, life in the woods.* Ticknor & Fields.

Trnka, R., Balcar, K., Kuška, M., & Hnilca, K. (2012). Neuroticism and valence of negative emotional concepts. *Social Behavior & Personality*, *40*(5), 843–44.

Tobias-Webb, J., Limbrick-Oldfield, E. H., Gillan, C. M., Moore, J. W., Aitken, M. R. F., & Clark, L. (2017). Let me take the wheel: Illusory control and sense of agency. *Quarterly Journal of Experimental Psychology*, *70*(8), 1732–46.

Toblin, R. L., Riviere, L. A., Thomas, J. L., Adler, A. B., Kok, B. C., & Hoge, C. W. (2012). Grief and physical health outcomes in U.S. soldiers returning from combat. *Journal of Affective Disorders*, *136*(3), 469–75.

Truszczynski, N., Singh, A. A., & Hansen, N. (2022). The discrimination experiences and coping responses of non-binary and trans people. *Journal of Homosexuality*, *69*(4), 741–55

Tuckman, B. W, & Jensen, M. A. (1977). Stages of small-group development revisited. *Group & Organization Studies*, *2*(4), 419–27.

Tugade, M. M., & Fredrickson, B. L. (2004). Resilient individuals use positive emotions to bounce back from negative emotional experiences. *Journal of Personality & Social Psychology*, *86*(2), 320.

Tupes, E. C., & Christal, R. E. (1961). Recurrent personality factors based on trait ratings. *USAF ASD Technical Report* (No. 61–97). U.S. Air Force.

Turner, M. E., & Pratkanis, A. R. (1998). Twenty-five years of groupthink theory and research: Lessons from the evaluation of a theory. *Organizational Behaviour & Human Decision Processes*, *73*(2/3), 105–15.

Urbaniak, G. C., & Kilmann, P. R. (2003). Physical attractiveness and the nice guy paradox: Do nice guys really finish last? *Sex Roles*, *49*(9–10), 413–26.

Vaes, J., & Leyens, J., & Paladino, M. P., & Miranda, M. P. (2012). We are human, they are not: Driving forces behind outgroup dehumanisation and the humanisation of the ingroup. *European Review of Social Psychology*, *23*(1), 64–106.

Vaillant, G. E. (1977). *Adaptation to life*. Little, Brown.

Van der Horst, M., & Coffé, H. (2012). How friendship network characteristics influence subjective well-being. *Social Indicators Research*, *107*(3), 509–29.

Van Inwagen, P. (2000). Free will remains a mystery. *Philosophical Perspectives 14*(1), 1–19.

Van Swearingen, J. M., Cohn, J. F., & Bajaj-Luthra, A. (1999). Specific impairment of smiling increases the severity of depressive symptoms in patients with facial neuromuscular disorders. *Aesthetic Plastic Surgery*, *23*(6), 416–23.

Van Tongeren, D. R., Green, J. D., & Richmond, T. (2022). In the valley of the shadow of death: The existential benefits of imbuing life and death with meaning. *Psychology of Religion & Spirituality*, *14*(3), 395–405.

Vygotsky, L. S. (1931/1997). The history of the development of higher mental functions. In L. S. Vygotsky (Ed.), *Razvitie vysshikh psikhicheskikh funktsij* (pp. 13-223). APN

Von Hippel, W., Vasey, M. W., Gonda, T., & Stern, T. (2008). Executive function deficits, rumination and late-onset depressive symptoms in older adults. *Cognitive Therapy & Research, 32*(4), 474–87.

Voskuil, P. (2013). Diagnosing Vincent van Gogh, an expedition from the sources to the present "mer à boire." *Epilepsy & Behavior, 28*(2), 177–80.

Wacker, J., Chavanon, M., & Stemmler, G. (2006). Investigating the dopaminergic basis of extraversion in humans: A multilevel approach. *Journal of Personality & Social Psychology, 91*(1), 171–87.

Walters, G. D. (2001). Development of a Fear-of-Change scale for the Psychology Inventory of Criminal Thinking Styles. *Journal of Offender Rehabilitation, 34*(1), 1–8.

Wang, L., Shi, Z., & Li, H. (2009). Neuroticism, extraversion, emotion regulation, negative affect and positive affect: The mediating role of reappraisal and suppression. *Social Behavior & Personality, 37*(2), 193–94.

Ware, B. (2012). *The top five regrets of the dying: A life transformed by the dearly departing.* Hay House.

Watson, D. (2004). Stability versus change, dependability versus error: Issues in the assessment of personality over time. *Journal of Research in Personality, 38*(4), 319–50.

Webster, R. (1995). *Why Freud was wrong: Sin, science, and psychoanalysis.* Orwell.

Wegner, D. M. (1989). *White bears and other unwanted thoughts: Suppression, obsession, and the psychology of mental control.* Guilford.

Wegner, D. M., Schneider, D. J., Carter, S. R., & White, T. L. (1987). Paradoxical effects of thought suppression. *Journal of Personality & Social Psychology, 53*(1), 5–13.

Wertheimer, M. (1987). *A brief history of psychology* (3rd ed.). Holt, Rinehart & Winston.

Weissensteiner, J. R., Abernethy, B., Farrow, D., & Gross, J. (2012). Distinguishing psychological characteristics of expert cricket batsmen. *Journal of Science & Medicine in Sport, 15*(1), 74–79.

Wells, D. L. (2009). The effects of animals on human health and well-being. *Journal of Social Issues, 65*(3), 523–543.

Wernick, L. J., Espinoza-Kulick, A., Inglehart, M., Bolgatz, J., & Dessel, A. B. (2021). Influence of multicultural curriculum and role models on high school students' willingness to intervene in anti-LGBTQ harassment. *Children & Youth Services Review ,129*, Artl. 106211.

Whitbourne, S. K. (2001). Stability and change in adult personality: Contributions of process-oriented perspectives. *Psychology Inquiry, 12*(2), 101–3.

WhoLife! (2018, February 17). *Doctor & Romana were romantically involved.* TARDIS Data Core. https://tardis.fandom.com/f/p/3100000000000153157

Williams, K. D., & Forges, J. P., & von Hippel, W. (Eds.) (2005). *The social outcast: Ostracism, social exclusion, rejection, and bullying.* Psychology Press.

Wilson, L. C. (2015). A systematic review of probable posttraumatic stress disorder in first responders following man-made mass violence. *Psychiatry Research, 229*(1–2), 21–26.

Winfrey, O, (2000, May. Oprah talks to Maya Angelou. *O, The Oprah Magazine, 14*(5), 154. Online: https://www.oprah.com/omagazine/oprah-interviews-maya-angelou/9

Wing, R. R., & Jeffery, R. W. (1999). Benefits of recruiting participants with friends and increasing social support for weight loss and maintenance. *Journal of Consulting & Clinical Psychology, 67*(1), 132.

Winthrop, H. (1949). Two concepts of personality disintegration: I. Attitude-inconsistency as failure to order values; II. Schizophrenic disturbances of thinking as failure to order meanings. *Journal of General Psychology, 40*, 177–218.

Witelson, S. F., Kigar, D. L., & Harvey, T. (1999). The exceptional brain of Albert Einstein. *The Lancet, 353*(9170), 2149–53.

Wong, P. T., Reker, G. T., & Gesser, G. (1994). Death Attitude Profile—Revised: A multidimensional measure of attitudes toward death (pp. 121–28). In R. A. Niemeyer (Ed.), *Death anxiety handbook: Research, instrumentation, and application.* Taylor & Francis.

Woodworth, R. S. (1917). Some criticisms of the Freudian psychology. *Journal of Abnormal Psychology, 12*(3), 174–94.

Wooten Thomas, C. (2010). Grandparent perspectives on raising their grandchildren: Protection, obligation, and sense of loss. *Dissertation Abstracts International Section A: Humanities & Social Sciences 70*(10-A), 3806.

World Health Organization (2022). *International classification of diseases and related health problems* (11th ed.). World Health Organization.

Wright, P. H. (1989). Gender differences in adults' same- and cross-gender friendships. In R. G. Adams & R. Blieszner (Eds.), *Older adult friendship: Structure and process.* SAGE.

Yalom, I. (1970). *Theory and practice of group psychotherapy.* Basic.

Yalom, I. (2008). *From staring at the sun: Overcoming the terror of death.* Jossey-Bass.

Young, I. M. (2003). The logic of masculinist protection: Reflections on the current security state. *Signs: Journal of Women in Culture & Society, 29*(1), 2–25.

Young, L., Camprodon, J. A., Hauser, M., Pascual-Leone, A., & Saxe, R. (2010). Disruption of the right temporoparietal junction with transcranial magnetic stimulation reduces the role of beliefs in moral judgments. *Proceedings of the National Academy of Sciences, 107*(15), 6753–58.

Young-Bruehl, E. (2008). *Anna Freud: A biography* (2nd ed.). Yale University Press.

Zak, P. J., Kurzban, R., Ahmadi, S., Swerdloff, R. S., Park, J., Efremidze, L., Redwine, K., Morgan, K., & Matzner, W. (2009). Testosterone administration decreases generosity in the ultimatum game. *PLOS One, 4*(12), e8330.

Zak, P. J., Stanton, A. A., & Ahmadi, S. (2007). Oxytocin increases generosity in humans. *PLOS One, 2*(11), e1128.

Zeigarnik, B. (1927/1938). On finished and unfinished tasks. In W. D. Ellis (Ed.), *A source book of Gestalt psychology* (pp. 300–14). Kegan Paul, Trench, Trübner.

Zhao, J., Li, X., Barnett, D., Lin, X., Fang, X., Zhao, G., Naar-King, S., & Stanton, B. (2011). Parental loss, trusting relationship with current caregivers, and psychosocial adjustment among children affected by AIDS in China. *Psychology, Health, & Medicine, 16*(4), 437–49.

Zhong, C.-B., Bohns, V. K., & Gino, F. (2010). Good lamps are the best police: Darkness increases dishonesty and self-interested behavior. *Psychological Science, 21*(3), 311–14.

Zhou, Y., Si, X., Chen, Y., Chao, Y., Lin, C.-P., Li, S., Zhang, X., Ming, D., & Li, Q. (2022). Hippocampus- and thalamus-related fiber-specific white matter reductions in mild cognitive impairment. *Cerebral Cortex, 32*(15), 3159–74.

Zimbardo, P. G. (2007). *The Lucifer effect: Understanding how good people turn evil.* Random House.

Index